WOODROW WILSON AND THE NEW AMERICA recreates in unique fashion the life of a great American and the era upon which he left his imprint. Told through the skillful use of original speeches, letters, official documents, journalistic commentary and the words and writings of close friends and bitter adversaries—all interspersed with an incisive running text by the author—the volume provides a remarkable insight into the excitement and controversy, the hopes and fears of an age in transition. It also offers a vivid and dramatic portrait of Woodrow Wilson the man, his joys and sorrows, his triumphs and defeats, and the eventual vindication of his principles.

Alfred B. Rollins, Jr., has been a Fellow of the Fund for the Advancement of Education. A member of the faculty of Harpur College of the State University of New York, he is the author of **Franklin D. Roosevelt and the Age of Action** and **Roosevelt and Howe.**

WOODROW WILSON AND THE NEW AMERICA

ALFRED B. ROLLINS, JR.

A LAUREL EDITION

Published by Dell Publishing Co., Inc.
750 Third Avenue, New York, N.Y. 10017
Copyright © 1965 by Alfred B. Rollins, Jr.
Laurel ® TM 674623, Dell Publishing Co., Inc.
First printing—February, 1965
Printed in U.S.A.

ACKNOWLEDGMENTS: Grateful acknowledgment is made to the authors, publishers and agents listed below for their permission to use the material reprinted in this volume:

Ray Stannard Baker, WOODROW WILSON: LIFE AND LETTERS, Doubleday, Doran & Co., 1927. Reprinted by permission of Mrs. Rachel Baker Napier.

Baker & Dodds, THE PUBLIC PAPERS OF WOODROW WILSON, Harper & Brothers, 1925-1927. Reprinted by permission of Harper & Row, Inc.

H. F. C. Bell, WOODROW WILSON AND THE PEOPLE, Doubleday, Doran & Co., Inc., 1945. Copyright 1945 by H. F. C. Bell. Reprinted by permission of Doubleday & Co., Inc.

Paul Birdsall, VERSAILLES TWENTY YEARS AFTER, Reynall & Hitchcock, 1941. Reprinted by permission of Harcourt, Brace & World, Inc.

John Blum, JOE TUMULTY AND THE WILSON ERA, Houghton Mifflin Co., 1951. Reprinted by permission of Houghton Mifflin Co.

Stephen Bonsal, UNFINISHED BUSINESS, Doubleday, Doran & Co., 1944. Copyright 1944 by Stephen Bonsal. Reprinted by permission of Doubleday & Co., Inc.

L. Brownlow, A PASSION FOR POLITICS, The University of Chicago Press, 1955. Reprinted by permission of The University of Chicago Press.

John Buchan, A HISTORY OF THE GREAT WAR, Thomas Nelson & Sons, Ltd., 1923. Reprinted by permission of Thomas Nelson & Sons, Ltd.

Ruth Cranston, THE STORY OF WOODROW WILSON. Copyright 1945 by Ruth Cranston. Reprinted by permission of Simon & Schuster, Inc.

George Creel, REBEL AT LARGE, G. P. Putnam's Sons, 1947. Reprinted by permission of G. P. Putnam's Sons.

C. Cruttwell, A HISTORY OF THE GREAT WAR, 1914-1918, Oxford University Press, 1936. Reprinted by permission of Oxford University Press, Inc.

Merle Curti, BRYAN AND WORLD PEACE, Smith College Studies in History, XXI (3-4), April-July 1931. Reprinted by permission of Smith College Studies in History.

Joseph Dorfman, THE ECONOMIC MIND IN AMERICAN CIVILIZATION, The Viking Press, 1948. Copyright 1949 by Joseph Dorfman. Reprinted by permission of the Viking Press, Inc.

John A. Garraty, HENRY CABOT LODGE: A BIOGRAPHY, Alfred A. Knopf, 1953. Reprinted by permission of Alfred A. Knopf, Inc.

George & George, WOODROW WILSON AND COLONEL HOUSE, John Day & Co., Inc., 1956. Reprinted by permission of Alexander L. George and Juliette L. George.

Louis L. Gerson, WOODROW WILSON AND THE REBIRTH OF POLAND, 1914-1920, Yale University Press, 1953. Reprinted by permission of The Yale University Press.

Cary T. Grayson, WOODROW WILSON: AN INTIMATE MEMOIR, Holt, Rinehart & Winston, Inc. Reprinted by permission of Holt, Rinehart & Winston, Inc.

Oscar Handlin, CHANCE OR DESTINY, Little, Brown & Co., Inc., 1954. Copyright 1954, 1955 by Oscar Handlin. Reprinted by permission of Little, Brown & Co., Inc., and of Willis Kingsley Wing.

Richard Hofstadter, THE AMERICAN POLITICAL TRADITION AND THE MEN WHO MADE IT, Alfred A. Knopf, Inc., 1948. Reprinted by permission of Alfred A. Knopf, Inc.

W. Stull Holt, TREATIES DEFEATED BY THE SENATE, The Johns Hopkins Press, 1933. Reprinted by permission of The Johns Hopkins Press.

Marc Karson, AMERICAN LABOR UNIONS AND POLITICS, 1900-1918, Southern Illinois University Press, 1958. Reprinted by permission of Southern Illinois University Press.

Robert Lansing, WAR MEMOIRS, Bobbs-Merrill Co., Inc., 1935. Copyright 1935 by The Bobbs-Merrill Co., Inc. Reprinted by permission of The Bobbs-Merrill Co., Inc.

Arthur S. Link, WILSON: THE ROAD TO THE WHITE HOUSE, Princeton University Press, 1947. Reprinted by permission of Princeton University Press.

for ARVILLA C. JACK
Who has lived with
dignity and kindness, with
integrity and courage,
over ninety years of
the American Epic

CONTENTS

PREFACE

This book is both a narrative history and an anthology.
The reader will find excerpts from significant source
materials and from some of the best historical
writing about Woodrow Wilson and his age. I have
attempted to be objective, but I have not sought to
avoid the historian's obligation to give meaning to the
facts. There are interpretations and judgments;
this is a book with a point of view.

Any author incurs almost innumerable obligations to
friends and colleagues. My special debt runs to two
whole generations of Wilson scholars, without whom,
in a very special sense, such a volume as this could
never have been written. It is my hope that readers
who discover for the first time here the rich literature
on this period will go on to read more deeply. No
decade was more filled with significance for America's
future than this. No personality has inspired more
vivid controversy than Woodrow Wilson. No literature in
American history is more significant and exciting.

Alfred B. Rollins, Jr.
Harpur College, State University of New York

WOODROW WILSON AND
THE NEW AMERICA

1. 1912

Sea Girt, New Jersey, in 1912, was an island of peace in a world full of trouble. Fresh Atlantic breezes tempered the sultry summer heat. Life moved gently with the pace of horse-drawn carriages. Gentlemen of leisure and of wealth strolled across the fairways of the country club. Their ladies swept along the sea-road of an afternoon in handsome open carriages or walked majestically in ankle-length tea-gowns, beneath the shade of parasols. Later, as the sun slanted to the west, there would be the genteel challenge of croquet on the broad lawns.

Occasionally a clumsy, raucous automobile, or a telephone bell would break the peace. Newspapers brought faint echoes of the distant National Conventions in Chicago and Baltimore, of the even more distant wars and rumors of wars. For the gentleman who would catch up quickly with the world, the popular Review of Reviews provided a capsule of news. It was a bumper year for basic farm crops; steel reported the largest shipments in its history; Harriet Quimby, America's first woman pilot, had fallen to her death in Dorchester Bay; the Akron, Melvin Vaniman's "enormous balloon," had exploded and destroyed its eleven-man crew. There were great American triumphs in the Olympic games at Stockholm; the Panama Canal was nearly finished. The threat of war was far away, in the Mediterranean and the Balkans. And the photos told other stories: the tough old Bull Moose, Teddy Roosevelt, lecturing a crowd from the balcony of Chicago's Congress Hotel; a young and cherub-faced Winston Churchill calling at the War Office in London; and "a new portrait of the popular German Kaiser and some of his family," showing that modest gentleman "in one of his favorite roles—that of family man."

But on the broad porches facing the ocean were rows of high-backed rocking chairs. Later gentlemen and ladies would rock quietly through the cooling evening— with no radios, no television, no traffic to break the peace. Evenings were for conversation; and, on one of these broad porches, evenings were often for poetry, as Woodrow Wilson recited for his gracious, sensitive wife, for his gay and fun-loving daughters, the romantic verse of Wordsworth, the ballads of Robert Burns, the sonnets of Shakespeare. This man of grim and sharp features seemed cold to many who met him. But among his family and friends he was a warm, emotional romantic, devoted to the eternal truths of his deep religious faith, devoted to the eternal dreams of the good and simple life that his beloved English poets had ceaselessly spun out.

In a few weeks, Woodrow Wilson would be marked for destiny: he stood, in 1912, at the threshold of a new America and a new world. Already America was caught in the deep tensions of a change that neither Wilson nor most of his countrymen understood. They would forge a new way of life without knowing it, as the factory, the city, the automobile and telegraph, the rumors of war and the perils of empire engulfed their rural institutions. But it was almost by inadvertence that they built, for Americans looked backward in their moment of challenge. As they edged almost imperceptibly into the modern world, they fought to save old institutions or mend them, to make the old values they had learned in country schools and in sober families live again in the world of machines and speed and perilous interdependence.

For most Americans the articles of faith were clear, but general. Individualism was the spark of the good life. The great steel magnate, Andrew Carnegie, had written in 1886: "There is not one shred of privilege to be met with anywhere in all the laws. One man's right is every man's right. The flag is the guarantor and symbol of equality."[1] Carnegie, as he was fond of noting, seemed a preeminent example of the success that came to those who struggled vigorously with their "equals." It all went back to the Declaration of Independence: " . . . all men are created equal . . . ." But it all went back, too, to Social Darwinism, that strangely unmoral dogma that man, like the jungle animals, was the product of struggle—of ruthless struggle against competitors, of kill or be killed, of succeed or be crushed. It was comforting, in a way. What could a man do but adapt to environment? If God was in his heaven—and few doubted it; if the struggle to achieve was nature's way—and few doubted that; if the way to achieve was to be ambitious and tough, but honest and virtuous—and few admitted to doubting that; then how could one escape the relentless logic that made Mr. Carnegie seem the very embodiment of God's will, the master achiever, who had risen by wit and honesty, ambition and integrity? For decades American boys had read the simple version of this pleasant myth in the stories of Horatio Alger. Ragged Dick, the prototype of all Alger heroes, rose from bootblack to bookkeeper in six months:

> "I should like nothing better," he said, his eyes sparkling with delight, "if you really think I could discharge the duties satisfactorily."
>
> "I think you could. I believe you have the ability, and of your fidelity I feel assured."
>
> "Thank you sir; you are very kind to me," said Dick gratefully.
>
> "I have reason to be," said Mr. Rockwell, taking his

hand. "Under God it is to your courage that I owe the life of my dear boy. I shall never forget it. One thing more. I intend Michael to undertake most of your present duties. . . . Do you think he will answer?"

"I think so," said Dick. "He has been a rough customer, but then he has never had a chance. I believe in giving everybody a chance."

"So do I," said Mr. Rockwell. "Michael shall have his chance. Let us hope he will improve it."[2]

Within three years, Dick was a junior partner in the firm, well married, and well-heeled, thanks to thrift and to a lucky real estate deal. "So Dick achieved *FAME AND FORTUNE,*—the fame of an honorable and enterprising man of business, and a fortune which promises to be very large. But I am glad to say that Dick has not been spoiled by prosperity. He never forgets his humble beginnings, and tries to show his sense of God's goodness by extending a helping hand to the poor and needy boys, whose trials and privations he understands well from his own past experience."[2]

It was all very simple, as well as comforting. And there were other simple articles of faith. Optimism was one. As late as 1915, clergyman Russell Conwell, would assure the nation: "Now then, I say again that the opportunity to get rich . . . is here in Philadelphia now, within the reach of almost every man and woman who hears me speak tonight . . . you ought to get rich, and it is your duty to get rich."[3] And Americans were optimistic about their nation too. This was a nation with a glorious future —to lead the world, in business, in culture, in morals— and particularly in democracy. It was this which made empire believable in a democracy. It was the nation's destiny, even its duty, to "lift up" the backward areas of the world, to lead the world to democratic institutions.

There were other values to add to the gospel of hard

work, self-reliance, ambition and success. America believed in the solid virtues: moderation, peace, temperance, generosity and philanthropy on earth, and a hope of Heaven beyond. And America believed in justice: man's justice, equality before the law, the rights of property and the rights of person—and God's justice, the inexorable victory of the Right. Sometimes God's justice was interpreted in a shabbily comforting fashion. As Conwell said: "I sympathize with the poor, but the number of poor who are to be sympathized with is very small. To sympathize with a man whom God has punished for his sins, thus to help him when God would still continue a just punishment, is to do wrong, no doubt about it."[3]

The nation believed in itself. And it was chronically suspicious of others. Three-quarters of the globe remained veiled in mystery for most Americans, easily dismissed as backward and heathen lands that American business might someday "open" and American missionaries "civilize." And even Europe seemed the hotbed of reaction, monarchy, feudalism, of decadent aristocracy, of ignorant and vicious masses, of war, poverty and evil.

For most Americans there was no cynicism in all this. The virtues were simple, unquestionable, abstract, undefined, easily related to each other. Most boys from Presque Isle or Pottawattamie, Valdosta or Valatie, knew what was right, knew how to get ahead, had no doubts that a man could rise if he would, and that if he fell, it was his own fault. And they had no doubt that the Stars and Stripes waved over a nation of virtue, equality, opportunity—the greatest nation in the world, with a deep destiny to save the world from evil and from barbarism.

There was much to boast about: the highest material standard of living in the world, the most rapidly developing industry, the most rapidly expanding economy; an emerging mass culture such as the globe had never seen; a viable democracy, the most stable and successful republican government in history; a remarkable system of public education, in most places; the "Americanization" of millions of immigrants; the freedom of the slaves; the constant miracle of today's millionaire who was yesterday's bootblack. As yet there was little fear that material progress would endanger the old virtues. There was practically no one who could imagine that democracy could be expected to include actual, complete equality for all races; there were few who could grasp the fact that, if the world's trade came to America, the world's troubles would also. There were few who could see inconsistency between military occupation of the Philippines and a crusade for democracy; there were few who even questioned the vicious, but common, assumption that America's destiny was high because America was the home of a chosen and superior "Anglo-Saxon" race.

There were few who could see the future. But there were already many who could feel and resent the frictions the new age was producing. Farmers on the Western plains had led the way. Resentful at exploitation by the "trusts," and the railroads and the grain exchanges, they had clamored for rate-regulation, trust-busting, and even government ownership—a curious crusade that sought limits on business individualism to preserve the individualism and opportunity of the farmer. An Interstate Commerce Act and a Sherman Anti-Trust Act stood as half-built monuments to their fight. Across the Great Plains and through the small-farm South, even more radical farmer demands swept like flames during the Populist rage of the 1890s. Now William Jennings Bryan, the "Boy Orator of the Platte," the Free-Silver Democrat of the 1896 and 1904 elections, stood as the symbol of challenge, not to the American Way, but to the concentration of economic power that made the plaint of individualism and equality a mockery.

Since the 1880s, organized labor had been reasserting its struggle to make the workingman the equal of the businessman in the competition of industry. But not all laboring men would enter the struggle. Arch-conservative William McKinley would enlist the votes of millions of shopworkers on the simple proposition that only bosses could give jobs, and that only a government favorable to the bosses would therefore create conditions favorable to labor. There were radicals: Henry George, with his magic potion, the Single Tax: socialists in varied ideological coats; Henry Demarest Lloyd, with his dream of a corporate commonwealth. They would arouse much interest, much activity, but their specific ideas would have less appeal than the emotional impact of their language.

Above all, there were the Progressives, substantially middle class, believing in the old virtues, fearful of socialism and anarchism, largely religious, incorrigibly optimistic—but deeply resentful of evil, deeply aroused by the mounting evidence of decay and injustice. They were predominately city and town men; eventually they would unite for a moment with the prairie radicals, even with labor, but chiefly they were interested in making the old system just, ethical, honest, as they knew it ought to be. And they were aroused by the muckraking journalism that swept the country in the first decade of the new century. Lincoln Steffens documented in fascinating detail the collusion of crooked bosses and substantial businessmen to sell out self-government for a fortune. Ida Tarbell ferreted into the questionable tactics of Standard Oil. David Graham Phillips wrote of the "Treason" of the United States Senate. Upton Sinclair brought disgust in both heads and stomachs with his relentless descriptions of conditions in the meat-packing industry. It was bad enough to know that street railway franchises and judgeships might be sold on the auction block. It was unpardonable that there might be rats in the sausage. And even conservatives in New York legislature were galvanized into action—a ten-hour day for bakers, when one of them, in exhaustion, fell into the mixers; a whole spate of safety laws, when over a hundred women were trapped like vermin in the Triangle factory fire.

Revulsion, fear, and concern among the middle class had led them to join the practiced phalanxes of western rebels in the progressive movement, and heroes had arisen in every State to carry the fight to Washington. Mostly they were Republicans: George Norris of Nebraska, Hiram Johnson of California, Charles Evans Hughes and Theodore Roosevelt of New York, and scores of others. The redoubtable Teddy had made himself the living symbol of the progressive rebellion. He had talked as few others ever did. That he did less than he talked was, for the moment, unnoticed, as the country thrilled to his crusades for the conservation of natural resources, for the busting of the "bad" trusts, for the reassertion of clean government. And in state after state, his allies led the way to initiative, referendum, recall, commission government for the cities, direct election of senators—devices that, it was hoped, would give the parties and the government back to the people. Always there was the faith that the people were sound in their instincts, loyal in their stewardship to democracy. And always there was the faith that an improved system, a smoother mechanics, would make the agrarian values of a Thomas Jefferson, the simple, rural ideals of an Abraham Lincoln, work in an industrial age.

But there were problems that mechanical tinkering could not resolve. Economic problems: How to maintain individual opportunity, and yet use the advantages of big production? How to concentrate the economic process, yet prevent its bosses from controlling the government and the culture? How to accumulate wealth for expansion, but at the same time deal justly with the millions in slums, on shabby farms, in the dull and brutal mining towns, around the fringes of ten thousand villages, the millions who lived in poverty without the gaslight and "mission" furniture, the carpets, carriages and magazines that stood for middle-class success, without even the Sears Roebuck catalogues that brought culture and goods to the prosperous farm, without even the food and decent clothing to guarantee human dignity? And political problems: How to boast democracy, while there was racial segregation? How to wed efficiency and representation? How to make the people want to take their government back?

For the moment the deep problems were sensed only in odd moments of introspection. Official, small-town America spent its energies on the symptoms. And in 1912 most Americans were hypnotized by the antics of Teddy Roosevelt—back from a hunting trip to excoriate the timidity and conservatism of William Howard Taft, whom he himself had placed in the White House—back to start a new Progressive Party under the rampant sign of the Bull Moose. As Henry May suggests, Roosevelt "...had been a compelling symbol of the country's regeneration. After thirty years of frock-coated pomposity and backstairs shabbiness, the presidency itself had furnished the model for right-thinking American youth. Roosevelt the rough-rider or bear-hunter, Roosevelt the civic reformer or trust-buster, Roosevelt the indulgent father, fond of a pillow fight but serious about essentials, reflected exactly the country's image of itself, combining the old virtues with the new, breezy, twentieth-century methods."[4] In Chicago that summer of 1912, Teddy left the Republican Convention and called for supporters in the Battle of Armageddon.

At Sea Girt that June, there was no sign of the tumult to come, except for the telephone on the Governor's desk that was connected directly to the Democratic National Convention hall in Baltimore. In the study of his substantial Georgian house, the New Jersey Governor's official summer "cottage," Woodrow Wilson sat down to write an old friend and confidant:

> Two weeks from to-day we shall either have this sweet Sunday calm again or an army of reporters camped on the lawn and an all-day reception. . . . Now that the possibility is immediately at hand . . . I find myself dreading it and wishing most devoutly that I may escape. Not that I dread what would be really big and essential and worth while in the whole thing, but all that would go with [it]—all that is non-essential. . . . May the Lord have mercy on me! . . . I am well . . . and underneath, deep down, my soul is quiet.[5]

Wilson had played many roles in his day: struggling lawyer, sharp and incisive commentator on American government, college professor, President of Princeton University, now Governor of New Jersey. And Wilson had fought many battles, and bitter ones. Now he must wait while friends fought for him the battle for the Democratic presidential nomination. The friends were too few, he often feared. They would have less than a third of the votes to show on the first ballot. The convention would be a brawling ordeal. Since Teddy had split the Republican Party, the chances of Democratic victory would be better than they had been for decades. But Teddy had also created the terms of the campaign. Democrats at Baltimore must choose to make their party conservative and risk losing progressives to Roosevelt, or to make their party progressive and risk losing conservatives to Taft. And Wilson's fate was in the hands of men who did not love him, whom he did not respect. His leading opponent was Speaker of the House Champ Clark, whom he had once privately called "a sort of elephantine 'smart aleck.'"[6] William Jennings Bryan, still adored by many, still a power in the party, was vaguely friendly to Wilson now, but once had been embittered by Wilson's careless and hostile remarks. Bosses like Charlie Murphy of New York, who had sworn enmity to the New Jersey reformer, and like Jim Nugent of Wilson's own state, who had suffered the Governor's lash, until, bitter and hostile, he had pledged a public toast to "The Governor of the State of New Jersey—a liar and an ingrate!"[7] And other bosses, like Thomas Taggart of Indiana, who had politely put off the blandishments of Wilson's managers; they might be won, but only if Champ Clark were stopped. Happily the etiquette of politics called for candidates to stay away from Convention Hall. In any case, he must trust his friends; this kind of management was not his special skill.

But Woodrow Wilson knew the kind of candidate the convention ought to want. Four years earlier, he had written: "A man who will be and who will seem to the country in some sort an embodiment of the character and purpose it wishes its government to have,—a man who understands his own day and the needs of the country, and who has the personality and the initiative to enforce his views upon the people and upon the Congress."[8] And, as for the country, he had written:

What the country will demand of the candidate will be, not that he be an astute politician, skilled and practiced in affairs, but that he be a man such as it can trust, in character, in intention, in knowledge of its needs, in perception of the best means by which those needs may be met, in capacity to prevail by reason of his own weight and integrity.... For he is also the political leader of the nation, or has it in his choice to be. . . . When he speaks in his true character, he speaks for no special interest. If he rightly interpret the national thought and boldly insist upon it, he is irresistible.[9]

And of this leadership, he had written in an unpublished essay:

In what, then, does political leadership consist? It is leadership in conduct, and leadership in conduct must discern and strengthen the tendencies that make for development. The legislative leader must perceive the direction of the nation's permanent forces, and must feel the speed of their operation. There is initiative here, but not novelty; there are old thoughts, but a progressive application of them. . . . Practical leadership may not beckon to the slow masses of men from beyond some dim, unexplored space or some intervening chasm; it must daily feel the road that leads to the goal proposed, knowing that it is a slow, a very slow, evolution to wings, and that for the present, and for the very long future also, Society must walk.[10]

In some ways he was a strange man to be running for President. He had shown at Princeton, and at Trenton, that he knew how politics could be managed. His record in New Jersey, his speeches for the last four years, had made him a progressive to rival Teddy himself. But, for most of his life, he had sounded, and had intended to sound, like a conservative of the old Southern cast. An ex-professor, he looked unhappily like one. And he looked rigid, cold, harsh. Someone said his smile almost "creaked," as if it needed oiling. Capable of deep emotion and profound friendship, he was strangely shy with most people. He found it difficult to warm to individuals. Two years before, a reporter had described him for Manhattan readers:

Woodrow Wilson's face is narrow and curiously geometrical. It is a rectangle, one might say, the lines are so regular. His forehead is high and his iron gray hair retreats from it somewhat, which adds to this effect. His face is refined, a face that shows breeding and family in every line, but it is heavy boned. The cheek bones are rather high and the jaw thrusts forward in a challenging way. The mouth is small, sensitive, with full lips, a mouth almost too well shaped for a man, and a woman might envy the arched eyebrows. But the almost brutal strength of the general bony structure of the face, and the aggressive jaw promise an active, iron willed, fighting man. His eyes, blue-gray they looked in that light behind his nose glasses, are very penetrating. They have a way of narrowing when he talks that gives him a stern, almost grim expression.[11]

And one of his greatest admirers confessed:

When I met him, he gave me a hand that felt very much like a five-cent mackerel; cold, stiff, moist, unresponsive, extended something as though a clerk desiring a larger sale would casually poke the fish across a counter. He smiled, but I got the wrong side of his face, a side which gave me a certain impression of a reptilian personality—a strong sense of some essential treachery in the man![12]

It was significant that Wilson could joke about his face. His favorite limerick—and he had hundreds of them—was:

For beauty I'm not a star,
There are others more handsome by far.
But my face I don't mind it,
For I am behind it,
It's the people in front that I jar.[13]

But Wilson's frigid personality could warm with exuberance with either close and intimate friends, or great crowds of people whom he had never seen before. Many years earlier, he had written to Ellen Axson, who was to be his wife: "I have a sense of power in dealing with men collectively which I do not feel always in dealing with them singly.... One feels no sacrifice of pride necessary in courting the favour of an assembly of men such as he would have to make in seeking to please one man."[14] Thus conscious of his own limitations, he would write a few years later:

That the leader of men must have such sympathetic insight as shall enable him to know quite unerringly the motives which move other men in the mass is of course self-evident; but this insight which he must have is not the Shakespearean insight. It need not pierce the particular secrets of individual men: it need only know what it is that lies waiting to be stirred in the minds and purposes of groups and masses of men. Besides it is not a sympathy that serves, but is a sympathy whose power is to command, to command by knowing its instrument.... Men in the mass differ from men as individuals. A man who knows, and keenly knows, every man in town may yet fail to understand a mob or a mass-meeting of his fellow-townsmen.[15]

He could be tough and haughty after a fashion. He wrote of Robert E. Lee: "No man whom you deeply care for or look to for leadership is made altogether of gentle qualities."[16] He was proud. He was driven by a deep sense of duty, rooted in his Calvinist religion: "I shall make mistakes, but I do not think I shall sin against my knowledge of duty."[17] This was the same man who had written his fiancee twenty-seven years earlier: "...there is always satisfaction in hard, conscientious work, in the earnest pursuit of a clearly-seen, however distant ideal." And again: "There's duty in drudgery as well as in love and laughter. . . . In short, if a man does not find duty agreeable, he does not deserve gratification."[18]

He sometimes confused his pride and his duty, and when the two came together, he could be petty, even peevish. But he could be warm and gay, rollicking about the house in parlor games with his three daughters, singing old Scottish songs and the vigorous hymns of his Presbyterian church, reading endlessly in the evening, as he sprawled out on the hearthrug with his family about him to listen. His sense of humor was fine, broad, and enduring. He liked Irish and Negro stories, and practiced his dialects endlessly. He loved limericks. Even as presidential candidate, he could confess to reporters after a seasick voyage:

> I wish that my room had a floor;
> I don't care so much for a door;
> But this walking around
> Without touching the ground
> Is getting to be a damn bore.[19]

Even in his writing, where his dedication and earnestness were sometimes nearly deadly, there sparked an occasional flash of the wit that made living in Wilson's household a joy. He may now have been thinking of the description of a presidential candidate he had written a quarter of a century before: ". . . he should wear a clean and irreproachable insignificance. . . . the shoals of candidacy can be passed only by a light boat which carries little freight and can be turned readily about to suit the intricacies of the passage."[20]

He would have been hurt if anyone had seriously applied his own words to the Governor Wilson of 1912. But in a way they were curiously appropriate. One of the great advantages his managers would have in Baltimore this week would be the fact that there was little heavy freight on the Wilson craft. She carried a large cargo of light and airy statement that placed Wilson beyond all doubt in the progressive camp. But how far he was committed not even he knew. Southern and Western agrarians would like him, as well as solid, middle-class progressives. Yet it was not beyond all hope that even the stolid men of business would come to accept him.

Once his friends called him from Baltimore to warn that hope was gone. He authorized a strategic withdrawal, and then, with hectic advice from others, he repudiated this authority. And now word came, on July 2 at 3:30 in the afternoon, that Woodrow Wilson would be the Democratic candidate for the presidency against Taft and Roosevelt. It had taken much maneuvering, horse trading, and old fashioned offers of patronage and position. But Wilson knew of none of this as he sat down happily to write his nephew: "The nomination has been won in such a way as to leave me absolutely free of private obligations." He would go to the people in the role of crusader, independent, the man above the machine. But for the moment the people came to him, in distressing numbers.

He squirmed in rebellion as political impresarios, news reporters, brass bands, photographers, and autograph hunters swarmed over the lawn, up on the porch, and even into the house. Outside of his bedroom the Governor had no privacy. Some ten thousand letters came in—more than half from people who said that they had prayed for the nomination of Wilson. He was awed by the trust of the masses and frightened by the pathetic faith of individuals in the omnipotence of their ruler.... "The life I am leading now can't keep up," he wrote.... "Not a moment am I left free to do what I would. I thought last night that I should go crazy with the strain and confusion of it." Coming out dripping from a hot room in which he had been sealed up to make phonograph records for the coming campaign, he exclaimed: "If any man ever tries to get me to run for president again, I'll break his neck!" ... To compose his acceptance speech in tranquillity ... he ran away early in July from the buzz and glare of Sea Girt, put himself "in retreat" at the home of a friend, and then escaped by sea for six days on [Cleveland] Dodge's yacht, carrying under his arm a copy of the party platform and an editorial from the *World* entitled "Planks to be Broken."[21]

Ahead lay an inspired and tough campaign. Ahead lay a victory for which he dared only mildly to hope. And ahead also lay the day when Woodrow and Ellen Wilson would leave what had been the best years of their life.

On Monday morning, March 3, 1913, [they] ... walked down Library Place in Princeton, New Jersey. They had just left the little house in Cleveland Lane— the artist's studio—where they had been living for two years and they were on their way, a generous half-mile, to the railroad station. They exchanged scarcely a word during the walk. It was a time too deeply charged with emotion. There on the right was the old house where they had lived when they came to Princeton twenty-one years before. There also on the right, next door, was the house they themselves had built. How they had struggled and worked and saved to pay for it! Mrs. Wilson had herself drawn the plans, had brooded over every timber that went into it, had laid out and planted the garden.

The street was full of memories—memories and friends. ... They walked down the hill past the beautiful buildings of the University. Just over there in old Witherspoon, Wilson, years ago as a student, had "found himself," had come first to "know who he was and what he had to do." What friends he had made there!

Into these newer piles of stone and mortar, and all that they signified, the man had built most of his life—his aspirations, his affections, his ambitions. . . .

They could not see from the hill where they walked the beautiful old home at the heart of the university—Prospect—where they had lived for so many years. But how could they forget it? They had lived richly there, their family had grown to maturity within its gray walls; there they had welcomed their friends. They were never to enter it again. They were never even to spend another night in the old town itself, where Wilson, as student, teacher, president, and governor, had lived for more than a quarter of a century. For he was on his way to become President of the United States. . . . his deep inner reaction was one of anxiety.

"We are not as light-hearted as we might be. Much as we have suffered in Princeton, deep as are the wounds our hearts have received here, it goes hard with us to leave it. . . ."

And on the day before he left Princeton he wrote:

"This is our last evening in this little house, and we find our hearts very heavy. We leave familiar scenes, which we may possibly never know again, and go out to new adventures, amongst strangers."[22]

NOTES, CHAPTER 1

1. Andrew Carnegie, **Triumphant Democracy** (N.Y.: Charles Scribners' Sons, 1890), p. 19.
2. Horatio Alger, **Fame and Fortune.**
3. Russell H. Conwell, **Acres of Diamonds** (N.Y.: Harper and Brothers, 1915), pp. 17–18, 21.
4. Henry F. May, **The End of American Innocence** (N.Y.: Alfred A. Knopf, Inc., 1959), pp. 107–08.
5. Arthur S. Link, **Wilson: The Road to the White House** (Princeton, N.J.: Princeton University Press, 1947), p. 431.

6. Ray Stannard Baker, **Woodrow Wilson: Life and Letters** (N.Y.: Doubleday, Doran and Company, 1927–39), III, 196.

7. **Ibid.**, p. 238.

8. Woodrow Wilson, **Constitutional Government in the United States** (N.Y.: Columbia University Press, 1908), p. 65.

9. **Ibid.**, pp. 66, 68.

10. Woodrow Wilson, **Leaders of Men** (Princeton, N.J.: Princeton University Press, 1952), pp. 43–45.

11. **New York World,** December 18, 1920.

12. William Allen White, **Woodrow Wilson: The Man, His Times, and His Task** (Boston: Houghton Mifflin Company, 1924), p. xiii.

13. Joseph P. Tumulty, **Woodrow Wilson as I Know Him** (N.Y.: Doubleday, Page and Company, 1921), p. 476.

14. Baker, **op. cit.,** I, 199.

15. Wilson, **Leaders of Men, op. cit.,** pp. 23–24, 26.

16. Baker, **op. cit.,** IV, 1.

17. **Ibid.,** III, 134–35.

18. **Ibid.,** I, 182–83.

19. Arthur Walworth, **Woodrow Wilson** (London: Longmans, Green and Company, 1958), I, 237.

20. Woodrow Wilson, **Congressional Government: A Study in American Politics** (N.Y.: Meridian Books, Inc., 1956), p. 48.

21. Walworth, **op. cit.,** pp 234, 235, 237.

22. Baker, **op. cit.,** IV, 1–3.

2. "WHEN A MAN FINDS HIMSELF"

In 1904, Thomas Woodrow Wilson had stood before his Princeton seniors and let his thoughts run back forty years and more to the sleepy Georgia town where "Tommy" Wilson had first heard rumors of civil war, as he listened to the street gossipers at his father's gate. "The child," he said, " . . . stands upon a place apart, a little spectator of the world, before whom . . . years open their slow story and are noted or let go as his mood chances to serve them. The play touches him not. He but looks on, thinks his own thought, and turns away, not even expecting his cue to enter the plot and speak. He waits, he knows not for what. The days tell upon him like rain and air and the succession of the seasons, and seem long, very long, to his dreaming senses."[1]

But Tommy Wilson had "noted" more than he had "let go." The play had touched him more than he thought. And the people and events that flitted across his childhood stage left an impact that would be felt in Princeton, Trenton, Washington, and Versailles a half century later. For one thing, he was a Southern boy— Virginia born, in 1856—a Georgia boy, who heard with deep concern of Lincoln's election to the presidency, who watched his family's friends fight the just cause of the Confederacy, who lived in his teens among the crushed and bitter people of the Reconstruction. He would always know that he was a man of the South: " . . . the only place in the world where nothing has to be explained to me."[2] But Tommy Wilson would not be a bitter Southerner, and his idol beyond all compare in later years would be Abraham Lincoln.

Perhaps it was partly that Wilson's family were of Midwestern roots. Living and working in the planter South, they had never really belonged to it. Theirs was the heritage of the Scotch-Irish frontier, the same culture that had produced Lincoln and Andrew Jackson, a culture shot through with pride of individualism and with the vigor of rebellion. Wilson would be conscious all his life of this heritage. He thought it a matter of race and of inheritance. A man was made by the roots from which he came. He spoke constantly of his Scotch "blood," and his Irish; he preferred to think himself Irish.

Thomas Woodrow Wilson was a Presbyterian—the son of a minister, heir of many ministers, a boy who lived in and with the church as closely as a clergyman's son ever did. His faith was one that went back to John Calvin, to the same roots that had produced the New England Puritans and the rebellious Huguenots of France. It was a faith that stressed the sober and harsh side of the Christian tradition. Duty was the watchword, reinforced constantly with the reminder of men's evil nature, a firm faith in God's ordering of all things, a fear of Hell and a hope of Heaven. It was a God of wrath, of harsh and even-handed justice, a God who demanded rigid, patterned behavior, that Tommy Wilson came to know in the Manse and in the tall, brick church in Augusta.

But these Wilsons and this faith were no somber parody of Puritan New England. Happiness was also a virtue and a duty, the clean and harmless joy of games and singing, funny stories, good horses, on occasion parties, and on every occasion good literature, and even good tobacco. As Tommy Wilson's father worked on his brisk Sunday sermons, the smoke billowed from the long clay pipe that was always with him. And pride was a virtue—pride in a job well done, and relentless remorse when it was not well done. And so was independent thought. The faith these Wilsons held demanded no easy, rigid acceptance of what was past and done and said. Faith was the partner of thought; a man's business was to make the two work together.

And Tommy Wilson was the son of Joseph Ruggles Wilson and Jessie Woodrow. This was more important than anything else; he lived under their benevolent shadow until the day in 1924 when, tired, defeated, desperately ill, he turned to his doctor and said, "I am ready."

Dr. Wilson was an extraordinary man. A person—a notability. He was not only a fine preacher ... but he was a scholar, a wit, a gentleman. He was a large man, powerful, full-bodied and square, though not quite as tall as his son. ... he was an unusually handsome man, his head crowned with a great shock of hair which he tossed back from his broad forehead. In later years, it turned, not white in the ordinary way, but a silky, sea-island cotton white with a yellow tinge in it. A thing to mark! ... His eyes were brown and piercing bright, full of fire. He had the distinctive Wilson nose, long and straight, with a flexible tip, especially marked during animated conversation. His son inherited this unusual characteristic. But above all—the sum of all—he had an indescribable quality of presence.

"If I had my father's face and figure," Woodrow Wilson once remarked, "it wouldn't make any difference what I said."

He was a distinguished figure in any company. He was courtly, as became a Southern gentleman, he had a gift of repartee that was often devastating. His joking and teasing sometimes left barbs in the wounds he made. ...

The boy's mother was more sedate and reserved, with

a firmer knit texture of character. She had received a better formal education than most of the women of her day. As a girl, she made a strong impression upon those who knew her. It was not so much beauty, certainly not prettiness, though she had the charm of remarkably fine gray eyes and sunny curls, as it was the sense of vivid life she gave. . . .

It was . . . a rarely devoted, loyal, and cultivated family in which the boy Tommy Wilson grew up. There were two older sisters, Marion, six years, and Anne, two years, his senior. His younger brother, Joseph Ruggles, Jr., was not born until after the Civil War; he was ten years Woodrow Wilson's junior. . . . It was a family much given to reading aloud. While some of the books were serious, there were also novels, books of travel and poetry—"anything good." Dickens was then the joy of the world. We catch glimpses of the family sitting together, the mother characteristically erect in her chair, knitting, the two sisters side by side, and the little boy Tommy flat on his back on the floor while the doctor read aloud with vast delight from *Pickwick Papers* or from Scott's novels. . . .

Every day there were prayers: the reading of the Word, and all the family kneeling while the minister talked with God. On Sunday evenings before the lamps were lighted, and often at other times, they would sing together some of the great old hymns, just voices, for there was no instrument in the house. . . .

. . . The boy . . . himself was backward—"lazy" he called himself. He did not even learn his letters until he was nine years old: and could not read readily until he was eleven. What need was there when a boy could spend such hours in delightful listening while others read aloud? He loved always the spoken word, the roll of language. Years later, in answer to a query as to his favourite fairy story, he wrote:

"The truth is that I was so voracious of fairy tales

when I was a small boy, that I loved them all almost equally well.... All was grist that came to my mill."[3]

Tommy's confession that he was "lazy" may have been only the patent escape of the boy from whom too much was always expected. His formal education was sketchy —a little now and then at some one-room private school. Mostly he was taught by his father, and the old gentleman was masterful, relentless. Nothing but perfection would do; never a second of doubt but what Tommy must be an extraordinary boy and man. There was no room for the ordinary, no pity for the inadequate.

He never permitted the use of an incorrect word or sentence. If there was any doubt, the boy was sent flying for the dictionary, and there was often great discussion of the exact meaning of a word or a phrase....

"What do you mean by that?" the Doctor would ask the boy when he fumbled a sentence.

Tommy would explain.

"Then why don't you say so?"

... The Doctor believed that there could be no clear thought without clear expression. And back of clear thought lay accurate observation, the activity of an alert mind. An idea must not be left ragged at the edges.... [Wilson later explained] "The best teacher I ever had used to say to me:

" 'When you frame a sentence don't do it as if you were loading a shotgun, but as if you were loading a rifle. Don't fire in such a way and with such a load that while you hit the thing you aim at you will hit a lot of things in the neighborhood besides; but shoot with a single bullet and hit that one thing alone.' "[4]

But Doctor Wilson knew that an education was something more than filling a boy with fact. Years later his son would remember his warning: " ' ... the mind is not a prolix gut to be stuffed!' That is not the object of it. It is not a vessel made to contain something; it is a vessel made to transmute something. The process of digestion is of the essence, and the only part of the food that is of any consequence is the part that is turned into blood and fructifies the whole frame."[5]

Life with Doctor Wilson would produce an unusual boy and man. Tommy Wilson must be an individual. "He was never schooled in the habits of the crowd," said Ray Stannard Baker. And Baker went on to note:

> He began early to think his own thoughts, cherish his own visions, go his own way. The world was utterly chaotic, incomprehensible; he must struggle to his own conclusions regarding it. . . .

Many of the causes which combined to make Tommy Wilson different also operated to make him thoughtful; to give him the scholar's or philosopher's steady point of view. He had his father always at his side, a cultivated man with a broad outlook, a religious man setting forth principles that lay deep beneath the surface conflicts. . . . What was the church for, and what religion, if not for law, order, forbearance, steadiness, the long look ahead? "Eternal things!"[6]

Tommy Wilson must be on the side of the "Eternal Things," on the side of The Right. But Tommy Wilson must also be an extraordinary man. He would be his own man; he must leave his mark on the world he had inherited. But Tommy Wilson would suffer deeply three confusions. If Wilson must be on the side of The Right, he would sometimes too easily assume that, if it was his side, it must be right. And William Allen White would later insist: "All his life Woodrow Wilson's major delusion was that he had a first-class mind. . . . What he had was a clear, clean, strong brain. . . . He wrote well. He had a capacity for research. . . . But he was not in the

world's first or second class of thinkers or writers."[7]
There would always be a dispute about this. But there
would be no dispute about the last of these dilemmas.
Wilson must always feel that he had done well. He
would search endlessly for the pride that could come
with a job well done. But he could never afford to be
proud for long. He was eternally committed to a struggle for success he could never gain, because once it came
he could not admit it. He yearned for pride; he could
not be proud. When his first book was accepted for publication, he privately admitted: "Success does not flush
or elate me, except for the moment. I could almost
wish it did.... I must push on; to linger would be
fatal."[8] Later he would be fond of quoting: "A Yankee
always thinks that he is right, a Scotch-Irishman knows
that he is right."[9] But Tommy Wilson would drive himself endlessly, as if to rest were a sin. In public, he would
always be sure beyond doubt of his rightness; in private
he would never be sure enough that he was right.

Yet there were three things of which he never had
doubts: his "incomparable father," his God, and his
country. He could say: " ...so far as religion is concerned discussion is adjourned." As Ray Stannard Baker
later noted: "He had an absolutely immovable faith in
God.... He believed absolutely in the immortality of
the soul."[10] And, as Herbert Bell has written: "He was
too fastidious to talk of 'God's own country'; but he was
certain God had not made its equal."[11]

Despite all his later vigor, fire and direction, the days
did seem "long, very long" for the younger Tommy
Wilson, and sometimes curiously pointless. When he
was fourteen, his family left Augusta, Georgia, for
Columbia, South Carolina. To the old Doctor it was a
fine promotion. To his shy son it was the beginning of
a search for direction and purpose. For thirteen years he
would wander in quest of himself, often plagued with
near physical collapse, often doubting there was a direc-

tion at all. But for the moment he attended William Barnwell's little school for boys, just an ordinary student, "extremely dignified," a bit exotic: "He was not like other boys," one of his friends said. "He had a queer way of going off by himself."[12] He was preparing for college, perhaps only because it was the obvious thing to do. He hung a picture of the statesman Gladstone over his desk, but his family intended him for the church. There was a year at tiny Davidson College, where his haphazard preparation at home hindered his work in everything except English and oratory. One friend remembered him as being "witty, genial, superior, but languid." Another recalled him chiefly on the baseball field: "Tommy Wilson would be a good player if he weren't so damn lazy!"[13]

After a year, physically exhausted, he went home for good. And then there were fifteen months with his family, as they moved to Wilmington, North Carolina. These were months of study as the "old young man"[14] buried himself in books, reading some to prepare himself firmly for college work, reading more because his deep curiosity drove him to it. And then, in the fall of 1875, he went north to Princeton College, the ancient stronghold of Presbyterian education in America.

Princeton in 1875 was vigorous, growing intellectually, and Wilson found it almost too challenging. He was still deficient in Greek and mathematics. The first year was a struggle. The second was a revelation. He began to find his interests, to read widely on his own, to write some. And he determined to make himself an orator. At Princeton he became a master-debater; in the summers, he practiced his speeches in his father's empty church. But his would not be the oratory of the pulpit, for he had discovered politics and loved it—not the practical politics of elections and management, but the politics of statesmanship and skillful persuasion. Old Doctor Wilson was crushed; he would never master his grief that Tommy would not enter the pulpit. But Tommy was discovering that Woodrow Wilson must go his own way. Years later he would write: "The rule for every man is, not to depend on the education which other men prepare for him,—not even to consent to it; but to strive to see things as they are, and to be himself as he is. Defeat lies in self-surrender."[15]

He studied government on his own and published an essay, "Cabinet Government in the United States."[16] He learned to love the New York theater; he spent endless nights in arguments with college friends; he still attended church, regularly and with deep commitment, but he was in love with politics. Statesmanship, religion, and ambition were deeply entwined. With one friend he concluded a "solemn covenant" that, as he later described it, "we would school all our powers and passions for the work of establishing the principles we held in common; that we would acquire knowledge that we might have power; and that we would drill ourselves in all the arts of persuasion, but especially in oratory . . . that we might have facility in leading others into our ways of thinking and enlisting them in our purposes." One of his favorite rejoinders was: "When I meet you in the Senate, I'll argue that out with you." He carefully lettered some calling cards: "Thomas Woodrow Wilson, Senator from Virginia."[17] There was more than a joke in this.

From Princeton he went directly to the University of Virginia to study law. He explained his decision later to his wife: "The profession I chose was politics; the profession I entered was the law. I entered the one because I thought it would lead to the other. It was once the sure road; and Congress is still full of lawyers."[18] Much of it was a bore. He did not really love the law. Worse yet, Virginia seemed to assume that the mind was a "prolix gut" to be stuffed: "This excellent thing, the Law, gets as monotonous as that other immortal article of food, Hash."[19] But he could read the things he wanted, too; he could debate; and there was a chance to write a constitution for a student organization. This he always loved. Yet, by December, 1880, his health had broken again, and he returned home, discouraged and uneasy. He taught his younger brother Latin, practiced "elocution" daily, doggedly read law by himself. And, in the spring of 1882, at age twenty-five, he struck out to practice law.

He joined another young attorney, Edward I. Renick, in Atlanta. It proved a hopeless business. Renick & Wilson had few clients. There was time to study, and he was delighted with his endless reading in the English poets and in government and history. There was time to write a little. Old Joseph Wilson complained: "That boy down in Atlanta isn't making a cent."[20] And there was time, too, to fall in love with Ellen Axson.

Wilson saw her in church, when he visited cousins in Rome, Georgia: " . . . what a bright, pretty face; what splendid, mischievous, laughing eyes! I'll lay a wager that this demure little lady has lots of life and fun in her!" he later wrote of the experience.[21] He called at once on her clergyman-father, and met Ellen. This was in April, 1883. By September, they were engaged. Ellen was a hugely sympathetic, tender person. Her love of literature and painting supplemented his passion for politics. "I am the only one who can rest him," she once said. "My salvation is in being loved," he told her.[22] He could at once confide in her: "I am proud and wilful beyond all measure."[23] And again; "I have not yet proved myself possessed of any extraordinary talents; and I cannot claim the possession until I have put away certain discursive habits and brought all the powers I have into the line of some concentrated effort."[24]

Woodrow Wilson would have been married at once if it had been his to decide. But Wilson also believed, as he later wrote: "A man may be defeated by his own secondary successes."[25] And Ellen Axson had the wit and feeling to know that her man had at last, in 1883, ceased wandering. His plan was to abandon the law. That spring he had written a close friend: ". . . the practice of the law, when conducted for purposes of gain, is antagonistic to the best interests of the intellectual life. . . . The philosophical study of the law—which must be a pleasure to any thoughtful man—is a very different matter from its scheming and haggling practice."[26] Frustrated in the law, seeing clearly for the first time that an ordinary practice no longer led inexorably to the Senate, he had decided to make his contribution to politics an intellectual one. He must study further; and he would teach.

If it had not been for Ellen and for lack of money, he would have followed the familiar path of American intellectuals to one of the German universities. Instead he chose The Johns Hopkins University in Baltimore, new, patterned on the German model, the first American institution to make its chief business the development of graduate study. And Johns Hopkins was already a pioneer in the scholarly study of history and politics.

Later he could joke with Ellen: "Why is it that the mere fact of being connected with a college gives grave gentlemen of almost thirty leave to sing in public songs which, under other circumstances, they would not dream of singing? For my part, I rejoice in the chance. The older I get, the more does a boy's spirit seem to possess me and I chafe often not a little under the necessity of having to preserve the dignified demeanour of a man. That's the reason, you see, that I've determined to live at college all my life!"[27]

The University was sheer joy, despite his protests against "cut and dried courses" and his uneasy complaint: "I can't cram!"[28] There were great men on all sides. There was a fine library. He was soon encouraged to go his own way, and within a month was working on what would be his greatest book: Congressional Government. Ellen encouraged him. He must continue his work; he must complete it. He had written her: "I want to contribute to our literature what no American has ever contributed."[29] She would wait, as it turned out, for two long years.

But life at Baltimore was not all study and writing for the engaged Woodrow Wilson. There was fun that he felt free to share with his Ellen: "We had a very jolly time, and I am afraid that I was not as dignified as I might have been.... I had ... numerous frolics with the young lady aforesaid and had been three times locked up in the pantry, each time gaining my freedom by making demonstrations towards demolishing the larder...."[30] And later: "It may shock you—it ought to —but I'm afraid it will not, to learn that I have a reputation (?) amongst most of my kin and certain of my friends ... for being irrepressible, in select circles, as a maker of grotesque addresses from the precarious elevation of chair seats, as a wearer of all varieties of comic grimaces, as a simulator of sundry unnatural, burlesque styles of voice and speech, as a lover of farces—even as a dancer of the 'can-can'!"[31]

It was not the formal work of graduate school, but his own study of Congressional Government that dominated his life at Johns Hopkins. He wanted to produce something unique: "... studies in the philosophy of our institutions, not the abstract and occult, but the practical and suggestive.... I want to ... present their weakness and their strength without disguise."[32] This was unusual in the 1880s, when the first political scientists were bemusing themselves with abstract discussions of definitions and concepts that seemed to have little relation to the way government actually worked. And Wilson helped lead the way to the modern study of government as it actually is. He gave the nation one of its first scholarly and incisive pictures of Congress at work, although, curiously enough, he never went to see it, never talked with a congressman or practical politician. Working always from documents, he saw, nevertheless, more clearly than other scholars had. The manuscript was accepted for publication long before he had completed his graduate work. It made a stunning impact. Gamaliel Bradford of Harvard said: "... this is one of the most important books, dealing with political subjects which have ever issued from the American press."[33]

It was a realistic book, and yet Wilson's great guide was Walter Bagehot, whose studies of the English Constitution he venerated. And he tended to judge the American government by the standards set in England's parliamentary system. But he saw the peculiar structure of Congress clearly:

> I know not how better to describe our form of government in a single phrase than by calling it a government by the chairmen of the Standing Committees of Congress. This disintegrate ministry ... has many peculiarities. In the first place, it is made up of the elders of the assembly ... in the second place, it is constituted of selfish and warring elements ... in the third place, instead of being composed of the associated leaders of Congress, it consists of the dissociated heads of forty-eight "little legislatures". .... and, in the fourth place, it is instituted by appointment from Mr. Speaker, who is, by intention, the chief judicial, rather than the chief political, officer of the House.[34]

And he was critical: "Congress spends its time working, in sections, at preparing plans, instead of confining itself to what is for a numerous assembly manifestly the much more useful and proper function of debating and revising plans prepared beforehand for its consideration by a commission of skilled men, old in political practice and in legislative habit, whose official life is apart from its own, though dependent upon its will."[35]

The lack of continuity was a major problem: "... even Americans are not Presidents in their cradles. One cannot have too much preparatory training and experience who is to fill so high a magistracy.... Unhappily, however ... a President is dismissed almost as soon as he has learned the duties of his office, and a man who has served a dozen terms in Congress is a curiosity."[36]

But it was the whole system of federalism and separation of powers that drew his sharpest barbs:

> Each branch of the government is fitted out with a small section of responsibility, whose limited opportunities afford to the conscience of each man easy escapes. Every suspected culprit may shift the responsibility upon his fellows.... Moreover, it is impossible to deny that this division of authority and concealment of responsibility are calculated to subject the government to a very distressing paralysis in moments of emergency. ... Policy cannot be either prompt or straightforward when it must serve many masters. It must either equivocate, or hesitate, or fail altogether....
>
> If there be one principle clearer than another it is this: that in any business, whether of government or of mere merchandising, somebody must be trusted, in order that when things go wrong it may be quite plain who should be punished.[37]

This was strong medicine for a public nursed on a slavish admiration for the Founding Fathers and weaned on a strong national pride and patriotism. But young Woodrow Wilson knew that he was right; he would make no apologies. He would merely explain: "The charm of our constitutional ideal has now been long enough wound up to enable sober men who do not believe in political witchcraft to judge what it has accomplished, and is likely still to accomplish, without further winding. The Constitution is not honored by blind worship."[38]

It was a remarkable performance, almost too much so. Even before the book had been accepted for publication, Wilson had become so irritated with the routines of the University that he toyed with leaving without his degree. Within a single year there were teaching offers from Arkansas, Tulane, Michigan, and Bryn Mawr. His health was poor; he hated drudgery; he wanted to get married; he wanted to earn a living. But Johns Hopkins offered a Fellowship and, with Ellen's encouragement, he remained. Reluctantly he went through the motions of submitting his already published book as a doctoral dissertation that would give him the degree and make him "marketable."[39]

He accepted a professorship at Bryn Mawr, a new and tiny women's college. On June 24, 1885, he and his Ellen were married in the parlor of the old Presbyterian Manse in Savannah. There were two clergymen: Ellen's grandfather, and Woodrow's "incomparable father."

NOTES, CHAPTER 2

1. Ray Stannard Baker, **Woodrow Wilson: Life and Letters** (N.Y.: Doubleday, Page and Company, 1931), I, 28.
2. Ibid., p. 54.
3. Ibid., pp. 31–32, 35–36.
4. Ibid., pp. 37–38.
5. Ibid., p. 39.
6. Ibid., pp. 54–55.
7. William Allen White: **Woodrow Wilson: The Man, His Times, and His Task** (Boston: Houghton Mifflin Company, 1924), pp. 120–121.
8. Baker, **op. cit.**, p. 220.
9. Arthur Walworth, **Woodrow Wilson** (London: Longmans, Green and Company, 1958), I, 73.
10. Baker, **op. cit.**, pp. 207–08.
11. H. C. F. Bell, **Woodrow Wilson and the People** (N.Y.: Doubleday, Doran and Company, 1954), p. 9.

12. Baker, op. cit., p. 59.
13. Ibid., p. 74.
14. Ibid., p. 78.
15. Woodrow Wilson, Mere Literature, and Other Essays (Boston: Houghton Mifflin Company, 1896), p. 49.
16. International Review, August, 1879.
17. Baker, op. cit., pp. 103–04.
18. Ibid., p. 109.
19. Ibid., p. 116.
20. Ibid., p. 152.
21. Ibid., p. 162.
22. Ibid., p. 166.
23. Ibid., p. 165.
24. Ibid., p. 166.
25. Ibid., p. 247.
26. Ibid., p. 155.
27. Ibid., pp. 190–91.
28. Ibid., p. 182.
29. Ibid., p. 213.
30. Ibid., p. 192.
31. Ibid., p. 193.
32. Ibid., p. 213.
33. The Nation, February 12, 1885.
34. Woodrow Wilson, Congressional Government: A Study in American Politics (N.Y.: Meridian Books, Inc., 1956), pp. 82–83.
35. Ibid., p. 134.
36. Ibid., pp. 170–71.
37. Ibid., pp. 185–87.
38. Ibid., p. 215.
39. Baker, op. cit., p. 236.

3. "OLD MASTER"

Many years later, Ray Stannard Baker would write: "Nothing he does ... is an end in itself—but always for something beyond.... Fifty-four years of his life he spent in preparation, ten in living, three in dying."[1] There was always a certain uneasiness about Wilson the teacher, a faint and general restlessness, a yearning for influence, public service and prominence. But for the moment, he gave himself with a driving energy to his teaching and his writing.

At Bryn Mawr there was work enough for the most demanding appetite. Like young professors in all ages, he slaved far into the nights hammering out the formal, carefully styled papers that gave him an early reputation as a fascinating lecturer. He had to teach new fields and learn as he taught. He made an impression of dignity; he was known for his sharp wit; he performed well in faculty meetings. Home life was a joy; and there were two daughters born at Bryn Mawr, Margaret and Jessie. He wrote for money as well as to make a professional contribution. He lectured on the side at Johns Hopkins to piece out his salary of fifteen hundred dollars. But there were frustrations. He was "hungry for a class of men." He complained that teaching women "relaxes one's mental muscle." He thought them intellectually inferior. And there was more: "I don't see how a literary life can be built up on foundations of undergraduate instruction. That instruction ... keeps you on the dusty, century-travelled highroads of every subject, from which you get no outlooks except those that are catalogued and vulgarized in every guide-book."[2]

He was delighted to go to Wesleyan University in the fall of 1888. There would be men, a higher salary, a fine library, inspiring colleagues. He was a great lecturer there, but less successful in the give and take of class discussion. He was determined to "master" his classes. His own standards were relentless; he was endlessly dissatisfied with his work. But he was well liked. He entered into student life here as he never had before, helping to coach the football team, cheering them on as he waved his umbrella from the sidelines. He was an inspiring chapel speaker. But his real zest went into the Wesleyan House of Commons, which he initiated, a student debating society structured along the lines of the British parliament. His enthusiasm was infectious. Students took hold of this practice in formal government with real fun.

His writing pace increased. He often escaped to a little room in the chapel tower, where he could pull up a ladder behind him and work, undisturbed, by candle-light. In the spring of 1889, he finished a textbook, The State. He started at once on his first piece of formal history, Division and Reunion. He tried literary essays. He watched national politics closely. His articles proved him a conservative, despite his "new" look at Congress years before. He thought things must move slowly; he admired immensely the precedents of the British tradition:

> The government which we founded one hundred years ago was no type of an experiment in advanced democracy . . . . it was simply an adaptation of English constitutional government. . . . we shall preserve our institutions in their integrity and efficiency only so long as we keep true in our practice to the traditions from which our first strength was derived.[3]

"Monarchies may be made," he said, "but democracies must grow." And he warned: "America is now sauntering through her resources and through the mazes of her politics with easy nonchalance; but presently there will come a time when she will be surprised to find herself grown old,—a country crowded, strained, perplexed,—when she will be obliged to fall back upon her conservatism . . . trust her best, not her average, members."[4]

He was happy at Wesleyan, but he found it "not . . . sufficiently stimulating."[5] And he knew now that he wanted to work in political science, not history. He was delighted at the chance to return to Princeton, in the fall of 1890, as a professor. He would lecture now on the law and on public administration. Princeton was growing and changing from a great stronghold of traditional Presbyterianism into a greater, many-sided modern university. Here Wilson found challenge and scope for his restless mind.

He continued to teach in his successful fashion, demanding of both student and instructor. He lectured avidly, at Johns Hopkins, at New York Law School, and throughout the country. The pace was killing—twenty-five off-campus lectures each spring term, and others in the fall. There was money in this, and also the much-coveted feeling that he might influence public affairs. While he was at Princeton he was offered the presidency of seven different universities. With it all, he made himself a power on the Princeton campus. A strong voice in its faculty meetings, a skillful fighter against the stuffy orthodoxy of his older colleagues, he led the battle for a student honor system and sought everywhere to breathe new life into the Princeton classroom.

He still wrote history, a biography of George Washington and a massive History of the American People. But this was clearly not his forte. His research was not dogged enough to root out the little inaccuracies; his literary style often carried him away. He confessed himself that he wrote his big work "to learn history."[6] He could not stand with the master craftsmen of his generation.

His most incisive writing of the period was in the science of government. Here his concern and his imagination helped him to break the stuffy abstractions and cut through to new ideas. He flailed out at the structural weaknesses and mediocrity of American government, at the lack of sound leadership. Much of this thinking was summed up in his book Constitutional Government in the United States, a series of essays. He balked at the old concept of checks and balances: " . . . government is not a machine, but a living thing. It falls, not under the theory of the universe, but under the theory of organic life. . . . No living thing can have its organs offset against each other as checks, and live."[7] Government must grow and change; it must conform to the needs of the human beings it serves.

Much as he loved the law, he could proclaim, courageously for that time, that there was no such thing as "a government of laws and not of men." "Constitute them how you will, governments are always governments of men, and no part of any government is better than the men to whom that part is intrusted."[8] He had caught by 1909 the picture of a changing America: "Ideas, motives, standards of conduct, subtle items of interest, airs from out every region travel with the news, with the passenger on the express train, with the merchant's goods and the farmer's grain. Invisible shuttles of suggestion weave the thoughts and purposes of separate communities together, and a nation which will some day know itself as a single community is a-making in the warp and woof of the fabric. The extraordinary way in which the powers of the federal government have been suffered to grow in recent years is evidence of the process."[9]

But he was no progressive, and he was certainly no radical. He could warn: "... there are natural limits beyond which such a development cannot go, and our state governments are likely to become, not less, but more vital units in our system as the natural scope and limits of their powers are more clearly and permanently established."[10]

Yet above all he remained a nationalist and an American. Nothing was more revealing of his ideas than his admiration for Lincoln:

> He never ceased to be a common man: that was his source of strength. But he was a common man with ... a genius for things American, for insight into the common thought. ... The whole country is summed up in him: the rude Western strength, tempered with shrewdness and a broad and human wit; the Eastern conservatism, regardful of law and devoted to fixed standards of duty. He even understood the South, as no other Northern man of his generation did.[11]

Despite all this activity, Wilson remained in poor health, constantly courting the breakdown that might bring disaster to his career. And he remained the tense, driving personality, who needed the support of confidants and the unending love of his family. At Princeton, as in Middletown and Bryn Mawr, Ellen Wilson maintained a "quiet place" for him, reassured him, buffed gently at the rough edges of his temper. Arthur Walworth has described their life at Princeton:

> When there was occasion to meet strangers ... Wilson often turned shy and made excuses. Ellen would have to coax him; but, once introduced, he enjoyed himself and dominated the talk. ... In one breath he could be witty, ridiculous and profound. He could listen well, too, to talk worthy of his mettle. Emotional

reactions showed in his face, and usually he could respond with an anecdote or comment that was pat. When his mind worked at its highest pitch, he dazzled even those who knew him best.

His powers of talk ran riot in the presence of ladies whom he thought "charming and conversable"; and it often happened that he thought the more charming the more conversable. He liked to air his literary fancies before what he regarded as the "deeper sensibilities" and "finer understanding" of intelligent women. He particularly enjoyed the "lightly turned laughter" of ladies of the South. When he discovered feminine charm, he would write to his Ellen about it with the ardor of a prospector striking gold. Like his father, he enjoyed playing the lion with women who could crack the whip of conversation sharply and deftly. But at a hint of sensuality, heaviness or petty jealousies he revolted. There were only a few women quick enough in word and understanding to hold his friendship through the years.

Feeling that she was not by nature "gamesome," Ellen Wilson encouraged and shared her husband's friendships with brilliant ladies. And his gallant adventures served only to raise the pedestal on which he kept his Ellen enthroned. ("I am not a fellow to be imposed upon, Madam, by superficial charms or a first impression. Very few people, alas! wear well with me; but your charm deepens with every year.") They kept their covenant, made before their marriage, to be quite open with each other in everything. All their treasures were held in common—books, money, pleasures, and friends, both men and women. Their opinions often differed, but even their closest relatives never heard them quarrel. His letters courted her constantly. Sometimes she would read them to her daughters, occasionally skipping a page or two saying with a smile, "This part is sacred." . . .

Life in the household moved with a smooth rhythm. Fresh flowers were kept in their bedroom. Nothing was

out of place; not so much as one stocking was allowed
to lie on the floor. Ellen Wilson made dresses for herself
and her girls and one year took pride in spending less for
clothes than her husband spent for books. She trained
two white servants, who stood loyally by her for decades.
Drawling softly, she imparted to the cook the secrets of
the Southern dishes that her husband relished. Sitting at
lunch with him after a morning of proofreading, they
would make a game of their labors. "I dare not have the
blues!" she wrote to a girlhood friend. "If I am just a
little sky blue he immediately becomes blue-black!"[12]

Aside from Ellen Wilson, his favorite companion was
his typewriter. It would go with him to the White House
and to Versailles. They had fought many a battle together, for Wilson was no wanderer at work. Tough with
himself, when he could not make the right word come,
he later confessed: "I never stir from my key-board. I
sit and hold my hand up and concentrate until the word
comes!"[13] But in the disciplined Wilson household,
there was a time for everything, for work and for fun:

In his composition, as in his professional
appointments, the professor was a clock of regularity.
... He never demanded absolute quiet in the house
while he worked; but when quarreling broke out, he
would call the girls to his study, ask them what the
trouble was, and explain gently the rights and wrongs
of the case. Once, when the little Wilsons and Cleve-
lands fought with neighbors of Republican heritage, he
said: "You must never quarrel about religion or politics.
Both are very private, and you will never change anyone's mind." When the children tried to divide the world
among themselves, he arranged straws for them to draw.
When the roll top of their father's desk slammed, the
lock clicked and the youngsters heard a soft whistle and
a jangling of keys, they knew then that their choicest

playfellow might join them for merry-making. They voted their father "the world's greatest orator" and thought him capable of being president of the United States or of anything else. . . .

Growing older, the Wilson girls sat up evenings with the family in the central living room, where their father would prance and jig with them. Or he might take off a drunk, or a stuffy, monocled Englishman. . . . Dressing up for a charade, he would put on a lady's hat and a feather boa, wrap himself in a long velvet curtain, hold one hand high for a "social" handshake, and gush in high falsetto in burlesque of a grand dame. Sometimes it would be the "heavy villain" of melodrama, or a Fourth of July orator who gestured with his legs instead of his arms. . . . Often his clear tenor would pour out "The Kerry Dance" or "The Duke of Plaza-Toro," a Scottish ballad or an old hymn of the kirk. He liked quaint sayings such as "Good Lord deliver us from witches and warlords and from things that say woo-oo in the night."

On New Year's Eve, in Scottish fashion, the clan gathered in the dining room, drank a toast, sang "Auld Lang Syne," standing each with one foot on a chair, and the other on the table, and then ran to open the front door so that the old year might go and the new year enter. . . . Sometimes he feared the very momentum of his own spirits, once confessing that he "dared not let himself go because he did not know where to stop."[14]

There was also fatigue and illness, particularly the painful neuritis that cramped his writing hand and made him practice like a boy before he could manage a fair script again. Travel always helped, and he went to England and Scotland twice in the 1850s, worshipping at the shrines of the romantic literature he and Ellen loved so well, searching out the homes and churches of his ancestors. Yet there was also the old restlessness. In

January, 1902, he confessed: "I was forty-five three weeks ago, and between forty-five and fifty-five, I take it, is when a man ought to do the work into which he expects to put most of himself. I love history.... But, after all, I was born a politician, and must be at the task for which ... I have all these years been in training. If I finish at fifty-five, shall I not have fifteen richly contemplative years left, if the Lord be good to me! But, then, the Lord may prefer to be good to the world!"[15]

In June there came another step in the unfolding, half-seen pathway of ambition. He was chosen president of his university. He didn't expect it; few on campus did. It was strangely done. There were problems in the university; the old president, Francis Patton, suddenly announced his resignation and suggested Wilson. A motion for his election was made—and, astoundingly enough, a unanimous one. He was well-known; he was a leader; his speeches had made him a favorite with alumni; his articles and books had given him a national reputation among scholars. And he had ideas about education. As he had viewed the scattered accretion of new courses, odds and ends of new disciplines that had grown upon the colleges with the vast expansion of learning, he had complained eight years earlier that reorganization was needed. The curriculum must be unified and brought into some kind of logical arrangement. "The graduates of our universities no longer go forth with a common training which will enable them to hold together in a community of thought."[16] Now he would have his chance to lead this reorganization, and also to practice the arts about which he had written endlessly as a "literary politician."

Princeton wanted leadership, and Wilson had a plan before he had been inaugurated. He challenged the Trustees to make it a real university, as great or greater than Harvard and Yale. They accepted the challenge. He gave them a blueprint: a Graduate School, a Law School, a Natural History Museum, a School of Electrical Engineering, all with a six-and-a-half-million-dollar price tag attached. And, more important, he would have a complete reorganization of the undergraduate college, its curriculum, buildings, staff, and spirit. He told a distinguished group of Manhattan alumni: "Gentlemen, we have dreamed a dream in Princeton."[17] The dream envisaged a community of scholars, professors and students, and above all young preceptors, serving their apprenticeship for college teaching, a lively group, constantly changing, acting as intimate tutors for the undergraduates, knowing their minds closely, being constantly with them. Like the English system from which the idea was drawn, there would be residential quadrangles to house the scholars, tutors and students together, to build an intimate atmosphere of intellectual endeavor. Wilson would choose the young preceptors himself; these were the people who would breathe new life into the ancient campus.

He was a vigorous, outlandish money-raiser: "I suspect there are gentlemen in this room who are going to give me two millions and a quarter to get rid of me. They will be able to get rid of me in no other way that I know of."[18] This kind of inspired performance helped smooth the way with his faculty. Wilson personally guided the faculty meetings that reorganized the curriculum. He proved his mettle. Later he could report to Ellen: ". . . we began a group of individuals and ended a body agreed in common counsel. . . . It took only four meetings to put it through all its stages. . . . It is not, as it stands now, exactly the scheme I at the outset proposed, but it is much better."[19]

The man had courage, and he could lead an enthusiastic team as few others could, but also he could be tough when principles were at stake. The stories of his sharp integrity multiplied. For example, he once said to one of the innumerable pleaders for special consideration in admission: "I want you to understand that if the angel Gabriel applied for admission to Princeton University and could not pass the entrance examinations, he would not be admitted." When a mother pleaded her poor health as an excuse to prevent her son's dismissal for cheating: "Madam, . . . if I had to choose between your life or my life or anybody's life and the good of this college, I should choose the good of the college."[20]

The first great victory came with the reorganized curriculum; the second in 1905, when the preceptorial system went into operation. But as the remainder of the program unfolded, there grew problems and distractions on all sides. Illness was one. In May, 1906, a stroke took the sight of his left eye, affected his shoulder and leg. His wife confided to a friend: "He has lived too tensely . . . It is an awful thing—dying by inches,—and incurable."[21] They took him to England, where rest restored part of his vision and all of his determination. He would not be kept down by hardening of the arteries. In September, he was back at work.

And there was politics. Already Wilson had been discovered by a political promoter. When he addressed the Lotus Club in New York in February, 1906, George Harvey astoundingly proposed to the distinguished audience that he should be nominated for the presidency. Harvey was a journalist who knew everybody. Most important at the moment, he knew the Wall Street bankers, including J. P. Morgan. And he was in a position to shape public opinion as head of the Harper publishing firm and as editor of Harper's Weekly. But, as Arthur Link concludes:

> . . . apparently only Wilson took Harvey seriously; he was emotionally stirred by Harvey's speech and hastened to write the editor that it was "most delightful to have such thoughts uttered about me." . . . Harvey,

on the contrary, was in dead earnest. On March 10, *Harper's Weekly* carried a full-page picture of Wilson on its front page, and Harvey reprinted his Lotus Club address and assured the *Weekly's* readers that his speech was not "a hasty or ill-considered utterance...."

Harvey obviously was sending up trial balloons, and he must have been gratified when newspapers all over the country discussed his proposal of nominating Wilson for President and when many editors gave the idea enthusiastic endorsement. It was natural that most of the commendations of Wilson's candidacy came from conservative editors.... as a midwestern editor wrote, "The nomination of Mr. Wilson would be a good thing for the country as betokening a return of his party to historic party ideals and first principles, and a sobering up after the radical 'crazes' "

... Had Harvey deliberately attempted to enlist the support of a more typical group of political and economic conservatives, who represented better the very things against which the progressives had long been struggling, he could not have been more successful. Wall Street bankers, utilities magnates, conservative editors, representing these interests, even Cleveland's secretary of the treasury, hated by agrarian radicals for his success in maintaining the gold standard—all of these were among Wilson's early supporters. Wilson observed this singular fact... and commented favorably upon it.[22]

But the major distractions would appear on his own campus. As the reformer must, Wilson soon faced a growing opposition. He proved less able to mend the frictions than to lead the first sallies of an enthusiastic crusade. The friction soon concentrated on the issues of the quadrangles and the Graduate College. The latter was the special project of Dean Andrew F. West, with whom Wilson frequently clashed over policy. West was a strong man in his own right. But Wilson too had advocated the Graduate College, frequently and ardently. While West worked out his plans, Wilson pressed his own crusade for the quadrangles, which would divide students in the university vertically into small residential groups, each with its quota of seniors, juniors, sophomores, freshmen, and graduate students. The first major hurdle would be Princeton's exclusive upper-class eating clubs. Deeply entrenched, traditional, jealous of their prerogatives, they held the firm loyalty of their alumni. They must be gradually displaced, if the quadrangle plan were to work. And Wilson objected to them anyway, distracting as they did from the intellectual life of the campus, introducing as they did artificial social distinctions and tensions.

In the spring of 1907, Wilson received the approval of his trustees. But there were sharp objections from the alumni. In the fall, the faculty divided vigorously over the proposals, with some of Wilson's oldest friends leading the opposition. In October, the trustees revoked their decision and left the matter for further study. Wilson was mortified and incensed. He decided on an appeal to the alumni, and even to the nation. Through the winter he traveled widely to talk with alumni clubs, hammering over and over the theme he had first raised in 1896, "Princeton in the Service of the Nation." He saw it more and more as a struggle against artificial social discrimination, as a fight for democracy. As wealthy supporters and trustees began to take the other side, he spoke frequently of the struggle against entrenched privilege and power within the university and the nation. He nearly collapsed at midwinter and had to go for a month's rest in Bermuda.

Now it was a personal vendetta. Sometimes the kernel of the issues was all but lost among the husks of personal bitterness. Faculty, alumni, trustees were disastrously divided; Woodrow Wilson as a man and a leader lay at the heart of the division. Unanimous choice of

1902, he was by 1908 an embittered partisan in a warring camp. The next two years would be agony. The battle of the quadrangles carried over into the fight for a graduate school. Wilson sharply opposed gifts for a graduate college at the edge of the campus. This would segregate the graduate students to everyone's detriment. The school must be the physical and intellectual center of university life. He opposed the plush living arrangements being planned for these scholars. He suspected the men of wealth who were supporting the plan. Above all, he suspected the ambitions of Dean West. Throughout 1909 and 1910, the maneuvering between West and Wilson became more devious and more bitter. Wilson again appealed to the country. At Pittsburgh in April, 1910, his fervor carried him away:

> What we cry out against is that a handful of conspicuous men have thrust cruel hands among the heartstrings of the masses of men upon whose blood and energy they are subsisting. . . . I have dedicated every power that there is in me to bring the colleges that I have anything to do with to an absolutely democratic regeneration in spirit.[23]

And there was a broader significance in all of this. Wilson himself was applying his concept of the Princeton struggle to national affairs. As early as the spring of 1908, he had blasted out against "predatory wealth in stock markets." And, as Arthur Walworth tells it:

> . . . in January of 1910, he told bankers assembled in the Waldorf-Astoria Hotel that they had allowed their minds to narrow and took no interest in the small businessmen. "You don't know the country or what is going on in it and the country doesn't trust you," he charged. "You are not interested in the development of the country, but in what has been devel-

oped." At the head table J. P. Morgan puffed at his cigar and looked glum.[24]

"No speeches of Wilson's life had in them more fire than those of the early months of 1910," said Ray Stannard Baker. "They bespoke his own internal wrath, the turbulence of balked purpose."[25] For Wilson was facing the kind of defeat that neither his pride nor his concept of duty could accept. The desperate, muddy struggle was strangely, but perhaps mercifully, resolved by the death, in May of 1910, of an old man in Salem, Massachusetts. His will, it appeared, provided a fortune for Princeton—perhaps as much as eight or ten million dollars. It was designed partly for the Graduate College. Dean Andrew West was made an executor of the estate. West with control of ten million dollars was too much for even Wilson to fight. He held up the telegram from his old enemy, the Dean, and said to his wife sadly: "We have beaten the living; but we cannot fight the dead. The game is up."[26]

It was only a question of time, and timing. Princeton was much too small for both a West and a Wilson. Neither man could compromise gracefully his principles or his pride. Wilson was already well on the way to the governorship of New Jersey. When the election came, and the Princeton trustees received his resignation, there were few regrets.

Students had proved poor prophets that June commencement, when they had sung their traditional popsongs:

> Here's to Woodrow, King divine,
> Who rules this place along with Fine.
> We have no fear he'll leave this town
> To try for anybody's crown.[27]

NOTES, CHAPTER 3

1. Ray Stannard Baker, Woodrow Wilson: Life and Letters (N.Y.: Doubleday, Page and Company, 1927), I, 247–49.
2. Ibid., pp. 290, 292, 295.
3. Woodrow Wilson, An Old Master, and Other Political Essays (N.Y.: Charles Scribners' Sons, 1893), pp. 104, 121.
4. Baker, op. cit., pp. 312, 314.
5. Ibid., p. 325.
6. Ibid., p. 247.
7. Woodrow Wilson, Constitutional Government in the United States (N.Y.: Columbia University Press, 1908), p. 56.
8. Ibid., p. 17.
9. Ibid., p. 47.
10. Ibid., p. 49.
11. H. C. F. Bell, Woodrow Wilson and the People (N.Y.: Doubleday, Doran and Company, 1945), p. 9.
12. Arthur Walworth, Woodrow Wilson (London: Longmans, Green and Company, 1958), pp. 70–72.
13. Baker, op. cit., II, 44.
14. Walworth, op. cit., I, 77–78
15. Baker, op. cit., p. 120.
16. Ray Stannard Baker and William E. Dodd (eds.), The Public Papers of Woodrow Wilson (N.Y.: Harper and Brothers, 1925–27), I, 248.
17. Baker, op. cit., II, 147.
18. Ibid., pp. 147–48.
19. Walworth, op. cit., I, 88.
20. Baker, op. cit., II, 151–52.
21. Walworth, op. cit., p. 98.
22. Arthur S. Link, Wilson: The Road to the White House (Princeton, N.J.: Princeton University Press, 1947), pp. 99–100, 102.
23. Ibid., pp. 83–84.
24. Walworth, op. cit., p. 135.
25. Baker, op. cit., III, 40.
26. Ibid., II, 346.
27. William Allen White, Woodrow Wilson: The Man, His Times, and His Tasks (Boston: Houghton Mifflin Company, 1924), p. 193.

4. PROGRESSIVE IN THE MAKING

Later Wilson would write gaily: "... as compared with the college politician, the real article seems like an amateur."[1] He had reason to know. Yet he faced the prospects of a political career in 1910 with serious disadvantages. In fact, he knew little about practical politics in the outside world. Of ward heelers, patronage, and vote-getting he was virtually innocent. What he did know, he hated. He had once told his readers: "The boss—a man elected by no votes, preferred by no open process of choice, occupying no office of responsibility —makes himself a veritable tyrant among us, and seems to cheat us of self-government."[2] Like the muckrakers of his age, he was against the sins of politics, but he had as little as they to offer in their place. And there was another problem, which Herbert Bell has described clearly: "Wilson had thought and written and lectured a good deal about the people. . . . But, more than many men of his profession, he had lived in the academic shades. . . . He had given the people his head but not his heart. Their hopes and fears, their joys and griefs, were outside his range."[3]

His views were evolving. He still distrusted violent change, extreme ideas; progress must come slowly and from deep roots. But there was also a strain of nineteenth-century liberalism, which stressed freedom of thought and intellectual combat, freedom to make up one's own mind and change one's mind. Wilson wrote of one instance: "For fifteen years I taught my classes *that the initiative and referendum wouldn't work. I can prove it now—but the trouble is they do!"*[4]

But this changing, uncertain character of Wilson's deep political philosophy might be an advantage under the circumstances. The strange thing would be the fact that the very bosses he had so vigorously assailed would be his sponsors in politics.

The organization men knew that only by enticing independent and progressive voters in large numbers could they avoid more impotent and jobless years. The conservatives were anxious to draw such voters away from Bryan, Roosevelt and La Follette, all very dangerous to established ways in business and in politics. . . . Wilson, loyal to his party as he was to any organization or group which could lay legitimate claim to him, made speeches and wrote articles in which both reformers and conservatives could find things to approve.

Take, for example, a speech he made at the Waldorf, in November, 1904, when stinging realization of his party's latest humiliation at the polls gave him the emotional stimulus he needed for the best of his performances. He called for the rejuvenation of the party; but what he demanded was revolt. "Unsafe" leaders (one could supply the name of Bryan instantly) were to be driven out: "It is now high time that the South which has endured most by way of humiliation at the hands of this faction should demand that it be utterly and once for all thrust out of Democratic counsels. . . . the historic party has always stood for moderation in affairs and a careful use of the powers of the federal government in the interest of the whole people. . . ."

That was exactly the sort of language that the conservative and much-organized Democrats of New York liked best. . . . It was not the sort of language to be expected from a potential leader of progressives and liberals; but the left-wing Democrats must have realized that he was not so much denouncing Bryan's extreme liberalism as his quackery. Many of them . . . may . . . have remembered passages from an article called "Democracy and Efficiency," which he had published in the *Atlantic* three years before. He had struck at privilege, boasting the way in which America had taught the world that every government should look after the welfare of all its people, not that of any special class.[5]

He might have alienated J. P. Morgan, but there were many men of wealth who still respected this fighting crusader who carried the comfortable dignity of a Presbyterian parson. And his Princeton crusade made it easy for progressives to see in him a new champion. For Wilson himself, there had been little choice, little debate. He might joke about Finley Peter Dunne's warning: "If anny Dimmicrat has a stiddy job he'd better shtick to it."[6] He might be concerned about Ellen's fear for their home life and his health, and her distaste for the crudeness and dirt of practical politics. But every thread of personality led to the State House. There was duty—the man who had called for reform for twenty-five years could hardly now refuse to lead. There was intellectual commitment—to make a great contribution to American statesmanship. There was his pride of achievement—grievously shocked in the miserable climax at Princeton. It could be saved only in a new and different arena. There was ambition, lifelong, deep, impossible to submerge. And there was a kind of fateful, martyr feeling. In 1908, he told a close friend that he might have a chance for the presidency and solemnly proclaimed: "The life of the next Democratic President will be hell and it would probably kill me." He told an ancient aunt a little later: "If I am nominated, I'll be elected, and, if I'm elected, I won't come out of the White House alive."[7]

But Wilson's practical dilemma was deep. It was the bosses who offered the nomination; it was the progressives who held him in suspicion. Wilson would have to make a bridge between them, and it would be difficult at best, given the reputation of his sponsors. The most important was James Smith, Jr. Baker has described him succinctly:

Smith was an extraordinary character. A Chesterfield of a man! Six feet tall, immaculately groomed, crowned with a silk hat, he was the veritable pattern of suave distinction that befitted a man of power and place. He had "the face of an innocent child." His rise had been characteristically American. He had begun as a grocer's clerk, had become the owner of two newspapers, the director of several manufacturing plants, and finally a bank president. Though without much formal education himself, having come from the family of an Irish Catholic immigrant, he sent three sons to Princeton, and had come on several occasions under Wilson's spell. He was of the genuine breed of the city boss—"generous to a fault," dispensing the money he received from great corporations or from the liquor interests among the little leaders and henchmen upon whom he depended to carry their precincts for the organization. He was recognized, generally as political overlord by Nugent of Newark and Bob Davis of Jersey City, themselves autocratic local bosses. He was on friendly terms with the equally influential, though more secretive bosses of the Republican Party. Both were controlled by, or worked in harmony with, business leaders, lobbyists, "Black-Horse Cavalry," who sought privileges and immunities at Trenton. He was as powerful in New Jersey as Richard Croker of Tammany Hall in New York —more powerful than elected senators or governors. He was, in short, besides being a human and likeable man, a shining exemplification of all that was worst, most hopeless, in American political life.[8]

The other sponsor, more remote, behind the scenes, was George Harvey. Harvey's pen was powerful, but his personality could gain few friends for Wilson. " 'Fascinatingly ugly,' one observer had thought him, a man arrogant, with defiant inferiority, carrying upon a scrawny neck a death's-head whose eye sockets were dark as inkwells and whose thin tight lips smiled superciliously."[9] The problem was more complicated because progressives had already raised rebellion within Republican ranks and were waving the banner of the "New Idea" in Jersey politics.

But in this deep challenge, Wilson's old integrity weighed the balance over:

> On July 12, Harvey invited influential politicians and a corporation attorney to meet Wilson at luncheon at the Lawyer's Club in New York. . . . When Smith, thinking it essential that he have the support of the liquor interest, bade a lieutenant to sound out the candidate on this issue, Wilson did not mince words. "I am not a prohibitionist," he declared. "I believe that the question is outside of politics. I believe in home rule, and that the issue should be settled by local option in each community." When reminded that Smith and the party had been fighting against local option for years, he said: "Well, that is my attitude and my conviction. I cannot change it." Later he gave the same reply to the Anti-Saloon League, and it coincided with what he had written some twenty years before: "The state ought not to supervise private morals."[10]

But all of this was private and off the record. Wilson wanted nothing that would make it appear that he sought the nomination. He broke his silence only once, when he felt his record on labor had been misconstrued. The chief trouble would be in Smith's own ranks. James Nugent privately cursed about that "damn dude from Princeton."[11] Others were cool. And Smith himself may have been uneasy. But he already had the private, elaborately relayed assurance of Wilson: "I would be perfectly willing to assure Mr. Smith that I would not, if elected Governor, set about 'fighting and breaking down the existing Democratic organization and replacing it with one of my own.' . . . I should deem myself inexcusable for antagonizing it, so long as I was left absolutely free in the matter of measures and men."[12]

Wilson understood neither the organization nor the full meaning of his promise. But, for the moment, it was enough. Smith's machine rolled inexorably over the protests from lieutenants and outlying satellites to prepare the steamrollered convention. Later, William Allen White described the mob scene from which Wilson's political career emerged:

At two-thirty, hot, red-faced, full of heavy food and too much rebellious liquor, came the delegates stamping into the close, stuffy opera house. Tension made their hearts beat quicker. Their nerves were raw. A thousand fans fluttered. Men let down their wet suspenders and unbuttoned their sweaty shirt fronts. The nominating speeches began. The speech for Wilson was greeted with enthusiasm; that was a part of the machine programme. Enthusiasm is one of the things in a convention that a machine always can produce. . . . At the end of . . . [the] speech, in the midst of the mechanical demonstration for Wilson, John J. Crandall, an old and picturesque lawyer in the Atlantic City delegation, arose to protest the nomination of Wilson. The Atlantic City delegation was divided. . . . A man slumping in a chair near by woke up, hearing the row in the Atlantic City delegation, rose, and tried to pull down Crandall.

The waking delegate failed. He tried again. Crandall, white with rage, broke his cane across the head of the Wilson man, and as the crowd howled its joy at the fight, the claquers went on with the demonstration. It was a great day for Mr. Wilson's "thoughtful Democrats." . . .

. . . J. Thompson Baker, unknown to those controlling the convention, rose and began to make "a man who" speech, setting forth glowingly the virtues of his candidate, but withholding his name. The tired, sweaty, nervous delegates rebelled. "Name him!" they cried, and, "Put 'im out!" and other disrespectful yowlings. The little old, bald-headed man, hurt and scared, answered, "His name is Woodrow Wilson." The tension snapped. The convention roared, then howled, then organized a demonstration of its own, and the opposition knew by the spontaneity of the clamor that Wilson had the votes. They came in the first ballot: Smith's 800 prediction was only a little short. Wilson got 747 and a half, the opposition got 665 and a half. Wilson had forty more than a majority, a narrow squeak![13]

Joseph Tumulty, later Wilson's secretary, has explained the dilemma of the progressive Democrats: "Every progressive Democrat in the Convention was opposed to the nomination of the Princetonian, and every stand-patter and Old Guardsman was in favour of Woodrow Wilson. . . . The Convention is at an end. . . . the delegates, bitter and resentful, are about to withdraw. . . . when the clerk of the Convention . . . announces in a most dramatic fashion: 'We have just received word that Mr. Wilson, the candidate for the governorship, and the next President of the United States . . . is now on his way to the Convention.' Excellent stage work . . . the deft hand behind this clever move was that of Colonel Harvey. . . ."[14]

It had not been easy for the bosses. There had been

moments during their long night's work of preparation when they feared it might not go. Once Harvey and Smith had found themselves wondering how Wilson would take defeat. But at Princeton that afternoon, Wilson met his escorts calmly, confidently. Now he

. . . appeared upon the stage of the crowded Opera House—a slim, well-knit figure still wearing his golf jacket. . . .

It was a speech wholly without the familiar oratorical clap-trap, but delivered with that peculiar sense of direct contact with his hearers which was the essence of Wilson's genius.

"As you know, I did not seek this nomination. It has come to me absolutely unsolicited, with the consequence that I shall enter upon the duties of the office of Governor, if elected, with absolutely no pledges of any kind to prevent me from serving the people of the State with singleness of purpose. Not only have no pledges of any kind been given, but none have been proposed or desired. . . .

"The future is not for parties 'playing politics,' but for measures conceived in the largest spirit, pushed by parties whose leaders are statesmen not demagogues, who love, not their offices but their duty and their opportunity for service. We are witnessing a renaissance of public spirit, a reawakening of sober public opinion, a revival of the power of the people, the beginning of an age of thoughtful reconstruction that makes our thought hark back to the great age in which democracy was set up in America. With the new age we shall show a new spirit. We shall serve justice and candour and all things that make for right. . . ."

. . . It was not so much what the man said, as it was the sense of power and of sincerity that he gave. . . . He literally brought around his bitterest opponents. Young Tumulty and his friends were converted on the spot.... "old John Crandall, of Atlantic City, ... a bitter, implacable foe of Woodrow Wilson ... was waving his hat and cane in the air, and yelling at the top of his voice, 'I am sixty-five years old, and still a damn fool!' "[15]

It was a vigorous and dangerous campaign. At first Wilson found it difficult to manage. He confessed: "I have been asking audiences all my life to accept certain ideas and principles, and I have a curious hesitation about asking anyone to vote for me. It smacks of a personal appeal when I want to bring about a change of view."[16] It was a bitter campaign, as Wilson, who sought to reform government, found himself attacked as an unwitting tool of the bosses. But his old skill, integrity and good humor asserted themselves. As Baker has noted:

He began to strike off the kind of phrases that stick and cling in the popular mind ... "corporation joy-riding" ... "pitiless publicity".... He had extraordinary aptness in swift repartee. Speaking of "political optimists," someone in the audience called out, "What is an optimist?"

"An optimist," he responded instantly, "is a man who is able to make pink lemonade out of the lemons handed him by his enemies in politics."[17]

He reached a climax of the campaign when he decided to meet George L. Record, New Jersey's sharpest and most popular progressive, on his own ground. Record posed questions for Wilson to answer, and Wilson did, publicly, at length, with great political skill. Typical of the score or more was Record's question 14:

"Do you admit that the boss system exists as I have described it? If so how do you propose to abolish it?"

Wilson's answer:

"Of course, I admit it. Its existence is notorious. I have made it my business for many years to observe and understand that system, and I hate it as thoroughly as I understand it. You are quite right in saying that the system is bi-partisan; that it constitutes 'the most dangerous condition in the public life of our state and nation to-day;' and that it has virtually, for the time being, 'destroyed representative government and in its place set up a government of privilege.' I would propose to abolish it by the above reforms, by the election of men who will refuse to submit to it and bend all their energies to break it up, and by pitiless publicity. . . . I should deem myself forever disgraced should I in even the slightest degree cooperate in any such system or any such transactions as you describe in your characterization of the 'boss' system. . . ."[18]

At the beginning of the campaign, Wilson had seemed a wishy-washy front man for the bosses. At the end, his image was firm. He was a progressive, a spokesman for reform, an enemy of the bosses who had made him. He had written many years before: ". . . I do not conceive the leader a trimmer, weak to yield what clamour claims, but the deeply human man, quick to know and to do the things that the hour and his nation need."[19]

He swept into the State House with a fifty-thousand-vote majority; he carried with him the control of the lower house of the legislature. But he also carried with him "Sugar Jim" Smith, "Planked Shad" Thompson, Jim Nugent, and old Bob Davis, the Jersey bosses. And the day after the election, a progressive New Jersey newsman reminded him publicly of his campaign commitments:

The insurgency-progressivism of New Jersey, long repressed, burst out into nominal Democracy, but it is Democratic only in name. . . . Governor Wilson has been given the commission by the people of the state to redeem the political reputation of New Jersey and to reconstruct the character of the controlling forces in the State House at Trenton.[20]

The showdown at Trenton would be with the leaders of his own party, not with Republicans, and it began to shape up even before inauguration. The first engagement was crucial, for it involved the election of a United States Senator by the State Legislature. In the September primaries, the Democratic voters had given a huge majority to James E. Martine. Ex-Senator "Sugar Jim" Smith had not even entered the primaries, but now, after election, it became clear that Smith wanted to go back to the Senate, that he expected to. A new Governor might well stay clear of this brawl—it was the legislature's business. But to Wilson it was a prime test of his leadership; since the primaries were involved, the issue of clean government was clearly joined. And it was a personal issue, for Wilson had thought he had Smith's firm assurance during the campaign that he was not a candidate for office. Martine would not have been Wilson's choice, but it was the principle, not the man— the principle of popular control against boss control.

He hoped the public would rise in wrath; meanwhile he tried diplomacy. But the boss was adamant, and angry. And the new Governor began to line up the votes with the young progressive Joseph P. Tumulty to help him. By early December, he could boast that Smith would be crushed. He called on the boss, gave him an ultimatum, and then issued a public statement: "I know that the people of New Jersey do not desire Mr. James Smith, Jr., to be sent again to the Senate. If he should be, he will not go as their representative. . . . "[21]

Smith replied at once: "The Governor-elect has given striking evidence of his aptitude in the art of foul play.

Gratitude was not expected of him, but fairness was, and his act denies it...." Wilson remained cool: "I am told by the press that I have been called a liar. The only one disturbed by being called a liar is the liar himself. I beg you will observe the equanimity of my disposition."[22]

Wilson proved himself, for the moment, the master of the rough politics he had only written about before. When the time came in mid-January, Martine had 40 votes, and Smith only ten. Smith retired to the background. Wilson was sympathetic with him: "It is a pitiless game, in which, it would seem, one takes one's life in one's hands,—and for me it has only begun!" But his own friend Cleveland Dodge wrote: "You poor dear scholar and amateur in politics! I feel so sorry for you. Why don't you get an expert like Smith to advise you?"[23]

This was merely the first skirmish. What really counted was the legislative program, and Wilson had begun to line up his henchmen even before Smith had been crushed. On the day before his inauguration he had held in New York City a small meeting of potential legislative leaders and supporters. There were some Republicans; there was George Record, the progressive, and there were some regulars, who promptly reported back to the bosses. Wilson talked about initiative, referendum, and recall, to which he had recently been won; the group agreed on a short list of bills, and Record was asked to draft them for submission to the legislature. This "secret" conference was attacked at once by the bosses. The next day at his inauguration, Wilson hinted easily that he would be the kind of prime minister who would take the legislative leadership into his own hands. To an old friend he wrote of his feelings at the inauguration: "All sorts and conditions of people came, men, women, and children, and I felt very close to all of them, and very much touched by the thought that I was their ... spokesman."[24]

The first major test was a bill to reform election practices, written by Record, endorsed by Wilson, formally introduced by E. H. Geran. When the crucial party caucus on this bill was scheduled, the Governor astounded both friends and enemies by coming to the meeting as if, as the leader, he belonged there:

> ... he walked in, brisk, persuasive (even the holster of the pistol was invisible), and with everything mapped out. His position, to say nothing of his air of assurance and his certainty as to what he wanted, gave him the leadership at once. One rebellious member asked what business lawmaking was of his. And then, just as a professor of government would do, he pulled out a copy of the Constitution and began to read: "The Governor shall ... at such ... times as he may deem necessary ... recommend [to the legislature] such measures as he may deem expedient."

If this did not precisely explain his presence at the caucus, it answered the rebellious member's question; and vocal opposition was for the moment stilled. For three hours the Governor discussed the Geran bill, clause by clause, drawing upon all his knowledge of American history and government, including that of existent laws in other States. It seemed hardly fair, this unloosing of a flood of knowledge with which no antagonist was prepared to cope. He ended with a stirring appeal for loyalty to the State and to the party. One legislator, describing the whole affair, was emphatic as to its effect: "We all came out of that room with one conviction: that we had heard the most wonderful speech of our lives. ... That caucus settled the fate of the Geran bill, as well as the whole Democratic program."

Apparently it did. The Geran bill made it impossible for repeaters, for dead men, and for other phantoms to cast votes; for corporations to contribute to campaign funds; for bribes, even in such elegant form as liquor and tickets, to be used. Another law snatched still more power from the bosses, by establishing primaries for all elective offices in the State. Still another allowed municipalities to adopt the commission plan of government, including the initiative and referendum, if they wished. The regulation of public utilities was provided for; and industrial employees became entitled automatically to compensation on a fixed scale for injuries received in course of work. The country looked on admiringly; and Wilson's stock as a probable nominee went up.[25]

But the final break with the bosses had come. Wilson's last conference with Jim Nugent left nothing to be said between them:

"Don't you think, Mr. Nugent," said the Governor, "that you are making a grave mistake in opposing the election bill?"

"No," said Nugent, "and you can't pass it without using the state patronage."

Nugent could have said nothing that would have cut deeper. He was accusing the Governor of bribing the legislators with promises of offices. Wilson met the charge in white heat. He rose from his chair and pointed his hand at the door.

"Good-afternoon, Mr. Nugent."

The boss hesitated, trembling with passion.

"You're no gentleman!" he shouted.

"You're no judge!" responded the Governor.[26]

Wilson continued to show himself the master of conciliation and maneuver, of principle and timing. He would not budge from his major propositions; he knew precisely when and how to go to the press and the public with strong statements that made it impossible for his legislators to back down. And progressive Republicans delightedly worked in the press and the Senate to give him the votes he needed to carry his measures through the upper house. The bosses growled about his ingratitude. Later the New York World *would tell the voters: "... what we need in public life is a great deal more of discriminating ingratitude."*[27]

By April, Wilson was the acknowledged master of New Jersey politics. As the session ended, he could sit down to recapture all the pride and excitement and sober challenge of this remarkable four months:

> The Legislature adjourned yesterday morning at three o'clock with its work done. I got absolutely everything I strove for.... and besides them, I got certain fundamental school reforms and an act enabling any city in the State to adopt the commission form of government.... Everyone, the papers included, are saying that none of it could have been done, if it had not been for my influence and tact and hold upon the people. Be that as it may, the thing was done, and the result was as complete a victory as has ever been won, I venture to say, in the history of the country.... The strain has been immense, but the reward is great.... I am quietly and deeply happy that I should have been of just the kind of service I wished to be to those who elected and trusted me. I can look them in the face.... It's a great game, thoroughly worth playing![28]

From that moment, Trenton was merely a way-station on the trip to Washington. But he could take pride in what he had done. He had been given only three months to prove himself. He had made his national reputation; he had made it as a progressive; and he had transformed New Jersey's reputation. In 1910, she had long been known as a corruption-ridden stronghold of the bosses and the trusts. In 1911, she was a leader in the fight for clean government. Wilson's task now lay abroad and within. He must win votes. But he must also bring his own convictions under discipline. It was significant that, as he wrote out his notes for a speech early in 1911, he had been able to arrive at only the most shallow definitions of the political tags that were so liberally used:

RADICAL—one who goes too far.
CONSERVATIVE—one who does not go far enough.
REACTIONARY—one who does not go at all.
Hence we have invented the term, label,
PROGRESSIVE, to mean one who (a) recognizes new facts and adjusts law to them, and who (b) attempts to think ahead, constructively. Progress must build tissues, must be cohesive, must have a plan at its heart.[29]

1912 would prove a sad year for him in New Jersey. His party lost control of the Assembly. His own Democratic bosses were newly inspired. He could only slaughter their bills with vetoes. And balked, he reacted as he had at Princeton, and as he always did when matters in which his own prestige and pride were involved, were crushed by opposition. To a close friend, he wrote of the Columbia University teacher, and Senate majority leader, who crossed his path most frequently: "And what shall we say when we find the leader of the petty partisan band a learned and distinguished Professor in a great University . . . with plenty of independent means and plenty of brains, of a kind, but without a single moral principle to his name! I have never despised any other man quite so heartily. . . ."[30]

When he came back to his legislature in January, 1913, he wore the mantle of a President. He had at least technical Democratic control of both houses. He had enormous prestige. He carried the dedicated air of a man without ambition, bent on doing his last duty to his beloved State. And with these immense advantages, he drove through the legislature the spate of bills designed to destroy the special privileges that had made New Jersey the mother of the monopolies. Ray Stannard Baker describes them:

At his request a series of seven regulatory bills designed to curb the abuses of the great corporations in the state were drafted. They were aimed particularly at price-fixing and the restraint of trade and applied the doctrine that Wilson had long advocated: "Guilt is personal." Directors of corporations violating the law would be liable to fine and imprisonment. The "Seven Sisters" acts were hotly opposed in the legislature. . . . by the middle of February the battle was won. On the 19th he signed the bills.

While the "Seven Sisters" laws put New Jersey in the vanguard of states having rigid anti-trust laws, they were, as a matter of fact, too hastily drawn, and poorly considered even by Wilson himself . . . since he was then overwhelmed with national problems. Some of the opposition which Wilson, in the heat of conflict, had considered selfishly unreasonable had been based upon honest doubt as to the wisdom of the legislation proposed. The laws have since been repealed. But the determined and resourceful fight which Wilson carried on in securing their passage not only served to increase his power and prestige in his own party but further cemented the confidence of the country in his sincerity of purpose.[31]

He held on in Trenton until March 1, three days before his inauguration as President. He would risk no slips, no tarnish on his State record.

NOTES, CHAPTER 4

1. Arthur S. Link, **Wilson: The Road to the White House** (Princeton, N.J.: Princeton University Press, 1947), p. 91.
2. H. C. F. Bell, **Woodrow Wilson and the People** (N.Y.: Doubleday, Doran and Company, 1945), p. 42.
3. Ibid., p. 1.
4. Ibid., p. 61.
5. Ibid., pp. 41–42.
6. Arthur Walworth, **Woodrow Wilson** (London: Longmans, Green and Company, 1958), I, 152.
7. Ibid., pp. 146, 208.
8. Ray Stannard Baker, **Woodrow Wilson: Life and Letters** (N.Y.: Doubleday, Doran and Company, 1927–39), III, 43–44.
9. Walworth, **op. cit.**, pp. 143–44.
10. Ibid., p. 154.
11. John K. Sague, **Memoirs** (unpublished).
12. Baker, **op. cit.**, p. 53.
13. William Allen White, **Woodrow Wilson: The Man, His Times, and His Task** (Boston: Houghton Mifflin Company, 1924), pp. 208–10.
14. Joseph P. Tumulty, **Woodrow Wilson as I Know Him** (N.Y.: Doubleday, Page and Company, 1921), pp. 17–19.
15. Baker, **op. cit.**, pp. 78–80.
16. Ibid., p. 87.
17. Ibid., p. 103.
18. Ibid., pp. 98, 101.
19. Woodrow Wilson, **Leaders of Men** (Princeton, N.J.: Princeton University Press, 1952), p. 60.
20. **Newark Evening News**, November 9, 1910.
21. Baker, **op. cit.**, p. 120.
22. Ibid., pp. 120, 125.
23. Ibid., p. 127.
24. Ibid., p. 135.
25. Bell, **op. cit.**, pp. 65–66.
26. Baker, **op. cit.**, p. 143.
27. **New York World**, January 19, 1912.
28. Baker, **op. cit.**, pp. 169–71.
29. Ibid., p. 149.
30. Ibid., p. 292.
31. Ibid., p. 435.

5. WILSON MEN AND THE WILSON PARTY

As Wilson had looked forward toward the White House, he had faced a challenge with three major dimensions. He must make himself known to the country; he must come to grips with the great progressive wave that swept the nation. He must deal with a divided, warring Democratic Party and somehow wrest from its practiced professionals the nomination he so much coveted.

Only the first of these was easily met. The coast-to-coast headlines his reform crusade brought him made him a national figure in six months. And he worked to enlarge this publicity. He travelled widely throughout the country, accepting almost any opportunity for a major speech, popularizing not only Woodrow Wilson, but also the vaguely inspiring philosophy of reform he was only just developing. Years later, it would seem a little vacuous. Arthur Link has summed it up: "By and large he talked in generalities, about returning the government to the people, the need for trust control and tariff and banking reforms, and the iniquity of special privilege legislation."[1] And cynic, H. L. Mencken wrote brutally:

The Woodrovian style, at the height of the Wilson hallucination, was much praised by cornfed connoisseurs. . . . It is difficult to believe that even idiots ever succumbed to such transparent contradictions, to such gaudy processions of mere counter-words, to so vast and obvious a nonsensicality. . . . stuff quite as bad as the worst bosh of Warren Gamaliel Harding.[2]

But people liked this man and his words. Although he wrong-headedly misunderstood its meaning, even Mencken grasped clearly the man's magnetic attraction: "Woodrow knew how to conjure up . . . words. He knew how to make them glow, and weep. He wasted no time upon the heads of his dupes, but aimed directly at their ears, diaphragms and hearts."³ Yet there was more than a witchery of words in Wilson's new popularity. It was important that the words were progressive ones, but not radical, offering hope of reform without disaster. Walter Weyl, writing even while Wilson maneuvered for his nomination, caught the spirit of this progressivism:

What we dimly see to-day is . . . the native growth of a democratic spirit. . . .

That this democratic evolution is already preparing is overlooked by him who runs. The development is too multiform and bewildering, and we are too near. If we fix our gaze at one point in progress, we conclude that results are small. If, however, we look over the field and note progress in a succession of social efforts, we are amazed at our advance. A democratic reform is instituted in one of our States with a blazon of trumpets. Thereafter we hear rumors of its working ill or well. Then silence. A dozen years later, we are surprised to learn that half the States adopted the new institution, and soon we forget the evil conditions which preceded. . . .

The new spirit is social. Its base is broad. It involves common action and a common lot. It emphasizes social rather than private ethics, social rather than individual responsibility. . . . A new insistence is laid upon human life, upon human happiness. . . . The inner soul of our new democracy is not the unalienable rights, negatively and individualistically interpreted, but those same rights, "life, liberty, and the pursuit of happiness," extended and given a social interpretation.⁴

And Herbert Croly, three years earlier, had demanded a resolution of the old enmity between nationalists and states-righters in the interest of justice and progress: "... nationalism can be adapted to democracy without an essential injury to itself, but the ... democracy cannot be nationalized without being transformed.... It must cease to be a democracy of indiscriminate individualism ... its members must be united not by a sense of joint irresponsibility, but by a sense of joint responsibility for the success of their political and social ideal. They must become, that is, a democracy devoted to the welfare of the whole people by means of a conscious labor of individual and social improvement."[5]

And, as Wilson's men converged on Baltimore for the Democratic National Convention, Theodore Roosevelt worked at the speech with which he would challenge Wilson a month later:

> The old parties are husks, with no real soul within either, divided on artificial lines, boss-ridden and privilege-controlled, each a jumble of incongruous elements, and neither daring to speak out wisely and fearlessly what should be said on the vital issues of the day. This new movement is a movement of truth, sincerity, and wisdom, a movement which proposes to put at the service of all our people the collective power of the people through their governmental agencies....
>
> The prime need today is to face that fact that we are now in the midst of a great economic revolution....[6]

Teddy went on to demand presidential primaries, the popular election of senators, corrupt-practices laws, a broad program of labor legislation, the vote for women, currency reform, conservation. Then he proclaimed: "Surely there never was a fight better worth making than the one in which we are engaged. . . . We stand at Armageddon, and we battle for the Lord."[6]

Wilson himself could not accept the systematic reformism of these progressive prophets. Precisely because of this, he was attractive to many progressives. The description George Mowry has written of the "progressive mentality" fitted him closely:

> As the progressive looked at the sharply differentiated America of 1900, he saw "pyramids of money in a desert of want". . . . Supremely individualistic, the progressive could not impute class consciousness, or, as he would have phrased it, class selfishness, to himself. His talk was therefore full of moral self-judgments, of phrases like "the good men," "the better element," "the moral crowd". . . .
>
> The progressive mentality was a compound of many curious elements. It contained a reactionary as well as a reform impulse. It was imbued with a burning ethical strain which at times approached a missionary desire to create a heaven on earth. It had in it intense feelings of moral superiority over both elements of society above and below it economically. It emphasized individual dynamism and leadership. One part of it looked backward to an intensely democratic small America; another looked forward to a highly centralized nationalistic state. . . .
>
> The progressive mentality was generated in part from both a fear of the loss of group status and a confidence in man's ability to order the future.[7]

But Wilson, unlike most men of his age, was changing sharply with the press of new ideas and new challenges. Basically, he would always wish to restore the old America—always yearn to preserve individualism, to curb national government, to rely on the discipline of the marketplace. His fundamental aim would always be the restoration of rural conditions of freedom in the new urban environment. But he faced the burgeoning problems with a mind divided and learning. He knew the popular mood; an unimaginative conservatism would never bring Woodrow Wilson to the White House. He saw increasingly from the State House at Trenton the social evils spawned by traditions. He sensed the curious irony of a world in which competition destroyed competition, and individualism crushed the individual. As he worked through his personal adjustment, he sought also the moderate middle way that would appeal to broad masses of aroused but emotionally traditionalist American voters. In the process, during five short years, he had, at one moment or another, the enthusiastic support of every wing of the Democratic Party.

At first he had seemed the natural candidate for financiers and business tycoons. It was these men to whom George Harvey advocated his candidacy long before he had come to Trenton. The tempest in Trenton had disillusioned many of the early supporters Harvey had enlisted. Yet, in November, 1911, he blazoned Wilson's name on the masthead of Harper's Weekly as his journal's official candidate for the presidency. And for the conservatives who would read carefully there was still much hope from Woodrow Wilson. Joseph Dorfman has described it succinctly:

> . . . perhaps his general attitude toward business was best expressed by his warm approval of the Wisconsin legislation regulating public service corporations. The men controlling the corporations, he said, fought the regulatory plans of the state as they "would have fought the prospect of ruin; and what happened? Regulation of the most thoroughgoing sort was undertaken, and the result was that the securities of those companies were virtually guaranteed to purchasers. In-

stead of being speculative in value, they were known to be absolutely secure investments, because a disinterested agency, a commission representing the community, looked into the conditions of this business, guaranteed that there was not water enough to drown in, guaranteed that there was business enough and plant enough to justify the charges and to secure a return of legitimate profit; and every thoughtful man connected with such enterprises in Wisconsin now takes off his hat to the men who originated the measures once so much debated. The chief benefit was, not regulation, but frank disclosure and the absolutely open and frank relationship between business and government." To answer those who thought such measures the first steps toward socialism, Wilson made it clear that he did not believe in socialism. But "if you want to oust socialism, you have got to propose something better. It is a case . . . of 'put up or shut up.' You cannot oppose hopeful programs with negations."[8]

But there was something else that appealed to conservatives. As progressives went, Wilson was both polite and cautious, a "gentleman and a scholar." As Henry May has noted: "By 1912 Wilson had become a major champion of progress who could not possibly be feared by any believer in ideals or culture. . . . while Roosevelt was violent, Wilson was impeccably polite. . . . Wilson . . . assured his friends in Virginia, 'No man that I know of and trust, no man that I will consent to consort with, is trying to change anything fundamental in America.' "[9]

In this moderate image lay his chief hope for winning the support of the warring Democratic factions. But he must cut loose from the New York group that had first sponsored him. As early as 1910, he had been disturbed by Hearst headlines: "WALL STREET TO PUT UP W. WILSON FOR PRESIDENT."[10] By December,

1911, he was sufficiently upset to tell George Harvey frankly and directly that the support of Harper's Weekly was hurting his cause. Harvey removed the Wilson banner from his masthead; but Harvey was insulted and became one of Wilson's strongest enemies.

But Wilson's major problems lay before him. The Democratic Party had grown from widely disparate roots. Its branches spread broadly to cover every corner of American life. Even in a state like New York, victorious Democrats fought among themselves in 1911 more angrily than they had ever fought Republicans. Upstate progressives wanted a President who would help them beat Tammany; Tammany wanted a President who would be "regular"; the Manhattan reformers wanted a "good government" President who would both destroy Tammany and curb the excesses of their country cousins. New York was symptomatic of the general problems in the Northeast, but this was only the beginning. The sharp division between conservatives and progressives carried over into the industrialized states of the Midwest, and it jumped across the great plains to California. Regulation of business, the monetary system, the conservation movement all divided the Democracy. But the more fundamental divisions were between the industrialized East and the farmers, and again between the farmers of the West and of the South. West of the Mississippi, William Jennings Bryan was still a hero with an emotional but solid following, and progressivism for many was still the farmer program of the populists, the war against business, finance and the city, the war to preserve the American farm. In the South, rural populism was also strong, but here it was given a peculiar twist as the section turned in upon itself to stress states' rights, to preserve its peculiar values of white supremacy.

Wilson bargained heavily on his Southern origins, and he had reasons. Whatever their uneasiness about his ideas, many Southern politicians were enlisted by their confidence that a Virginia-born and Georgia-reared President must be a President with the South's interests at heart. Wilson offered the best prospects in sight for creating the first Southern President since the Civil War.

But Wilson's principal problem lay to the West. He must somehow win the allegiance of the farmer radicals who had thrilled to Bryan's oratory, but he must do it without endangering the support that moderate progressives might bring him, in disgust with Taft or fear of Roosevelt. And here he seemed fatefully at a disadvantage because of his own contempt for Bryan. He had often expressed it. Privately he had said in 1904: "... the man has no brains. It is a great pity that a man with his power of leadership should have no mental rudder."[11] Four years later, he had artlessly told a reporter that Bryan was "the most charming and lovable of men personally, but foolish and dangerous in his theoretical beliefs."[12] This was bad enough, but Wilson's cause seemed destroyed when in January, 1912, the hostile New York Sun published a private statement he had written to Adrian Joline five years earlier: "Would that we could do something, at once, dignified and effective, to knock Mr. Bryan, once for all, into a cocked hat."[13]

Bryan was outraged, but Bryan was also a cool political tactician and a man of considerable common sense. He could not help but remember the warm and friendly evening he had spent with the Wilsons at Princeton the previous April. As Herbert Bell explains, Ellen Wilson had carefully arranged this first meeting between her husband and the Great Commoner: "... the two men saw each other under conditions that made for perfect ease. They eschewed political talk; capped each others' stories; sized up each others' personalities; and parted with mutual liking. Tumulty, with characteristic enthusiasm and exaggeration, declared joyfully: 'You have nominated your husband, Mrs. Wilson.'"[14]

Whatever his emotions, Bryan now refused to jump to

the *Sun's* bait. Recognizing that a rift between Wilson and himself might destroy them both, and destroy their cause, he treated the whole business as a trick by the business interests to split the progressive wing of the party. And, on January 8, at the Jackson Day Dinner, Wilson healed the breach with drama and impeccable good taste:

" . . . while we have differed with Mr. Bryan upon this occasion and upon that in regard to the specific things to be done, he has gone serenely on pointing out to a more and more convinced people what it was that was the matter. . . . he has . . . not based his career upon calculation, but has based it upon principle. . . .

"Now, what has been the matter? The matter has been that the government of this country was privately controlled . . . that the people of this country did not have the control of their own affairs."[15]

The finishing touch was one of Wilson's triumphs of eloquence: "Let us apologize to each other that we ever suspected or antagonized one another; let us join hands once more all around the great circle of community of counsel and of interest which will show us at last to have been indeed the friends of our country and the friends of mankind."

The speech was spectacular, the applause tremendous! Bryan rose from his seat, put his hand affectionately on Wilson's shoulder, and murmured, "That was splendid, splendid."[16]

It would be many months before Bryan placed himself firmly in Wilson's camp, but from that moment on there was no danger of the Commoner's enmity. Yet, meanwhile, the Wilson cause would suffer throughout the spring of 1912 from both stiff competition and outrageous slander. In December, 1911, it had seemed possible that he might run away with the nomination. By

June, it seemed almost unbelievable that he could manage it at all. The campaign against him had been viciously personal, shot through with innuendo, distortions, unfair charges. Hearst was particularly violent against the Princeton "Professor." In March, 1912, he issued a statement in which he said among other things: "To my mind he is a perfect jackrabbit of politics, perched upon his little hillock of expediency, with ears erect and nostrils distended, keenly alert to every scent or sound and ready to run and double in any direction."[17]

Wilson was outraged: "God knows I want the . . . presidential nomination. . . . but if I am to grovel at Hearst's feet, I will never have it."[18]

But more damaging than all the propaganda and venom of his enemies were the simple facts of organization. His personal "machine" was one of the most narrowly restricted in the history of presidential campaigns. A small group, it was poorly financed and was led by amateurs. And it was a peculiar group—overwhelmingly Southerners who had found some prominence in the business world of New York—William G. McAdoo, William McCombs, Walter Hines Page, Dudley Field Malone, the shadowy Texas Colonel, Edward M. House—most of them young men, untested in politics.

They would face in the convention some of the toughest, most seasoned professional politicians the city machines and the Western and Southern congressional delegations could produce. And most of these professionals would be voting in the first ballots for Champ Clark, the Speaker of the House of Representatives. As Arthur Link has described him:

> Clark was an old-time war horse from Pike County, Missouri, who had served in the House since the 1890's. A politician of the Bryan type, he had accumulated a consistent progressive record over the

years. He had never originated any legislation or taken leadership in any important movement, however; and he was narrow and provincial in outlook, undistinguished by intellectual prowess, and temperamentally and for lack of experience in leadership unfitted for the presidency of a great nation. There is, therefore, little reason to doubt that the *New York World* was justified when it warned that Clark's nomination would spell disaster for the Democratic party and, if he were elected, for the United States.

. . . Clark made hardly any popular campaign for the nomination, except occasionally to recite his stock lecture, "The Signs of the Times." . . . one after another of the states went for the Speaker. Clark had inherited most of Bryan's following in the Middle and Far West. He had the fervid support of William Randolph Hearst, and the influence of the Hearst newspapers in his behalf in states like Illinois, California, and Massachusetts was decisive. Finally, Clark had the support of most of the time-serving Democratic politicians and state organizations, and their support was the critical factor in the success of his campaign.

, While Clark gathered some 436 delegates pledged to support his nomination at the national convention in Baltimore in June, Wilson could count at the most only 248. The best the Wilson managers could hope for was that the support of the uninstructed Wilson delegates would give him control of at least one-third of the total convention vote of 1088. Wilson had made an especially hard fight to win his native South, but had to divide the Southern delegations with Clark and Oscar W. Underwood of Alabama, chairman of the House Ways and Means Committee. For Wilson and his friends the days preceding the Baltimore Convention were disheartening indeed. Wilson himself was ready to quit. Colonel Edward M. House . . . became discouraged and advised his friends to find another candidate to support if it seemed Wilson could not be nominated.

It was easily the most critical time in the history of the Democratic Party since 1896 when the national convention opened at Baltimore on June 25, 1912, for nothing less than control of the party and also of the federal government was at stake.[19]

Baltimore was a riot of noise and confusion of milling crowds in the sweaty July heat, a riot of tedious oratory, monstrous demonstrations and quiet deals crossing each other in hopeless confusion among the tired, uncomfortable delegates. Wilson's men must somehow stop Clark before their own drive could even begin. And the great urban bosses, like Murphy of Tammany and Taggart of Indiana, held their delegates quietly aside from both camps to bargain for the best advantage. Wilson's own managers were divided. House had escaped to Europe. McAdoo was firm, driving, optimistic, but McCombs was ready to quit before the Convention had hardly begun. The fights were more bitter, the dangers greater, because the rewards seemed suddenly more certain. Only three days before, Theodore Roosevelt had launched his Progressive Party. In a three-way race, Democrats would have their best chance for victory since the Civil War.

And in all of this, Bryan, it proved, held the balance of power. He moved at once to control the temporary chairmanship, and with a flash of his old oratory he laid down the gauge to the bosses. He was beaten; but when it came time to choose a permanent chairman, the Wilson men won out. They won again in a dispute between two rival delegations from South Dakota, this time with support from Illinois's boss, Roger Sullivan, whom they had helped in a similar dispute. Wilson's managers were proving adept at the sharp, tough infighting.

Before the convention was two days old Bryan took the platform with a resolution that threatened to split the party as badly as the Republicans had been split two weeks before. Fearful of a deal between Clark and Tammany's Charles F. Murphy, he read to the howling mob of warring partisans:

" 'Resolved, That in this crisis in our party's career and in our country's history, this convention sends greetings to the people of the United States, and assures them that the party of Jefferson and of Jackson is still the champion of popular government and equality before the law. As proof of our fidelity to the people, we hereby declare ourselves opposed to the nomination of any candidate for President who is the representative of or under obligation to J. Pierpont Morgan, Thomas F. Ryan, August Belmont, or any other member of the privilege-hunting and favour-seeking class.

" 'Be it further resolved, That we demand the withdrawal from this convention of any delegate or delegates constituting or representing the above-named interests.' " . . .

Demanding a record vote, Bryan was in a strong strategic position, for any delegate voting "nay" was in effect declaring that he favoured the nomination of a candidate favourable to the "privilege-hunting and favour-seeking class."

It was a brilliant stroke, even New York and Virginia joining in support of the resolution. As the vote was being taken, Boss Murphy leaned over to Belmont and said:

"August, listen and hear yourself vote yourself out of the convention."

The resolution carried by a vote of 883 to 201½.[20]

Some thought Murphy had made Bryan look like a fool. The Old Commoner had been compelled to withdraw the "expulsion" section of his resolution to get this vote of approval. It all seemed like a joke when Murphy himself voted for it. But Bryan told his nation-wide newspaper audience: "Belmont and Ryan have been plowing with our heifer; they have been employing the methods usually resorted to by the predatory interests. . . . There is nothing more timid than a politician, except two politicians. The ratio of moral courage in the plain, everyday voter as compared with the courage of the average delegate to a national convention is about 16 to 1. . . . But the convention has done one thing, if nothing else. It has committed a great party more openly to opposition to the Plunderbund than any great party was ever committed before by a national convention."[21]

The angry convention went on into the night of June 27. It was nearly midnight before the nominations began. It was seven in the morning before the first vote was taken: Clark 440½—Wilson 324—Governor Judson Harmon of Ohio: 148—the rest scattered among favorite sons. Someone voted for Bryan, but only one. Arthur Link has described the tense struggle for the prize:

> When the delegates assembled in the afternoon of June 28, the lines were tightly drawn for the coming battle. . . . During the first nine ballots little change in the voting occurred. . . . The Wilson men knew that the knockout blow was yet to come. They expected that New York's ninety votes would be delivered to Clark on the third or fourth ballot but were forewarned by their friends in the New York delegation when Murphy decided to transfer the votes to Clark at a later time. The expected transfer came on the tenth ballot when the Tammany boss electrified the convention by shifting his state's votes from Harmon to Clark. It was the signal for the Clark landslide, for New York's votes gave Clark 556 votes, well over a majority

of the convention. Clark ... had already prepared a telegram of acceptance. ... Not since 1844 had a Democrat obtained a majority of the national convention and then failed of nomination by the necessary two-thirds. At Sea Girt, Wilson lost his nerve and was anxious to quit the fight. ... Fortunately for Wilson and his followers, McCombs refused to release the Wilson delegates.[22]

The convention became a mob as Clark delegates whooped and paraded in premature celebration of their "victory." The hall reechoed with the inane strains of their Missouri campaign song: "I doan' keer if he is a houn'—You gotta quit kickin' my dawg aroun'." And the Wilson Men—McCombs, McAdoo, Albert Burleson of Texas, A. Mitchell Palmer of Pennsylvania—scooted about the crowded hall desperately trying to dam the tide. Their hard work and the resentment against Tammany and Murphy paid off. Their block, and Oscar Underwood's, stood firm, on the tenth ballot, and the eleventh. At four in the morning of June 29, the convention adjourned again. It had been Underwood who had made the difference. He wanted the presidency only —he refused Clark offers of the second position. He had bent finally to Wilson managers' promise that, if Wilson failed, they would do everything they could to nominate Underwood.

There yet remained the danger that McCombs, often nervous and panic-stricken, might take a fatal step that would ruin Wilson's chances for the nomination. . . . Early Saturday morning McCombs called Wilson on the telephone. He was very discouraged and suggested that Wilson authorize him to withdraw his name from the balloting; Wilson accordingly sent a telegram to that effect and considered sending Clark a message of congratulations. The Wilsons even began to make plans for a visit to the lake country of England. . . . "Now we can see Rydal again," Mrs. Wilson told her husband.

Later in the morning . . . McAdoo . . . telephoned Wilson and urged him by no means to consider withdrawing because he was steadily gaining in strength and would eventually be nominated. Wilson authorized McAdoo to countermand the withdrawal authorization he had given McCombs and the danger was averted.[23]

The stalemate held, through the twelfth ballot and the thirteenth. And then Bryan's own Nebraska became restless; a private poll showed a majority for Wilson but they were still voting under the unit rule for Clark. On the fourteenth ballot, Senator Gilbert Hitchcock demanded an official poll, and Bryan, thus forced to the decision, demanded time to explain his vote: "I shall withhold my vote from Mr. Clark as long as New York's vote is recorded for him. . . . With the understanding that I shall stand ready to withdraw my vote from the one for whom I am going to cast it whenever New York casts her vote for him, I cast my vote for Nebraska's second choice, Governor Wilson."[24]

The reaction was violent on all sides. One New Yorker shouted that Bryan was "a money-grabbing, selfish, office-seeking, favor-hunting, publicity-loving marplot."[25] Clark rushed to Baltimore from his Washington office to fight with fury and bitterness. The deadlock went on, but Wilson gained tediously throughout the long day of voting. Sunday, June 30, provided a day for deals and tension, and little rest. Wilson made it more difficult for his manager by refusing to authorize any deals involving the vice-presidency or the cabinet. But his managers quietly went ahead without him, and they had to fight Murphy's attempt to lure away their own leaders with promises of the nomination.

On Monday, the logjam broke. Thomas Taggart threw Indiana into the Wilson camp—later their favorite son, Thomas Marshall, would be nominated for vice-president. Iowa, Vermont, Wyoming, Michigan all left Clark and Wilson began to outrun the Speaker. But the Wilson men had reached the end. The nomination could be made only by Roger Sullivan's 58 Illinois delegates or by Underwood's block. There was much Wilson support in both camps. Both leaders hated Hearst, and Hearst was supporting Clark. On Monday, Sullivan promised to help. On Tuesday morning he threw his delegates to Wilson. Virginia and West Virginia broke away from the Speaker. On the forty-sixth ballot, Underwood finally gave way to Wilson. Missouri refused to make it unanimous, but Wilson was nominated by 990 votes.

It had been Underwood and the tough machine bosses who had made Wilson's nomination possible. But Bryan's activities had made Wilson seem the white knight of progressivism, atilt with the forces of evil. The platform was a progressive document. The situation dictated a progressive campaign. The man to beat was Roosevelt, not Taft. Wilson was no economist, but the problems on which this campaign would pitch would be economic. As he turned away from the crowds of office-seekers to draft his acceptance speech, he worked out a document full of cheering promise for reform—of tariff and of trust laws—promise for protection of labor and of the nation's resources, but yet artfully vague and general. It must be. He must go to school that summer to liberal advisors like Louis D. Brandeis before he would be able to flesh out the bare bones of his campaign. It was a dull speech for his audience on the lawn of the great Georgian mansion at Sea Girt, and it was a hot day. But Wilson was speaking for a nation to read. Years before he had put into print his concept of the job he was undertaking. A President, he had written:

"... can dominate his party by being spokesman for the real sentiment and purpose of the country.... If he rightly interpret the national thought and boldly insist upon it, he is irresistible.... A President whom ... [the country] trusts can not only lead it, but form it to his own views."[26]

NOTES, CHAPTER 5

1. Arthur S. Link, **Woodrow Wilson and the Progressive Era, 1910–1917** (N.Y.: Harper and Brothers, 1954), p. 11.
2. H. L. Mencken, **A Mencken Chrestomathy** (N.Y.: Alfred A. Knopf, Inc., 1949), pp. 249–50.
3. **Ibid.**, p. 250.
4. Walter E. Weyl, **The New Democracy** (N.Y.: The Macmillan Company, 1912), pp. 158, 160–61.
5. Herbert Croly, **The Promise of American Life** (N.Y.: The Macmillan Company, 1909), p. 214.
6. Theodore Roosevelt, **Works** (National Edition; N.Y.: Charles Scribners' Sons, 1926), XVII, 254–55, 298–99.
7. George Mowry, **The Era of Theodore Roosevelt, 1900–1912** (N.Y.: Harper and Brothers, 1958), pp. 104–05.
8. Joseph Dorfman, **The Economic Mind in American Civilization, 1865–1918** (N.Y.: The Viking Press, 1949), pp. 337–38.
9. Henry F. May, **The End of American Innocence** (N.Y.: Alfred A. Knopf, Inc., 1959), pp. 115–16.
10. Ray Stannard Baker, **Woodrow Wilson: Life and Letters** (N.Y.: Doubleday, Doran and Company, 1927–39), III, 6.
11. **Ibid.**, p. 203.
12. **Ibid.**
13. **Ibid.**, p. 23.
14. H. C. F. Bell, **Woodrow Wilson and the People** (N.Y.: Doubleday, Doran and Company, 1945), p. 58.
15. Baker, **op. cit.**, pp. 264–65.
16. Arthur S. Link, **Wilson: The Road to the White House** (Princeton, N.J.: Princeton University Press, 1947), p. 356.
17. **Washington Post**, March 14, 1912.
18. Link, **op. cit.**, p. 382.
19. Link, **Wilson and the Progressive Era, op. cit.**, pp. 11–12.
20. Baker, **op. cit.**, pp. 343–345.

21. William Jennings Bryan, **A Tale of Two Conventions,** (N.Y.: Funk and Wagnalls Company, 1912), pp. 168–69.
22. Link, **Road to the White House, op. cit.,** pp. 448–49.
23. **Ibid.,** p. 451.
24. Baker, **op. cit.,** pp. 355–56.
25. Link, **op. cit.,** p. 454.
26. Woodrow Wilson, **Constitutional Government in the United States** (N.Y.: Columbia University Press, 1908), p. 68.

6. "THE NEW FREEDOM"

It was a campaign of personalities—the dynamic, sometimes violent, Teddy Roosevelt: candidate of the Bull Moose party, spirited prophet of Croly's New Nationalism—the taut "intellectual" but eloquent Wilson: spokesman for a divided Democracy, striving manfully to draft a campaign for the "New Freedom." Taft hardly counted, and Wilson ignored him. And Wilson sought a dignified campaign on the issues. He liked to tell the story of the Irishman digging a cellar, who explained, "I'm letting the darkness out."[1] He tried to avoid whistle-stopping about the country. He told his organization to keep away from millionaire financing—a warning they could only afford to ignore. But the vigorous Teddy forced Wilson to make three broad swings around the country. In one, he made over 30 speeches in seven different states. As he spoke, he learned. The "New Freedom" grew as it was explained.

Later William Allen White would say: "Between the New Nationalism and the New Freedom was that fantastic gulf that always existed between tweedle-dum and tweedle-dee."[2] But there were differences. Wilson would not accept Roosevelt's commitment to strong national government; Wilson would not make the Bull Moose assumption that "good" monopolies must be accepted. Wilson would not embrace the Progressive's broad, systematic program of reform on all sides. He sought limited reform, with states' rights, with individualism, with an emphasis on freedom. Wilson would not turn the nation inside out. Wilson would seek the specific, particular reforms essential to return the nation to its old values. And Wilson would seek, as he had promised in his acceptance speech: "an unentangled government, a government that cannot be used for private purposes, either in the field of business, or in the field of politics; a government . . . that will not permit legislation to be employed to further any private interests."[3]

As Richard Hofstadter has summarized it:

> Wilson emerged as the middle-of-the-road candidate, flanked on the right by Taft and on the left by Roosevelt in his new pose. The bulk of left-wing reform sentiment went with the Progressive Party, and many moderate Republicans seem to have deserted Taft for Wilson. . . . Wilson's program, the result of his first serious thinking on the trust problem, was taken from the preachings of Louis D. Brandeis and formulated with the lawyer's guidance. Wilson's speeches . . . sound like the collective wail of the American middle class.

What has happened in America, Wilson told the voters, is that industry has ceased to be free because the laws do not prevent the strong from crushing the weak. . . .

Those who criticize the competitive order assert that free competition itself has made it possible for the big to crush the little. This Wilson denied. "I reply, it is not free competition that has done that, it is illicit competition." A big business that survives competition through intelligence, efficiency, and economies deserves to survive. But the trust is "an arrangement to get rid of competition"; it "buys efficiency out of business." "I am for big business," said Wilson, succumbing to the equivocation that invariably creeps into politicians' discussions of the trust problem, "and I am against the trusts."

The interests that have squeezed out the middle class

are the same that control politics, Wilson went on. "The government of the United States at present is a foster-child of the special interests." But the people will regain control and return to their old competitive, democratic principles. . . .

The New Freedom would address itself to the fundamental problem of the present age. "What this country needs above everything else is a body of laws which will look after the men who are on the make rather than the men who are already made."[4]

Above all, Wilson staked his faith on Jefferson's proposition that the judgment of the people would be sound. It was necessary only to let them back into their government to "open up all the processes of politics. . . . We must substitute public for private·machinery . . . to give society command of its own economic life. . . . The best thing that you can do with anything that is crooked is to lift it up where people can see that it is crooked, and then it will either straighten itself out or disappear. Nothing checks all the bad practices of politics like public exposure. You can't be crooked in the light."[5]

And he sought a bridge between the old Jefferson and the new progressive:

I am . . . forced to be a progressive, if for no other reason, because we have not kept up with our changes of conditions, either in the economic field or in the political field. We have not kept up as well as other nations have. . . . If you do not adjust your laws to the facts, so much the worse for the laws, not for the facts, because law trails along after the facts. . . .

We used to think in the old-fashioned days when life was very simple that all that government had to do was to put on a policeman's uniform, and say "now don't anybody hurt anybody else." . . . That was the idea that obtained in Jefferson's time. . . . Freedom to-day is something more than being let alone. The program of a government of freedom must in these days be positive, not negative merely.

. . . Our purpose is the restoration of freedom. We propose to prevent private monopoly by law, to see to it that the methods by which monopolies have been built up are legally made impossible. We design that the limitations on private enterprise shall be removed, so that the next generation of youngsters, as they come along, will not have to become protégés of benevolent trusts, but will be free to go about making their own lives what they will; so that we shall taste again the full cup, not of charity, but of liberty,—the only wine that ever refreshed and renewed the spirit of a people.[6]

There were differences between the New Freedom and the New Nationalism, significant ones. But the chief distinctions between Wilson and Roosevelt were those of temper and manner, of symbol and slogan. While Roosevelt appealed for regulation of the great corporations, Wilson spoke for the little man. The American people were flattered when he told them that "Freemen need no Guardians." And he pilloried Roosevelt as a self-made "political saviour" who presumed a superiority that compelled him to protect the people: "I don't want a smug lot of experts to sit down behind closed doors in Washington and play Providence to me."[7] He rang the changes on the old faith. He talked of a "Parliament of the People"—"Our part is to lift so high the incomparable standards of the common interest and the common justice that all men with vision, all men with hope, all men with the convictions of America in their hearts, will crowd to the standard and a new day of achievement may come for the liberty which we love."[8] He boasted: "Life comes from the Soil." He wanted to "emancipate" business—to "liberate the vital energies" of the people. He demanded, above all, "justice," not "benevolence."[9]

For all his reputation for intellectualism, for all his desire to "let the darkness out," Wilson proved himself in 1912 chiefly a master of the glittering generality, a wizard at slogans and catchwords, a prophet of vague hopes and deep desires. There was no demagoguery here. He believed what he said. But there was a vagueness that betrayed his own uncertainty in his travels from tradition to reform. To avoid specifics was good campaigning, but, in any case, he did not yet know how he would resolve them. His speeches betrayed no understanding of the modern economy. There was no discussion of how, in practice, the elaborate process of government and business could be unveiled, or more important, how the people could be persuaded to take the opportunities they were offered. Citing his own stupendous victories in New Jersey, he assured the people: "The way to resume is to resume."[10]

It was a campaign filled with hazards and confusion. Wilson narrowly escaped serious injury when his Pullman was hit by a freight car in the West, again just before election when his head was gashed in a highway accident. There was much confusion among McAdoo, who took the lead at headquarters, House, who operated subtly behind the scenes, and scores of other leaders. In the complicated politics Wilson sometimes stubbed his toe, as he did too obviously by snubbing Boss Murphy at the New York State Fair. Then, following Colonel House's advice, he refused to support anti-boss rebels in New York and quietly allowed Murphy to control the state nominations through a carefully rigged "open" convention. Wilson's progressive supporters were sickened, but they still worked for him. There was no choice.

And, Southerner that he was, Wilson carefully dodged

requests that colored voters be recognized, that he reassure them of their future in the party. The most he would offer was a written statement that he desired for the Negro "justice executed with liberality and cordial good feeling."[11] A Democratic nominee must fear the wrath of the Southern white supremacists more than he did the resentments of the scattered and weak Northern Negro voters.

A month before the election, newspapers, gamblers and politicians had all concluded that Wilson would win. When the votes rolled in on November 5, he had a landslide in the Electoral College. But the popular vote told a significant story.* Wilson had six and a quarter million, Roosevelt a little over four million, Taft nearly three and a half million. Taft's votes and Roosevelt's combined would have beaten him. But, perhaps, if there had been only two candidates, Republicans would not have polled this total of seven and a quarter million. Another thing: both Wilson and the two Republicans fell short of their record party votes in the past. Perhaps some conservative Democrats had gone to Taft, perhaps some progressive Republicans to Wilson. But nearly one million progressives of various kinds had voted in protest for Eugene Debs, the Socialist candidate. There was one thing beyond all doubt. It was a vote for change, reform, progress—even Taft said he was a progressive. But it was also clear that there was immense national disagreement on the nature of that progress.

Yet Arthur Link has concluded:

> ...it was as much a political revolution as Jefferson's election had been.... 1912 effected an im-

*Wilson: 6,293,091
Roosevelt: 4,119,507
Taft: 3,484,956
Debs: 901,873

portant shift in the geographical control of the federal government. For one thing, Southern influence had been decisive in nominating Wilson and directing his campaign, and Southerners would soon be given the same share in formulating national policies that their grandfathers once enjoyed. But the most significant result of all the preceding three or four years of political ferment was the emergence of Woodrow Wilson as a national leader.... the Democratic party and the country now had a leader of resolution, ability and boldness. ... He would be embarrassed by no important political bargains. Few presidents have entered office so completely free to serve the general interest.[12]

And Wilson intended to lead. "The President is at liberty," he had once written, "both in law and conscience, to be as big a man as he can."[13] And he had seen that the President had tremendous potential advantages over Congress, if he chose to exercise them: "The true significance of the matter...," he had said, "is that the greatest power lies with that part of the government which is in most direct communication with the nation itself."[14] He knew the outrageous challenge of the job, and he had plans for simplifying it, for preventing his energies from being dispersed by the trivial. Only five years before he had laid out the blueprint: "... he need reserve for himself only the larger matters of counsel and that general oversight of the business.... most of our presidents have taken their duties too literally and have attempted the impossible. But we can safely predict that as the multitude of the President's duties increases ... the incumbents of the great office will more and more come to feel that they are administering it in its truest purpose and with greatest effect by regarding themselves as less and less executive officers and more and more directors of affairs and leaders of the nation."[15]

His fundamental concepts of leadership came from the British parliamentary system. In February, 1913, he wrote to his future Attorney-General of the President: "He must be prime minister, as much concerned with the guidance of legislation as with the just and orderly execution of law."[16] He would be a party leader; he would push through a party program. But he would be guided inexorably by his fundamental belief in political democracy.

When he came to face the realities of the White House, Wilson would grasp serious limitations to his preconceived theories. He would not be able to shuck off all the trivia, nor even a large part of it. The decentralization of the parties, the lack of discipline, the regional differences—and the rigid limits of the constitutional structure—would prevent him from ever being in a real sense the prime minister he had hoped to be. And he would find that there was more to the challenge of democracy than merely giving power to that political abstraction, the people. He would learn more of the importance of institutions during his White House years than he had ever known as a scholar.

But Wilson would also be helped and impeded by the strange personality that nature and experience had given him. He could arouse the deep emotional loyalties of people—at a distance—and now the partisans flocked to Trenton and to Sea Girt with all the zeal of converts to the faith of a new prophet. He could, and did, talk constantly of the need for advice, his commitment to common counsel, his desire to discuss everything widely and publicly. But the Wilson who had, as a teacher, found lectures rewarding and discussions difficult, still found it easier to educate those around him than to learn from them. He was a democrat; but he was also a moralist. He often seemed more Presbyterian preacher than politician.

Mencken would write bluntly of him: "Wilson was

a typical Puritan—of the better sort, perhaps, for he at least toyed with the ambition to appear as a gentleman, but nevertheless a true Puritan. Magnanimity was simply beyond him."[17] Years later, Felix Frankfurter, who as a young man had worked under him in several capacities, explained: "Wilson was very dogmatic. That was his great limitation, and he didn't believe in debating. He used phrases like 'laying mind against mind' and 'consulting the common council of the nation,' but he didn't carry that out in practice at all—quite the opposite."[18] And he went on to confess: "Wilson didn't appeal to me man to man. I didn't warm in his presence. I recognized then as I do now his great qualities, but he was not sympatico to me as a man. He was cold ... intolerant; fundamentally didn't like his kind. He believed in democracy in the abstract, but didn't care for people. That's true! And he'd cut off their heads with equanimity."[19]

With intimates, Wilson could relax, be genial, easy, gay. But there were few outside his family with whom he could reach these terms. He never could with McAdoo, one of his earliest supporters, later his son-in-law, for eight years a member of his Cabinet. To be really a Wilson intimate one must be discreet beyond all suspicion, one must be sensitive to the man's pride and moralism, one must be, above all, outside the official circles of command. By the end of the campaign, Wilson had found only one such man, Colonel Edward M. House. House was his only close personal friend.

House was ambitious, and in his own way a ruthless man. Wealthy, sophisticated, he had devoted himself to the search for and use of power. But he had also learned that he must work through others. He had come early in life to covet the quiet joy of pulling the puppet strings from behind the scenes. He was a great practical joker, and a great conspirator, as one scholar relates:

Once, for example [in preparatory school], a rather dull-witted lad who had cut classes and was desperate for an excuse to offer the headmaster asked House for advice. House suggested that he say he had gone sailing early in the morning and had been becalmed. This the boy did. The fact was, as the headmaster and practically everyone else knew, ice had choked the harbor for weeks. The errant "sailor" was properly chastised. House was enchanted. . . .

House played pranks which provided him with opportunities to feel superior in a very special way. By some small action of his, he set in motion a chain of events which he could then sit back and contemplate with quiet amusement, an amusement tinged with contempt. To "control" people, to be able, while himself seemingly calm and unruffled, to turn their emotions on and off at will, gratified him enormously.[20]

Leaving his native Texas behind him, House had moved to New York in a conscious quest for a man to make the President. He had hit upon Wilson after others had failed. And he had helped materially. But House also knew the limits of his own security. He could have immense ranges of secret pleasure as long as he could see his plots and plans working out through Wilson's office, his ideas flowing from Wilson's pen. But House also knew that the moment he became too prominent, the moment he claimed influence for himself, that very moment his house of power would collapse into a shambles. As one of his biographers bluntly explains:

"House quickly learned that in trying to influence Wilson it was expedient to appeal to his vanity. . . . If Wilson shied away from a recommendation it was House's practice simply to drop it without any indication of displeasure. The Colonel once told his biographer that he never argued with the President beyond a certain point. . . .

"When Wilson showed House the draft of a speech or outlined some plan or policy, he was certain of a sympathetic and admiring reception. House was an unfailingly good listener and, to Wilson, unfailingly reverential. . . . Most important of all, House was careful to nurture the impression that he was satisfied to work through Wilson, that he did not covet independent power in an official position. . . . As early as April, 1913, he wrote his brother-in-law, Sidney Mezes, with some concern (if also with some pleasure!) of the publicity he was getting. 'I do not know how much of this kind of thing W. W. can stand. The last edition of Harper's Weekly spoke of me as "Assistant President House." I think it is time for me to go to Europe or take to the woods.' "[21]

Wilson may not have thought much about the matter. He simply liked House; instinctively he could trust the man. And he found him immensely useful. Wilson's official biographer and personal friend has noted: " 'House . . . had qualities that Wilson lacked.' He liked to confer and adjust, and he had the time to do it. He was incurably confidential. . . . He was indefatigable, going about shrewd-eyed, silent, unobtrusive."[22]

During the hectic interim between election and inauguration, Wilson sometimes fled to House's home for relaxation. When he left for the isolation of a Bermuda vacation, he gave House his first important assignment—to round up raw material for the Cabinet. The group that House largely chose was generally competent, broadly representative of the various wings of the party, the disparate sections of the country. Bryan became Secretary of State, despite his general ignorance of foreign affairs. But prestige was important to him; and Bryan's prestige was important to Wilson's legislative success. Bryan's friend Josephus Daniels of North Carolina became Secretary of the Navy. McAdoo was rewarded handsomely with the Treasury Department. Franklin Lane of California became Secretary of the Interior. Lindley Garrison of New Jersey headed the War Department. And William B. Wilson, a dynamic organizer for the United Mine Workers, became the first Secretary of Labor. But, if there were progressives and old Bryanites here, there were also stolid conservatives—David F. Houston, economist and friend of Colonel House, in the Department of Agriculture; James C. McReynolds as Attorney-General; the tough old Texas professional Albert Burleson as Postmaster General; and an uninspiring product of the Brooklyn machine, William C. Redfield, in the Commerce Department. There was much give and take in the process of recruiting this Cabinet. Wilson himself stolidly refused to give his inadequate campaign manager, William McCombs, a Cabinet job. But in other matters he proved surprisingly docile. He was determined, for example, to have with him in Washington the brilliant lawyer who had done so much to shape his own ideas, Louis D. Brandeis. But, when House objected that Brandeis would raise controversy, that there would be political objections, Wilson backed down and accepted the difficult and conservative McReynolds, and the nonentity Redfield instead.

And Wilson, like many another strong President, would hold himself aloof from his Cabinet. It proved a dangerous place to reveal confidences; the secrets soon appeared in the press. And Wilson could not take easily the advice of his official subordinates. He sat at the driver's wheel. His Cabinet was viewed as a collection of administrative subordinates. There was never a whisper of the collective cabinet responsibility that might have been expected to go along with his British conception of the prime ministership.

While the Cabinet was being formed, Wilson spent much of his own time conferring with the congressional leaders whose help he would need. And he moved to strengthen the public image of his progressivism, an image he himself saw more clearly as each month passed:

Having won the election, he was free to speak his heart and conscience without fear that any man would accuse him of soliciting votes; and his tongue was loosed by the exposure in a Congressional investigation of methods by which bankers controlled vast industrial enterprises. . . .

At a dinner of the Southern Society of New York, whose leaders had promoted his candidacy, the prophet had loosed the indignation that had been festering in him ever since his frustration at Princeton. His tense, resonant voice had asserted, as the hall became quiet and people sat forward in their chairs; "Business cannot be disturbed unless the minds of those who conduct it are disturbed." To Wilson a panic—like hell—was merely "a state of mind," because, he said, "when a panic occurs there is just as much wealth in the country the day after the panic as the day before." Sometimes, he explained, "panics are said to occur because certain gentlemen want to create the impression that the wrong thing is going to be done." To any man living who dared to precipitate a panic in that way, Wilson promised "a gibbet . . . as high as Haman's." And then he added: "But that is only figuratively speaking. What I will do will be to direct the attention of the people to him, and I think that they will cut him to the quick."[23]

As he left for Washington, it was with a deep sense of mission. A prophet to his people, he had been chosen to lead them. In Bermuda he had carefully prepared the inaugural address whose measured phrases set the tone for one of the most dramatic, intensive legislative victories in the history of the Presidency:

March 4, 1913: a sparkling winter's day in gala Washington; festooned balconies, soldiers, bands, and gay banners—Princeton's orange and black almost as much in evidence as the national red, white, and blue.

Vast crowds thronged the plaza around the Capitol and the inauguration platform: Justices in black robes, diplomats and generals in brilliant uniforms, a sea of faces, a great shout of welcome—all centering upon a straight, spare figure in the tribunal with bared head, book in hand, to whom the Chief Justice of the United States was administering the oath.

The Bible used, at the President-elect's request, was Mrs. Wilson's. Opened at random for him to kiss, his lips brushed these verses of the 119th Psalm:

"And take not the word of truth utterly out of my mouth; for I have hoped in thy judgments.

"So I shall keep thy law continually for ever and ever.

"And I will walk at liberty: for I seek thy precepts.

"I will speak of thy testimonies also before kings and will not be ashamed."

At the beginning of the ceremonies, the President-elect, seeing that the people were crowded far back and that there was a large open space in front of the speaker's stand, called the guard and said: "Let the people come forward."

They came with a rush.[24]

There has been a change of government. . . . At last a vision has been vouchsafed us of our life as a whole.

...Our duty is to cleanse, to reconsider, to restore, to correct the evil without impairing the good, to purify and humanize every process of our common life without weakening or sentimentalizing it. There has been something crude and heartless and unfeeling in our haste to succeed and be great. Our thought has been "Let every man look out for himself, let every generation look out for itself," while we reared giant machinery which made it impossible that any but those who stood at the levers of control should have a chance to look out for themselves....

We have come now to the sober second thought. The scales of heedlessness have fallen from our eyes. We have made up our minds to square every process of our national life again with the standards we so proudly set up at the beginning and have always carried at our hearts. Our work is a work of restoration.... Justice, and only justice, shall always be our motto.... This is not a day of triumph; it is a day of dedication. Here muster not the forces of party but the forces of humanity.[25]

NOTES, CHAPTER 6

1. Joseph P. Tumulty, **Woodrow Wilson as I Know Him** (N.Y.: Doubleday, Page and Company, 1921), p. 36.
2. William Allen White, **Woodrow Wilson: The Man, His Times, and His Task** (Boston: Houghton Mifflin Company, 1924), p. 264.
3. Arthur S. Link, **Wilson: The Road to the White House** (Princeton, N.J.: Princeton University Press, 1947), p. 473.
4. Richard Hofstadter, **The American Political Tradition and the Men Who Made It** (Vintage Edition; N. Y.: Alfred A. Knopf, Inc., 1948), pp. 255–56.
5. Woodrow Wilson, **The New Freedom** (Spectrum Edition; N.Y.: Prentice-Hall, Inc., 1961), pp. 75, 77.
6. Ibid., pp. 27, 35, 36, 132, 164.
7. Ibid., p. 49.
8. Ibid., p. 74.
9. Ibid., pp. 59, 117, 151, 161.
10. Ibid., p. 133.

11. Link, op. cit., p. 505.
12. Arthur S. Link, Woodrow Wilson and the Progressive Era, 1910–1917 (N.Y.: Harper and Brothers, 1954), p. 24.
13. Woodrow Wilson, Constitutional Government in the United States (N.Y.: Columbia University Press, 1908), p. 70.
14. Ibid., pp. 108–09.
15. Ibid., p. 81.
16. Ray Stannard Baker, Woodrow Wilson: Life and Letters (N.Y.: Doubleday, Doran and Company, 1927–39), IV, 131.
17. H. L. Mencken, A Mencken Chrestomathy (N.Y.: Alfred A. Knopf, Inc., 1949), p. 248.
18. Felix Frankfurter, Felix Frankfurter Reminisces: Recorded in Talks with Dr. Harlan B. Phillips (Anchor Edition; Garden City, N.Y.: Doubleday and Company, 1962), p. 98.
19. Ibid, p. 100.
20. Alexander L. and Juliette L. George, Woodrow Wilson and Colonel House (N.Y.: The John Day Company, 1956), pp. 80–81.
21. Ibid., pp 125–26.
22. Baker, op. cit., III, 304.
23. Arthur Walworth, Woodrow Wilson (London: Longmans, Green and Company, 1958), I, 289.
24. Ruth Cranston, The Story of Woodrow Wilson: Twenty-eighth President of the United States, Pioneer of World Democracy (N.Y.: Simon and Schuster, 1945), pp. 109–10.
25. U. S. 63d. Congress, Special Session, Senate Documents (Washington, D. C.: 1913), No. 3, pp. 3–6.

7. "JUSTICE, NOT BENEVOLENCE"

Washington in 1913, while no longer the muddy village of Lincoln's day, was still more a sleepy southern town than the granite and marble metropolis of today. Only the climate has remained constant, and impossible—damp-cold, penetrating in winter; steaming-hot, enervating, at worst sickening in summer. Then as now, the city was romantically beautiful in the early spring, but it was an unhappy location for the seat of government. Where the imposing buildings of the government agencies now stand along Constitution Avenue, there was in 1913 little but swampy, rough land, scattered with rickety buildings. Just to the north, Pennsylvania Avenue, the axis between the White House and the Capitol, although known to the local people as "The Avenue," was an enormously wide, unattractive street lined largely by dilapidated residences and grimy stores.

Clattering streetcars swayed through Washington with more competition from balky horses than from the few automobiles. The hub of the fashionable district, DuPont Circle, not yet a traffic hazard, was an easy walk from the shops on F Street. Georgetown remained a distinct, typically southern town, and Chevy Chase, now a teeming dormitory of government workers, was a sparsely settled rural suburb.

To the city's permanent, voteless inhabitants, the administrations that came and went were a passing show, only rarely taken seriously as a part of life. In the eyes of the élite of Potomac society, still living in the shadowy tradition of the post-Civil War decades, the government worker, elected or appointed, remained somewhat disreputable, a notch, perhaps, above the tradesman. A few exceptions—the judiciary, the diplomats, the occasional Senator who had been in service for a generation—were received in fashionable parlors; even they, to their good fortune, were not subjected to the rigors of the cocktail party, then happily uninvented. . . .

The Wilsons found sleepy Washington agreeable. A southern family, they were at once at home in the provincial southern atmosphere. Local "Jim Crow" ordinances seemed as natural to them as did the soft drawl of clerks who dispensed yard goods to the girls. Never accustomed to the pace or diversions of urban life, they did not miss them. They were quickly busy. Mrs. Wilson, quiet, warm, efficient, gave endless hours to slum-clearance and settlement-house work. Margaret, the oldest daughter, setting a precedent for a later day, went on the concert stage. The two younger girls lost themselves in romance; Jessie soon married Francis Sayre, an able academician; Eleanor later married William Gibbs McAdoo, who seemed, to his critics, to be relying on matrimony as well as the patronage of the Treasury to further his career. Wilson himself, immersed in his office, must have found his life and surroundings somehow familiar. He had become accustomed, after all, while president of Princeton, to the limitations on privacy that presidencies impose. And to be in the South was to be in his native land.[1]

It was his warm and comforting family life that provided Wilson with an anchor against the tides of tension, with a bulwark against his nervousness, his faltering health, the irritations of office. "It is a good thing a President doesn't know in advance what it means, or we should never have any Presidents," he *said at one point. "He needs to have the constitution of an athlete, the patience of a mother, the endurance of an early Christian."*[2] Yet,

All was so jolly and novel during the first week in the new home that it was hard for the Wilsons to understand what Taft had meant when he said to the President-elect on Inauguration Day: "I'm glad to be going—this is the loneliest place in the world." Woodrow Wilson loved the swift pace of family life about him. He insisted that his wife and daughters preserve the candor and integrity of their own personalities. . . . The normality of their doings helped him to escape unhealthful moods. His new office demanded dignity, but he could not put it on without being conscious of acting and, therefore, a little ashamed of himself. He liked to think of himself as standing next to the chair of State, not sitting on it. "The old kink is still in me," he explained. . . . "Everything is persistently *impersonal*. I am administering a great office—no doubt the greatest in the world—but I do not seem to be identified with it. . . . This impersonality of my life is a very odd thing . . . but at least prevents me from becoming a fool and thinking myself *it*."

He kept his spirit young and humble by playing tag and rooster fighting with daughter Nellie in the White House corridors. Sometimes he would spend an evening at billiards. Adhering to the habits of earlier years, he punctually followed a daily schedule. Rising early, he sharpened his razor on a heavy leather strop and fancied that he could predict the weather by the sound. He retired at a discreet hour, as he had all his life; and when owls hooting in the magnolias awakened him, he would go to the window and hoot back, and then at breakfast boast that he had "hooted the hooters away." He refused to join the fashionable Chevy Chase Club, for fear that he might be buttonholed by lobbyists, and he best found relaxation at vaudeville shows, where he could himself become one of "the people" to whom he was devoting himself. . . .

The President loved to operate the little electric elevator in the White House, with its panel of mirrors, and his favorite apartments were the dining room and the Blue Room. Next to the Oval Room, where the immediate family spent their evenings, was his own study. In this sanctum he could be alone with his choicest books and with the old, familiar typewriter and its noisy clack—"it and I have gone through many thoughts together, and many emotions," he had written on it a month before taking office. His desk here, unlike the official one in the West Wing, was always piled high with documents."[3]

So far as he could, Wilson tried to maintain his warm relations with old friends. One visitor wrote: "It was just like the old times in Princeton. After dinner we drew up chairs round a fire in the drawing room and talked about books. Mr. Wilson stretched himself out on the hearth rug and recited poetry, as we had often heard him do. . . . The President of the United States rocked back and forth in the firelight, with his knees clasped between his hands, declaiming sonnets, while his face glowed with affection. I have never heard a man address a woman with a more perfect blending of love and respect than was present in the word 'Ellen' when Mr. Wilson addressed his wife."[4]

But, even with the warming influence of his family, there was the constant terror that the President might collapse, that the fragile health that had tyrannized him for over a decade might give out too soon. Cary Grayson, his physician, has described the problem he and his famous patient faced as they looked ahead to the monstrous demands of the Presidency:

When he entered the White House...
Dr. Weir Mitchell prophesied that the new President
could not possibly outlive his first term. Careful examin-
ation and all the medical tests revealed that there was no
organic disease, but much sedentary life had been bad for
a constitution not naturally vigorous, and he was below
par. It was a clear case for preventive medicine.

With his confidence and cooperation, four outstand-
ing elements of treatment and of his own personality
kept him going under conditions that would soon have
exhausted the powers of a younger and stronger man.
These four things were system, exercise, a sense of
humor, and food suited to his idiosyncracies. . . . The
remarkable thing is not that he broke down finally, but
that, with his constitution and his burdens, he kept well
by obedience to the simple laws of health.[5]

But, as Wilson learned to live with the White House,
he faced the problems that would blast his naive plans
for simplifying the office. The most significant was the
management of his party's vast and sprawling disagree-
ments. In 1912, they had been briefly united by the
hope of victory. Now they were desperately fighting
again, each segment hoping for Wilson's influence to
win its local victory. Only a little more difficult than
most situations were the tangled and interminable
fights in New York. A score of New York City congressmen raucously demanded the Wilson patronage for their
regular machines. But Tammany had opposed Wilson at
Baltimore, while a noisy and enthusiastic claque of upstate progressives had shouted and fought and helped
to organize the sweeping vote for Wilson in the state.
Now they too demanded recognition, and precisely for
that purpose of destroying Tammany. Their agents were
prominently placed—Secretary of the Treasury McAdoo,
Assistant Secretary of the Navy Franklin Roosevelt. Instinctively Wilson favored the reformers.

But there were other dimensions of the tangled problem. The reformers proved unable to discipline themselves, could never provide Wilson with a tough and efficient organization to replace the Tammany alliance. They needed Wilson's help to do it. But he could not afford to scrap the regular New York organization, until they could provide him with an alternative. And his power in local politics was weak, as a President's always is. Most important, he needed the votes of the New York congressmen, and he needed especially the support of strategically-placed oldsters like Brooklyn's John Fitzgerald, who chaired the Ways and Means Committee. If he sought to break Tammany, he courted defeat for his program. If he supported Tammany, he courted the disillusionment of the liberals. Faced with the impossible, Wilson simply withdrew. He left his subordinates to fight it out within his own administration. But he could not detach himself completely. He spent immense amounts of time carefully turning aside the appeals that were pushed relentlessly to his desk. And often he had to insist upon an appointment to ensure the votes on a strategic bill in Congress. Colonel House played constantly at New York politics, anonymously, erratically, behind the scenes. The confusion was immense. Some appointments went to the progressives, some to Tammany and its friends. Often the timing was bad. In the end, the hopes for a progressive Democracy in New York were crushed. By 1916, everyone in the New York party was angry with Wilson. Yet, by 1916, Wilson could also point quietly to the fact that New York congressmen had regularly and loyally supported his program.

This was only one of the scores of political tangles through which Wilson fought his way while his legislative program evolved and the problems of foreign policy pressed in upon him. His handling of post-office appointments was typical of his initial idealism, and his rapid *disillusionment. At the beginning he told the Post-master-General:*

> "Now Burleson, I want to say to you that my administration is going to be a progressive administration. I am not going to advise with reactionary or standpat senators or representatives in making these appointments. I am going to appoint forward-looking men and I am going to satisfy myself that they are honest and capable."

"When I heard that," remarked Burleson, "it paralyzed me. I never felt more depressed in my life. I knew it meant ruination for him. . . . I made up my mind to take my stand no matter what happened. I stayed with him over two hours. . . .

" 'Mr. President,' I said, 'if you pursue this policy, it means that your administration is going to be a failure. It means the defeat of the measures of reform that you have next to your heart. . . .'

"As your Postmaster General," said Burleson, "I am going to make 56,000 appointments. I will see honest and capable men in every office. But I will consult with the men on the Hill. I have been here a long time. . . . I know these congressmen and senators. They are mostly good men. If they are turned down, they will hate you and will not vote for any thing you want."

A full week passed before Wilson sent again for Burleson. As soon as he appeared, the President said:

"Well, Burleson, let's consider these cases."

Burleson took up the first in order, an appointment recommended by Congressman Moon of Tennessee, to which Wilson had received certain hot protests. Wilson detailed these objections, and then leaned back and threw up his arms.

"Burleson, I can't appoint a man like that!"

Burleson then went on to tell him the whole story, both sides, quite frankly, picturing the situation in the

little town in Tennessee, the Congressman's connection
with the local situation, all the intensely human and
even dramatic features which enter into such a situation. It was a long story but Wilson listened intently,
without saying a word. All of the complicated elements
of politics in a democracy were bound up in this one
trivial appointment. When Burleson stopped talking,
the President was silent for a moment and then said:
  "Well, Burleson, I will appoint him."[6]

*Even more time-consuming and difficult were the con-
stant pressures of the interest groups. Here again, Wilson's major guideline was the fate of his legislative program. Where the pressures were not directly related to
it, he tried to soften them and stall them off. But this
took time, and skill, and worry.*

*For this Southerner in the White House, perhaps the
most difficult of these problems was the pressure for
Negro rights:*

  As soon as he was settled in office he was
visited by various delegations of Negroes, uncertain of
the status of their race as office holders under a Democratic administration with a President who was a
Southerner by birth: and a little later there began to be
charges that coloured people were being segregated in
certain departments of the government. The appointment of a coloured Democrat of Oklahoma as Register
of the Treasury, a place traditionally held by a Negro,
had not been pushed. One of the most active friends
of the Coloured race was Oswald Garrison Villard, editor
of the *New York Evening Post*.... When Villard protested strongly, seconded by the National Association
for the Advancement of Colored People, the President
replied:
  "It is true that the segregation of the colored employees in the several departments was begun upon the

initiative and at the suggestion of several of the heads of departments, but as much in the interest of the Negroes as for any other reason, with the approval of some of the most influential Negroes I know, and with the idea that the friction, or rather the discontent and uneasiness, which had prevailed in many of the departments would thereby be removed. It is as far as possible from being a movement *against* the Negroes. I sincerely believe it to be in their interest. And what distresses me about your letter is to find that you look at it in so different a light. . . . My own feeling is, by putting certain bureaus and sections of the service in the charge of Negroes we are rendering them more safe in their possession of office and less likely to be discriminated against."

On the other hand Wilson soon found that he had to meet the protests of Southern senators and extreme Southern opinion against the appointment of any Negroes at all to public office. When Thomas Dixon, author of *The Clansman* and other novels dealing with the Negro problem from a bitterly Southern point of view, wrote protesting against the appointment of "a Negro to boss white girls as Register of the Treasury," the President replied:

"I do not think you know what is going on down here. We are handling the force of colored people who are now in the departments in just the way in which they ought to be handled. We are trying—and by degrees succeeding—a plan of concentration which will put them all together and will not in any one bureau mix the two races."[7]

And while Wilson dealt with the interminable and irritating tangles that seemed to him so irrelevant to his major purpose and his duty, he had also to manage the routine deskwork of a presidency that would expand monumentally during his years in the White House.

Perhaps because he was so used to the scholarly isolation of his study, without secretary, he did an appalling number of things himself. It became customary for officials at all levels to receive his personally typed "chits" and directives in response to the long letters their staffs had prepared for them to sign. Sometimes the sheer pressure overwhelmed this emotional, physically harrassed, horrendously serious man. When he had been in the White House only three months, he would sit down one morning to write to his wife of his distress at missing his own daughter's engagement party: "I can hardly keep back the tears as I write. . . . It is a bitter, bitter thing that I cannot come to my dear ones; but the duty is clear, and that ought to suffice. I cannot choose as an individual what I shall do; I must choose always as a President. . . . The President is a superior kind of slave, and must content himself with the reflection that the kind is superior! . . . I am too lonely. I must think quietly and not with rebellion. The big house is still: I must copy its stately peace, and try to be worthy of the trust of those whom I try to serve."[8]

This was, above all, a man of duty. Before his administration was two weeks old, he had begun the relentless drive to see his legislative program through Congress. For two long years, he drove himself, and he drove his Congress, and by the end of 1914, he had fulfilled the promises he had made in 1912. It was a most remarkable feat of legislative leadership. It was like the thunderous days at Princeton, on a larger and more significant scale. As Arthur Link has pointed out:

> No one who had read Wilson's writings could have doubted that he would inaugurate a new system of presidential leadership. . . . Wilson's strengthening and extension of the presidential powers constituted perhaps his most lasting contribution to American political practice. A strong believer in party government,

he decided to work through and with his party in Congress, rather than to govern by a coalition of progressives, as he might have done. . . .

Wilson's methods and practices of leadership were spectacularly successful, to be sure; but they succeeded in large measure because of the peculiar circumstances that prevailed during his first administration. To begin with, because of the Republican rupture, the Democrats had a majority of seventy-three in the House during the critical first two years of the administration. Moreover, many of the Democratic members were new and inexperienced—114 of the 290 had been elected for the first time in 1912—and Wilson easily dominated them. In addition, the old-line Democratic leaders like Oscar W. Underwood, William C. Adamson, or Henry D. Clayton realized that the fate of their party depended upon their performance, and they willingly co-operated with the President to prove that they were not, as Republicans often charged, "the organized incapacity of the country." Finally, most of the Democrats in the Senate were able, responsible, and progressive, as eager as Wilson himself to give the administration success. . . . Wilson's task was one mainly of uniting his forces and encouraging the strong Democratic determination to make good.[9]

It was not easily done. Sometimes he had to appeal directly to the people, in a desperate gamble that Congress would bend. He whipped them through a continuous session until his program was done, despite the summer heat, the restlessness, the fatigue. He threatened them with continuous special sessions if they adjourned. He worked constantly and closely with the leaders. He wielded the patronage with tough and inspired realism when he dealt with legislators whose constituents were howling for rewards. And he learned to compromise more than he had ever been willing to do before, to preserve the fundamentals. But he was still sure of himself, still certain that his was the side of The Right, still drastically impatient with opposition. In September, 1913, when tempers all over Washington were frayed thin by six continuous months of congressional sessions, he protested to an intimate confidant:

Do not believe anything you read in the newspapers.... Their lying is shameless and colossal! ... [They] represent me ... as master of the situation here, bending Congress to my indomitable individual will. That is, of course, silly. Congress is made up of thinking men who want the party to succeed as much as I do, and who wish to serve their country effectively and intelligently. They ... accept my guidance because they see that I am attempting only to mediate their own thoughts and purposes.... They are using me; I am not driving them.... And what a pleasure it is, what a deep human pleasure, to work with strong men, who do their own thinking and know how to put things in shape! Why a man should wish to be the whole show and surround himself with weak men, I cannot imagine! How dull it would be! ... Power consists in one's capacity to link his will with the purpose of others, to lead by reason and a gift for cooperation.[10]

Yet, a week later he could write to the same person:

The struggle goes on down here without intermission. Why it should be a struggle is hard (cynicism put on one side) to say. Why should public men, senators of the United States, have to be led and stimulated to what all the country knows to be their duty.[11]

But the results were magnificent. On April 7, he had called the special session to deal with the tariff reform. On June 23, deep in a fight against the tariff lobbies, he went to Congress again with his personal demand for banking and currency reform. And these were not mere "messages," tediously read by a clerk to a near-empty house. For Wilson dramatized his personal leadership by going to Congress personally to speak his views and to capture their support. This itself was as new as the President's conviction that the legislative program must start with him. On July 15, the Newlands Act went into effect, planned to relieve a major labor problem by providing a Board of Mediation and Conciliation for the railroad industry. On October 3, the Underwood-Simmons Tariff Act was finally passed, pointing a new and downward direction, a direction away from protection of already bloated special interests. On December 23, he signed the Federal Reserve Act. On January 20, 1914, he went to Congress to demand revision of the antitrust laws. On September 26, the Federal Trade Commission Act was passed, on October 15, the Clayton Anti-Trust Act.

Joseph Dorfman has described, in brief, the substance of the program:

Wilson considered the tariff the real problem. "Every business question in this country," he stated, "comes back, sooner or later, to the question of the tariff," and the tariff, he felt, should be cautiously reduced in such a manner as to revive the energies of the business community. . . .

Having succeeded in obtaining some reductions in it, he then asked for the reform of the banking and currency system. Congress must give the businessmen a banking and currency system, he said, which would enable them to "make use of the freedom of enterprise and of individual initiative which we are about to bestow upon them" through tariff reform. They should create a currency "readily, elastically responsive to sound credit." The control of the new system of bank-

ing and of issue must be vested in the "government itself, so that the banks may be the instruments, not the
masters, of business and of individual enterprise."

Following the broad terms laid down by Wilson,
Representative Carter Glass of Virginia and Senator
Robert L. Owen of Oklahoma pushed through the
measure that became the Federal Reserve Act. The
usual opposition to a central bank was avoided by setting up twelve regional Federal Reserve banks with the
stock owned by the national banks in the districts and
those state banks and trust companies that joined the
system. But at the head of the entire system was the
Federal Reserve Board appointed by the President with
Senate approval.

Under the scheme a member bank could rediscount
at its regional Federal Reserve Bank short-term commercial paper and paper issued for the purpose of carrying on trading in federal securities, but rediscounting of
paper issued for carrying on other trading in stocks,
bonds, or investment securities was prohibited. Through
rediscounting, the member banks would receive a new
currency, the Federal Reserve notes. These notes the
Federal Reserve Bank could obtain by pledging with the
Federal Reserve Agent—who would also be chairman
and a director of the Federal Reserve Bank—a 100 per
cent collateral consisting of gold and paper eligible for
rediscount. The Federal Reserve Bank would have to
maintain a 40 per cent gold reserve against Federal Reserve notes in circulation, but the gold given as collateral for the notes could be considered part of the
reserve. . . .

The measure seemed to please practically all interests. . . . There was considerable opposition, however, to
the third main step in Wilson's reform program on
trusts and monopolies. "Private monopoly is indefensi-
ble and intolerable," Wilson declared. His program, he
hoped, would be "comprehensive but not a radical or

unacceptable" one, and the items of reform would be those changes which "opinion deliberately sanctions and for which business waits," such as preventing "interlockings of the personnel of the directorships of great corporations—banks and railroads, industrial, commercial, and public service bodies." This would bring a "new spirit of initiative, new blood, into the management of our great business enterprises".... the country would, he thought, willingly accept a law empowering the Interstate Commerce Commission to superintend and regulate the financing of railroad development. Another forward step would be an explicit legislative definition of the existing anti-trust law. Nothing hampered business so much as uncertainty, he said; monopolistic practices, having been abundantly exposed, should be explicitly and specifically forbidden by statute. An interstate trade commission should be established, not to make terms with monopoly or to assume control of business, but to serve only as an indispensable instrument of information and publicity, as a clearing house for the facts by which both the public and the managers of great business undertakings could be guided. Holding companies should be prohibited, and holders of large blocks of stock in a number of companies might be allowed voting rights only in one company.

Congress refused to extend the power of the Interstate Commerce Commission, but it was willing to establish a Federal Trade Commission. This Commission, which superseded the Bureau of Corporations, was given the authority to order business engaged in interstate commerce to cease "unfair methods of competition" in commerce; that is, the Commission had the power to issue "cease and desist" orders, and it was authorized to seek aid from the courts when business failed to comply. Along with this, Congress passed the Clayton Act, which limited common directorships and forbade a variety of practices, including the acquisition of stock by one corporation in like enterprises in commerce when its effect "may be to substantially lessen competition . . . or tend to create a monopoly." It also declared it illegal for anyone engaged in commerce within the jurisdiction of the United States to discriminate in price between different purchasers of commodities. . . . The proponents recognized that "fair competition" was a shifting concept but to them this was no serious disadvantage, for the Commission would be composed of economists as well as lawyers and men experienced in industry.[12]

When he went to Congress early in December, 1914, Wilson could claim: "Our program of legislation with regard to the regulation of business is now virtually complete. . . . In it every honest man, every man who believes that the public interest is part of his own interest, may walk with perfect confidence."[13]

The reaction among progressives had been electric. The New Freedom was now law, at least it seemed to be. But in the enthusiasm over achievement, many observers failed to see that it had changed sharply in the process. Even Wilson did not yet sense that the best of his victories were past, that the future would see him trending onward toward goals he could not have seen and would have disowned in 1912. One of his biographers has set the turning point as early as Christmas, 1913, when Wilson had gone to Mississippi for a much-needed rest:

During the warm and sunny weeks at Pass Christian, health and vigor flowed back into Wilson. He felt gloriously relaxed, and so prepared to push ahead. But . . . those weeks proved to be something of a watershed in his life. Things were never again to be as they had been in 1913. Long before another year was out he was to lose the first Mrs. Wilson, whose companionship, whose care for his every interest, whose political instinct and gentle, moderating influence had been of such inestimable value.... And Wilson's public life was to be different, too. For one thing, his relations with Congress would not be quite the same as in his great year of triumph. He would keep control, and see to it that more important legislation was put through, but his leadership would not be quite so willingly or completely accepted as it had been. He had taken Congress by surprise, much as he had taken the legislators at Trenton; but dissenting elements would now have had time to consider ways of obstructing him or giving him trouble at any rate. Then, being a reformer, he inevitably trod on more and more toes. Even with the people he would not have quite the same success. The element of novelty would be lacking.... Other plans and problems stretched before him into the distance, like the wires of the telephone and telegraph systems which he once thought (though not for long) of trying to bring under government ownership.[14]

NOTES, CHAPTER 7

1. John Blum, **Joe Tumulty and the Wilson Era** (Boston: Houghton Mifflin Company, 1951), pp. 55–56.
2. Ruth Cranston, **The Story of Woodrow Wilson** (N.Y.: Simon and Schuster, 1945), p. 114.
3. Arthur Walworth, **Woodrow Wilson** (London: Longmans, Green and Company, 1958), I, 283–84.
4. Cranston, **op. cit.**, p. 157.
5. Cary T. Grayson, **Woodrow Wilson: An Intimate Memoir** (N.Y.: Holt, Rinehart and Winston, 1960), pp. 81–82.
6. Ray Stannard Baker, **Woodrow Wilson: Life and Letters** (N.Y.: Doubleday, Doran and Company, 1927–39), IV, 45–47.
7. **Ibid.**, pp. 220–22.
8. Walworth, **op. cit.**, pp. 310–311.
9. Arthur S. Link, **Woodrow Wilson and the Progressive Era** (N.Y.: Harper and Brothers, 1954), pp. 34–35.
10. Baker, **op. cit.**, p. 183.

11. Ibid., p. 184.
12. Joseph Dorfman, **The Economic Mind in American Civilization: 1865–1918** (N.Y.: The Viking Press, 1949), pp. 338–41.
13. Baker, op. cit., V, 77.
14. H. C. F. Bell, **Woodrow Wilson and the People** (N.Y.: Doubleday, Doran and Company, 1945), p. 139.

8. TO A LAND DIMLY SEEN

On his first battle—for tariff reform—Wilson had proved brilliantly consistent and wondrously effective. This was the only part of his program on which he had maintained unchanged the view of his youth. He knew precisely what he wanted. He forced Congressman Oscar Underwood to adopt the free import of wool and to set merely nominal and temporary rates on sugar. He pressured recalcitrant congressmen personally, and, when Underwood's Committee reported its bill to the House, it stood for abolishing tariffs on most consumer items, goods made by the "trusts" that were being so sharply attacked, and the average rates had been reduced to about 29 percent from the existing averages of over 40 percent. But the major difficulties were outside Congress, not within. One newspaper reported: "Washington is fairly seething with tariff. . . . Hotels are crowded with businessmen from all over the country. . . . Wool men from as far west as Montana, fruit men from California, beet-sugar men from the West, and cane-sugar men from the South; New England manufacturers, woolen men from Pennsylvania, and representatives of many interests are on the ground to look after their own."[1]

As Herbert Bell has noted:

> . . . there was no one to lobby for the consumers, for the people as a whole. At least there did not seem to be, until Wilson made his . . . dramatic move. He was thoroughly aroused. Not only was the tariff act itself in danger, but the pressure of the lobbyists struck

at his own leadership, at his whole conception of the presidency, at his desire to bring system and responsibility into our legislative process. . . . After the manner of good strategists, the President quietly "estimated the situation," and then, at the end of May, struck suddenly and hard. Through the representatives of the press he appealed to the nation: "Washington has seldom seen so numerous, so industrious and so insidious a lobby. The newspapers are being filled with paid advertisements calculated to mislead the judgments of public men. . . . the people at large have no lobby . . . while great bodies of astute men seek to . . . overcome the interests of the public for their private profit."[2]

At first the Senate resented his interference, but, as progressives of both parties took up the advantage he had given them, the Senate turned to an elaborate investigation of lobbying that brought an immediate and irresistible wave of public reaction against the special interests. In the end, the Senate actually reduced the average rates further. Wilson was delighted, and so was the nation. There might be dispute about the precise effects of the tariff. But there was no dispute that it had been honest without precedent, that it cut deeply into the power of privileged groups. And it was straight in the channel Wilson had outlined during the campaign. Here was something concrete to help the "man on the make" rather than "the man who has already been made."

But, on other matters, Wilson had been forced to wander erratically from the central channel of his New Freedom. The income tax was a case in point. The prime battle had already been fought; the necessary constitutional amendment had been ratified before Wilson took office. But he must use an income tax for the first time. His influence lay on the side of low rates, and only slightly graduated ones. Only reluctantly did he give in to pressure from progressive Republicans like Robert La Follette and George Norris and help push through a compromise that hit the wealthy more heavily than he had intended. His campaign speeches could have justified a conscious use of the tax to redistribute income, to help restore equality of opportunity. But Wilson had no interest in carrying the reconstruction that far.

Yet, if he wandered to the right on income taxes, he tacked sharply to the left as his program for control of banks and currency developed. No one, least of all Wilson, could have predicted in 1912 the path he would take. He knew little of the issues, and his party was divided. The Taft administration had left a plan for banking and currency reform that had been charted by Senator Nelson W. Aldrich. It was supported strongly by the bankers themselves, and for good reason. It would have provided a central bank, controlled by the bankers, not the government, and charged with the issuance of new currency. Wilson's party was generally opposed to central banking of this kind, but they were sharply divided on the issue of control. Congressman Carter Glass favored banker-control. Over two months before the Inauguration, he had briefed Wilson on his plans and had the President-elect's guarded approval, except that Wilson insisted on a "capstone" governing board at the top to coordinate the work of the decentralized units. But when the plan became known, there were violent explosions on all sides. Bankers objected to decentralization and insisted that they must control it. Bryan and his progressive friends in Congress warned Wilson that they would never support it, and insisted instead on a government-controlled bank and government issuance of currency.

It was Brandeis who convinced the President that he must decide between the bankers and the public control. With the issue thus posed, he had little choice.

His own blasts at vested economic monopoly led the way. The dramatic revelations of the Pujo Committee in the House of Representatives in the fall of 1912 had demonstrated sharply to a shocked nation the already steepening concentration of wealth and economic power in the hands of a few New York bankers. On June 23, Wilson told Congress: "The control of the system of banking and of issue . . . must be public, not private, must be vested in Government itself, so that the banks may be the instruments, not the masters, of business and of individual enterprise and initiative."[3]

Wilson's concern was now thoroughly enlisted. He moved at the opposite flank to put down demands by rural congressmen that antitrust regulations be included and that guarantees of more liberal farm credit be written into the law. He failed in the latter, but in giving in to the farmers on this point, he gained Bryan's crucial support. Bryan's persuasion helped see the bill through the House. Wilson's relentless pressure, patronage and persuasion helped see it through the Senate. The Federal Reserve System finally enacted preserved Wilson's capstone board, appointed by the President, and it preserved Glass's local boards, with banker membership. It met Wilson's demands for a device to prevent concentration of monetary control in the hands of the city financiers. It met the demands of rural progressives for decentralization. It met the demands of business for a system that would assure adequate currency and credit, and adequate stability. But it had carried Wilson farther along the road toward government control of economic life than he could possibly have imagined in the fall of 1912.

The fight against the trusts carried him even farther. On this point the New Freedom had been clear, beyond all doubt. Wilson planned to destroy the trusts, by legislation that would make individual officers personally and criminally responsible for illegal acts, and above all by the white glare of publicity. On occasion, he had hinted vaguely that more government activity might be necessary. But the objective was clear. He would not, like T. R., tolerate the "good" trusts and enter the detailed business of regulating them. He would restore, he seemed sure he could restore, the old, segmented, competitive conditions.

That something had to be done at once was clear. Wilson himself had made the attack on economic concentration one of the major planks in his program. The Pujo Committee's investigators had told the nation that four New York banks held ". . . 341 directorships in 112 corporations having aggregate resources or capitalization of $22,245,000,000." That these included "150 directorships in 110 of the greater corporations."[4] But there was a fundamental difficulty with Wilson's initial approach that he was soon compelled to recognize. It might not be possible, or even desirable, to turn back the clock to the days of the small competitors. Wilson's New Freedom might indeed turn out to be the most hopeless kind of reaction. Walter Lippmann saw the problems clearly as he published, that same year, his widely-heralded book, Drift and Mastery:

The ideal is the old ideal, the ideal of Bryan, the method is the new one of governmental interference. . . . The New Freedom means the effort of small businessmen and farmers to use the government against the larger collective organization of industry. Wilson's power comes from them; his feeling is with them; his thinking is for them. Never a word of understanding for the new type of administrator, the specialist, the professionally trained business man; practically no mention of the consumer . . . no hint that it may be necessary to organize the fundamental industries of the country on some definite plan so that our resources may be developed by scientific method instead of by men "on the make"; no friendliness for the larger, collective life upon which the world is entering, only a constant return to the commercial chances of young men trying to set up in business. That is the push and force of this New Freedom, a freedom for the little profiteer, but no freedom for the nation from the narrowness, the poor incentives, the limited vision of small competitors,—no freedom from clamorous advertisement, from wasteful selling, from duplication of plants, from unnecessary enterprise, from the chaos, the welter, the strategy of industrial war . . . to what percentage of the population can he hold out . . . hope? . . . A few hundred at the outside. And for these few hundred sons whose "best energies . . . are inspired by the knowledge that they are their own masters with the paths of the world before them," we are asked to give up the hope of a sane, deliberate organization of national industry brought under democratic control.

I submit that it is an unworthy dream. I submit that the intelligent men of my generation can find a better outlet for their energies than in making themselves masters of little businesses.[5]

The problem was more complex than Wilson had ever dreamed. As Arthur Link has pointed out:

The most significant fact about the first Wilson administration is that the New Freedom, as it was originally conceived by its author, survived for only a few months. . . . In effect, what occurred from 1913 to 1917 adopted many of the assumptions and almost the whole platform of Theodore Roosevelt's New Nationalism. . . .

The philosophic foundations of the New Freedom were dealt . . . . [a] heavy blow during the formulation of antitrust policy by administration leaders. It was Wilson's original idea that all that was required was to define precisely what constituted an unfair trade practice or illegal restraint of trade, so far as to remove all element of doubt from the laws. . . . Brandeis, George L. Rublee, and Representative Stevens of New Hampshire visited the President and persuaded him to change the character of the antitrust program entirely. Under their direction, the Clayton bill was rewritten so as to provide for greater flexibility in defining an unfair trade practice and, more important, the interstate commerce commission was reconstituted as the Federal Trade Commission and given apparently vast authority over the day-to-day operations of the business world. . . . This . . . marked the complete adoption by the Wilson administration of Roosevelt's program for the regulation of business. . . . The Southern and Western Agrarian radicals, acting with a small labor bloc in the House, worked hard . . . to have a provision inserted in the Clayton bill exempting farm and labor unions from the operation and application of the antitrust laws. . . . Although Wilson was rapidly abandoning his New Freedom assumptions, he was not yet ready to go so far as to approve what was obviously legislation in the interest of particular classes. Since the first days of his administration he had resisted bitterly this move. . . . When the Clayton bill was under discussion in the House Committee, however, the Agrarian and Labor bloc declared that they would guarantee its defeat unless Wilson gave in to their demands.

Thus faced with another major revolt within his party, Wilson resolved his dilemma by resorting, it must be admitted, to one of the most artful dodges in the history of American politics. The famous labor provisions of the Clayton bill . . . represented Wilson's attitude perfectly. On the face of it, the new provisions did indeed seem to give the exemption and immunity from antitrust prosecution that the farm and labor spokesmen were demanding. Actually, this was not the case at all. Farm and labor organizations were not to be construed by the courts as being, per se, combinations in restraint of trade, but they were in no way freed from threats of prosecution if they violated the antitrust laws.[6]

In the elaborate maneuvers, Wilson had shifted ground sharply, but he had also weakened the terms of his original approach. Having suddenly shifted from merely clarifying the law to a reliance on the Federal Trade Commission, he stood aside while the Senate seriously weakened the whole Clayton Act by making the practices illegal only "where the effect may be to substantially lessen competition or tend to create a monopoly in any line of commerce." And, in accepting Brandeis's new concept of the Trade Commission, he had committed himself to just the kind of governmental surveillance of business that he had so strongly attacked in Roosevelt's program two years earlier. Years later, an historian would note bitterly ". . . the Clayton Act neither destroyed nor freed nor clarified much."[7]

But, if he was carried by the logic of events and politics well beyond his 1912 position on big business, Wilson disappointed his progressive supporters on a wide spectrum of the reforms they had demanded. As he looked backwards toward his idealized picture of the old America, he resisted more and more staunchly the demands that government support the interests of this or that specific group. He was no more pro-labor, pro-farmer, or pro-consumer than he was pro-business, perhaps less so in each case. He would be no broker among the interests. He boggled at once at governmental concern with anything less than the great, but necessarily vague "public interest." He refused to implement an act designed to prevent the prosecution of labor and farm organizations under the antitrust laws by withholding funds for this purpose. He fought bitterly against proposals for government-sponsored rural credit programs. He refused to support the drives for a Federal child labor law, for women's suffrage, for better opportunities for the Negro. He weakened the effectiveness of the Federal Trade Commission by appointment of men who were irresolute or hostile to its purposes. He loaded the Federal Reserve Board with big businessmen, even with some big bankers. He allowed Redfield to advertise the Federal Trade Commission widely as a "counsellor and friend" to business rather than a policeman. As the country moved into a dangerous recession, he cultivated a new atmosphere of friendship to business. He ostentatiously sought financial and business advice, as the 1916 election approached.

Progressives were shocked—and then sickened. Croly wrote: "Any man of President Wilson's intellectual equipment who seriously asserts that the fundamental wrongs of a modern society can be easily and quickly righted as a consequence of a few laws ... casts suspicion either upon his own sincerity or upon his grasp of the realities of modern social and industrial life."[8]

But there was a consistency within Wilson's own terms. If he opposed child labor legislation on constitutional grounds, he would veto a literacy test for immigrants on grounds of simple justice. If he refused to support ordinary labor legislation because it was "class legislation," he would avidly support the La Follette Seamen's Bill and sign it, despite international complications—because this was a matter of setting men free, free from the outrageous conditions of contracts in which they had no choice. And the exigencies of war would push him even further. Conservative himself on tax policy, he would be forced by budget needs to accept the increased income taxes, excess profits taxes, inheritance taxes that the agrarian leaders constructed. Because there seemed no other way to get on with the war, he would eventually accept a vast program of economic management, of price-setting and labor control, even direct government operation of railroads, telegraphs and express companies.

The press of events took him a long way from the simple, naive ambitions of the New Freedom. Joseph Dorfman has described how, in one of the several fields, Wilson became, almost despite himself, a prophet of the future rather than of the past:

> Labor made distinct gains during the Wilson administration. One event, the importance of which has generally been overlooked, was the establishment of a separate cabinet department of labor, which was "to foster, promote, and develop the welfare of the wage earners of the United States." ... Furthermore, Wilson had written into the Clayton Act a declaration which Samuel Gompers described as labor's "Magna Charta." In summary: "The labor of a human being is not a commodity or article of commerce"; ... injunctions were prohibited in labor disputes growing out of the "terms or conditions of employment, unless necessary to prevent irreparable injury to property."

This "Magna Charta" did not immediately grant the kind of freedom that Gompers had hoped for, because it was open to many interpretations. ... Equally controversial was Wilson's support of an eight-hour day for railroad trainmen. In 1916, after all efforts had failed to arbitrate the dispute between the railroad brotherhoods and the companies, he asked Congress to pass an eight-hour law. "The eight-hour day now undoubtedly has the sanction of the judgment of society in its favor," he declared. The "whole spirit of the time and the preponderant evidence of recent economic experience" clearly support it.[9]

And his own Industrial Commission dramatized to the country the labor conditions that would later compel action that he himself was not yet ready to take:

The wealth of the country between 1890 and 1912 increased ... 188 per cent, whereas the aggregate income of wage earners in manufacturing, mining, and transportation has risen ... only 95 per cent. ... Furthermore, the wage earners' share of the net product of industry in the case of manufactures was only 40.2 per cent in 1909, as compared with 44.9 per cent in 1889. ...

... This investigation secured detailed information regarding ... income and living conditions for 15,726 families.

It was found that the incomes of almost two-thirds of these families ... were less than $750 per year and of almost one-third ... were less than $500. ... the very least that a family of five persons can live upon in anything approaching decency is $700. ... between one-half and two-thirds of these families were living below the standards of decent subsistence, while about one-third were living in a state which can be described only as abject poverty. ... How do the children of American workers fare? ... The babies of the poor died at three times the rate of those who were in fairly well-to-do families. ... one-third of all the adult workmen reported ... earned less than $10 per week.[10]

Partly it was the pressure of rural radicals in his own party that pushed Wilson ahead, as Arthur Link has insisted. Partly it was the mere swapping of congressional support here, for presidential support there. Wilson soon learned that it was the practical and tough professionals of his party, and not the liberal talkers, whose support he would have to have. He told Burleson: "What you told me about the old standpatters is true. They at least will stand by the party and the administration. I can rely on them better than I can on some of my own crowd." And he told Tumulty: "My head is with the progressives in the Democratic party, but my heart, because of the way they stood by me, is with the so-called Old Guard in the Senate. They stand without hitching."[11]

But it had taken an oat-bag as well as a hitching post to keep the "Old Guard" in line. He had been compelled to put prohibitions against interlocking directorates into the Clayton Act in order to keep them out of the Federal Reserve Act. He had been compelled to approve some rural credit provisions in the Federal Reserve Act to avoid other, more radical approaches that he staunchly opposed. He had been compelled to accept a wealth-tax program early in the war to obtain the preparedness appropriations he must have.

But a recent scholar has demonstrated that it was less the pressure of the rural radicals than the pressure of events and the formlessness of Wilson's own views that drove him on. Once he cut loose from the too tight, too systematic ideology of the New Freedom, he himself was free to extemporize with the needs of the moment. Never a believer in expediency, he nevertheless demonstrated himself a master of the momentary maneuver. Richard Abrams says: "Wilson always subordinated his commitment to the New Freedom to his obligation—owed to himself, his country, and his party—to come out on top in both the international crisis and the election campaign of 1916. It was to fulfill this obligation that Wilson moved toward a more advanced progressivism during the years 1913–1916."[12]

The year 1913 had been the year of the New Freedom. But there had been other dramatic events that year that forecast in headlines the obsolescence of Wilson's philosophy in the very year of its birth. For 1913 was also the year in which Henry Ford introduced to America the modern assembly line; 1913 was the year in which the Armory Show in Manhattan marked the overturn of a thousand years of tradition in the arts; 1913 was the year in which Charles Beard published An Economic

Interpretation of the Constitution and signaled the economic and social interpretation of human events that would dominate twentieth-century American thought. And 1913 was the year George Norris of Nebraska entered the United States Senate as a liberal Republican. Twenty years later, Franklin Roosevelt's New Deal would enact the Tennessee Valley Authority for which Norris had long fought. The New Deal would build on the new understanding of American society that Beard and his generation had popularized so broadly. There would be little of the New Freedom. But there would be much in the New Deal of what Wilson had actually built. Even T.V.A. found its excuse in the dam constructed by Wilson's administration for the wartime production of nitrates. And the New Deal would carry to logical conclusions Wilson had never envisaged, and perhaps would never have approved, the directions set in the Federal Trade Commission Act, the Federal Reserve Act, the Underwood Tariff, the La Follette Seamen's Act and the Clayton Anti-Trust Act.

Wilson was growing while he led. The prophet of the old America in 1912, had become the prophet of the new America by 1914. But he led by instinct and necessity, and for Woodrow Wilson personally the land to which he led always remained a land only dimly seen.

NOTES, CHAPTER 8

1. **New York Evening Post,** quoted in H. C. F. Bell, **Woodrow Wilson and the People** (N.Y.: Doubleday, Doran and Company, 1945), p. 126.
2. Bell, **op. cit.,** p. 127.
3. Ray Stannard Baker and William E. Dodd (eds.), **The Public Papers of Woodrow Wilson** (N.Y.: Harper and Brothers, 1925–27), I, 39–40.
4. U. S. 62nd Congress, 3d Session, **House Reports,** (Washington D. C.: 1913), Doc. No. 1593, pp. 86–90.
5. Walter Lippmann, **Drift and Mastery** (Spectrum Edition; N.Y.: Prentice-Hall, Inc., 1961), pp. 82–85.
6. Arthur S. Link, "The South and the 'New Freedom': An Interpretation," **American Scholar,** XX (Summer, 1951), 315–16, 318–20.

7. John Blum, **Woodrow Wilson and the Politics of Morality** (Boston: Little, Brown and Company, 1956), p. 78.

8. **New Republic,** I (November 21, 1914), p. 7.

9. Joseph Dorfman, **The Economic Mind in American Civilization: 1865–1918** (N.Y.: The Viking Press, 1949), pp. 341–42.

10. U. S. 64th Congress, 1st Session, **Senate Documents** (Washington, D. C.: 1916), Doc. No. 415, I, 21–23.

11. Ray Stannard Baker, **Woodrow Wilson: Life and Letters** (N.Y.: Doubleday, Doran and Company, 1927–39), V, 92.

12. Richard Abrams, "Woodrow Wilson and the Southern Congressmen, 1913–1916," **Journal of Southern History,** XXII (1956), 437.

No one can say what would have been Woodrow Wilson's fate had there been no World War. He might have been a one-term president; he might have been considered by future generations much less a progressive. For it was Wilson's foreign policy that tipped the scales narrowly his way in the 1916 election. And it was the demands of the international scene that pushed him to some of the most significant domestic experiments upon which his reputation has ridden.

But the crises of foreign policy may have also impeded the development of a more logical and consistent domestic program. For not one single day was Woodrow Wilson freed from the worry of explosive international crisis.

It had been a peculiar fate that had forced this essentially political theorist to the solution of essentially economic problems. It was even more curious that this essentially domestic American must deal with the constant crises of international affairs. Even before his inauguration, he had confided to a friend: "It would be the irony of fate if my administration had to deal chiefly with foreign affairs."[1] He confessed that he had few ideas and little knowledge about the world overseas. But he knew the responsibility. In Constitutional Government he had written: "The initiative in foreign affairs, which the President possesses without any restriction whatever, is ... the power to control them absolutely."[2] And he knew the limitations: "The President can lead only as he can command the ear of both Congress and the country."[3] He also had certain firm commitments long before he had reached the White House. As early as 1901 he had warned: "Absorbed in our own development, we had fallen into a singular ignorance of the rest of the world."[4] He had thought about the problem of imperialism, and he had made his peace with it, as Arthur Link suggests:

> Wilson's rationalization of American Imperialism was a rather sophisticated and pseudo-religious expression of the idea of the "white man's burden." He insisted that self-government was not easily come by, and he proposed that the United States should give the Filipinos a government that would "moralize them" and "elevate and steady them" in preparation for self-government. . . .
>
> "Liberty is not itself government. In the wrong hands, —in hands unpracticed, undisciplined,—it is incompatible with government. . . . They can have liberty no cheaper than we got it. They must first take the discipline of law, must first love order and instinctively yield to it. . . . . We are old in this learning and must be their tutors."[5]

It was typical of Wilson's approach to life that he accepted inherently both the "supremacy" of the Anglo-Saxon peoples and the essentially moral nature of foreign affairs. The combination of the two led to a third assumption, that peace and order and the international good life must be imposed by the "superior" peoples.

It was this "moral imperialism" that "led the idealistic Wilson to use the club of armed intervention more frequently than any other American president."[6] But in the earliest stages of his administration it was William Jennings Bryan, not Wilson, who dominated American foreign policy. It was a curious product of accident that *this Nebraska isolationist, religious pacifist, provincial advocate of the American farmer, should suddenly become Secretary of State at the most crucial moment in modern American foreign policy. Bryan accepted the challenge, however, and the responsibility with depth of purpose, though with little understanding. Merle Curti has described the Great Commoner's personal crusade to make America the leader for world peace:*

At the very time that he assumed the responsibilities of this office, he publicly declared that he could never take part in any negotiations which would lead his country into any kind of foreign war. When had anyone vested with the direction of the foreign affairs of a major power ever made such a commitment?

Moreover, not a month had passed before friends of peace learned that he had taken carefully planned steps for the negotiation of treaties embodying his program. When the President elect had invited him to Princeton and offered him the first place in the cabinet, the peace leader had secured Wilson's approval for the cause so close to his heart.... Then, on April 24, 1913, he summoned the diplomatic corps and proposed the negotiation of treaties committing the parties to submit all questions, without exception, to an investigating commission, and to abstain from hostilities until the commission's report had been made. The commissions, appointed prior to the dispute and permanent in personnel, were to be composed of one subject or citizen from each nation, chosen by that nation, and one chosen by each nation from a foreign state, with a fifth commissioner to be selected by agreement of the two contracting parties. The right to act independently, after the commission had reported, was clearly stipulated....

On August 17, 1913, the first treaty was signed, with Salvador; the Netherlands was the first European country to come into the arrangement. Altogether thirty treaties were negotiated, and twenty ratifications exchanged. Bryan showed much greater skill in handling the senate than his predecessors; he submitted a statement in advance to the committee on foreign affairs, setting forth the interpretation that all disputed questions could be submitted directly to international commissions without previous consent of the senate. When twenty-seven nations had committed themselves to the plan, Bryan, in high spirits, celebrated the event by distributing to the respective diplomats souvenirs in the form of a paperweight representing a plowshare beaten out of an obsolete army sword provided by the war department. He took great pride in his achievement.... He regarded this as his greatest contribution to world peace.[7]

But Bryan was as irresolute and shallow in his grasp of international realities as he was sincere and devoted in purpose. Richard Hofstadter has seen this clearly:

Bryan had been a most eloquent Christian pacifist, and yet when the Spanish War came he had fulfilled his idea of "service" by enlisting in the First Nebraska Volunteers, rising to a colonelcy, and camping with his troops in a sinkhole near Jacksonville, Florida, until the war was over. The inconsistency between his participation in the war and his discipleship of the Prince of Peace seemed not to trouble him....

Bryan in power was like Bryan out of power: he made the same well-meant gestures, showed the same willingness under stress or confusion to drop ideas he had once been committed to, the same inability to see things through....

Bryan's inability to hold steadily to a line of principle was nowhere so well illustrated as in his imperialist policies in the Caribbean, where, as Selig Adler has shown, he was "chiefly responsible for a distinct acceleration of American penetration." Wilson ... gave Bryan a substantially free hand in Caribbean policy, and the former anti-imperialist, in dealing with Nicaragua, Haiti, and Santo Domingo, was fully as aggressive as his Republican predecessors. ...

Bryan also wanted to father a sweeping policy of financial intervention in Latin America, which he outlined in two memoranda to Wilson in 1913. He proposed to counteract the influence of European creditors of Latin-American nations by having the United States government go to their "rescue." ... This would so increase the nation's influence in Latin America "that we could prevent revolutions, promote education, and advance stable and just government." ...

It was neither courage nor sincerity but simply steadfast and self-confident intelligence that Bryan lacked.[8]

Wilson—and millions of Americans—shared the "missionary impulse"[9] of Bryan. But the missionary impulse ran parallel in their minds with the historic, Jeffersonian concept of equal rights of nations. In October, 1913, in a major speech at Mobile, Alabama, Wilson told his nation that a new attitude was needed toward the Latin-American republics: "You cannot be friends upon any other terms than upon the terms of equality. You cannot be friends at all except upon the terms of honor. We must show ourselves friends by comprehending their interest whether it squares with our own interest or not. It is a very perilous thing to determine the foreign policy of a nation in the terms of material interest."[10]

Yet missionary zeal, if carried to its logical ends, belied the very integrity of other peoples. And Wilson's Mobile speech ran counter to his own concept of Anglo-Saxon obligation. The two were not parallel no matter how hard he tried to make them so. This ambivalence he never resolved, except in the easy and prideful as-

sumption that he, personally, could speak better for
other peoples than they themselves could—that he
knew better than they did what was good for them. And
this ambivalence could cause no end of confusion
abroad. Latin Americans were led by the Mobile speech
to expect one policy, by Bryan's actions to fear another.

Nowhere were the dangers of this fundamental uncertainty more apparent than in American policy in the Far
East. In moral repugnance Wilson drew back from the
Dollar Diplomacy of the Six Power loan that was being
negotiated for Chinese railroads. But, in his own house,
he violated the basic regard for Japanese interests and
feelings that his Mobile speech had promised all nations.
The trouble grew from the determination of the California legislature to bar Japanese from land-ownership.
This was a second insult, hard pressed upon the prior
slap they had received when the United States had ex-
cluded Asians from citizenship. Wilson could, and did,
plead that under the American system of federalism, he
could do nothing about California's action. But, in fact,
he treated the matter lightly, not understanding its importance, not suspecting the danger until the country
stood on the verge of war with Japan. War was averted
in the spring of 1913, Wilson and Bryan went out of
their way to curb naval preparations that might have
offered an excuse. But the bitterness lingered in Japan.

And there were more problems. Wilson recognized
promptly the new Republic of China in May, 1913. But
he soon found that simple recognition was not enough
as an aggressive Japanese government stepped up its demands on the new Republic and threatened its political,
economic and geographic integrity. By the spring of
1913, Wilson and Bryan were anxious to cooperate with
Japan, naively hopeful of a pleasant solution. They
would apparently have been willing to see Japanese influence expand, short of danger to American interests.
But, as the Japanese stepped up their pressure, the ad-

ministration's policy hardened. The Japanese finally gave in, under tough warnings from Washington that the United States would never accept any Sino-Japanese agreement that threatened the open-door policy, or American interests in China. The Japanese remained bitter. The Chinese were hardly encouraged. The crisis was put off. But to the world at large, it seemed more a policy of imperialism than anything else. And the rankling resentment played a role in worsening Japanese-American relations during the next thirty years.

Sometimes the moralistic view of international affairs worked well. Such was the case with Wilson's insistence that the Congress repeal the Panama Ship Tolls Act, which gave exemption to American ships in outright violation of treaty obligations to Great Britain. To accomplish it, Wilson had to violate the Democratic platform on which he had run; he had to push roughshod over his own congressional leaders; he had to endanger the remainder of his legislative program by angering the anti-British and strategically placed Irish-Americans; he had to fight persistently for two months. But he did it. For Wilson it was a simple matter of honor and good faith, and he would not be put off.

But moralism was not enough in dealing with Latin America. In fact, it hopelessly endangered the prospect of good relations to the south. For Wilson was not always right, and he could fight as determinedly when he was wrong, as he had when he had been right. Furthermore, he had inherited a Latin-American policy built on naval domination of the Caribbean. It would be difficult at best to withdraw. It seemed reckless to endanger American security by sacrificing the essential naval bases. And it seemed to Wilson, Bryan, and Daniels the height of folly to invite European intervention by weakening American domination. Finally, for Wilson there were really no doubts. As with the Philippines, so with the Caribbean, it was America's obligation to do their thinking for them in their own best interests.

The result was a record of United States intervention that was to trouble the nation's relations with Latin America for the next half century: a continued control of Nicaraguan affairs—a sad mismanagement in Santo Domingo, which led eventually to the nation's political collapse and to occupation by American marines—the occupation of unstable Haiti in 1915. And, through it all, the influence of the American bankers ran in as unsavory a fashion as it had in the Taft administration. "Missionary Diplomacy" seemed little different from "Dollar Diplomacy," in practice. And American power was even less welcome to the south in the guise of the reformer and protector than it had been in the naked armor of imperialism.

Yet there were moments when a sounder judgment placed United States prestige in a more friendly light. Wilson worked hard, though he failed eventually, to gain hemisphere approval for a Pan-American Pact, that would have moved in the direction of the later, much-hailed Good Neighbor Policy. And Wilson moved rapidly to undo the damage that had been done by the Roosevelt administration's seizure of Panama. To be sure, he would not give back the Canal Zone, but he did sign a treaty with Colombia, providing reparations and publicly constituting an apology for T. R.'s actions.

Nothing, however, did more damage to American prestige to the south than the confused and arrogant policy into which Wilson fell in the handling of affairs with Mexico. As Robert E. Quirk has described it:

On April 21, 1914, United States military forces landed at Veracruz, Mexico, and occupied that port for more than six months. This act of hostility, President Woodrow Wilson said, was the direct result of the "studied contempt" of General Victoriano Huerta toward the American government and American nationals in Mexico. Specifically, it was in retaliation for three recent, but isolated, incidents: the arrest of several American sailors and their commanding officer at Tampico on April 9; the detention of a mail courier at Veracruz on April 11; and the delay of an official dispatch of the Department of State, also on April 11, at Mexico City. We may think the causes picayune, and indeed they were, since all three were seen subsequently to be understandable mistakes. But war is a serious and dreadful business, and to commit a country to hostilities against a weaker neighbor requires sound reasons and self-justifications, if only to salve one's conscience. It is true that Wilson had not anticipated bloodshed at Veracruz; he had convinced himself that the Mexicans would not resist the landing. And he was appalled by the reports of loss of life at Veracruz—nineteen American sailors and several hundred Mexicans. But it was equally true that Wilson had been looking for just such an excuse to intervene in Mexico. His entire Mexican policy turned upon the elimination of Victoriano Huerta.

Woodrow Wilson and Victoriano Huerta came to the presidency of their respective countries almost simultaneously.... The American president was chosen by the free vote of the people, but the Mexican seized control of the government after a bloody revolution and the assassination of the legally elected president and vice-president. Wilson never forgot the difference, nor would he permit Huerta to do so. From the moment of his inauguration he refused to recognize the regime of Huerta, who was, he said, a usurper and a murderer. ... He offended Wilson's sense of decency and fair play, his desire to see popular and democratic rule installed everywhere.... In the fall of 1913 ... [Wilson] told Sir William Tyrrell, the secretary of the British ambassador to Washington: "I am going to teach the South American republics to elect good men!" ... American public opinion was squarely behind Wilson. Most Mexicans hated and despised Huerta. Above all, Huerta was not an effective administrator, not even a competent army commander. Once Wilson had decided upon his elimination, Huerta had no chance whatsoever.[11]

On the eve of the American intervention, Huerta was already in desperate straits. Already he was being squeezed between the forces of Emiliano Zapata in the south, and the Constitutionalist armies of Venustiano Carranza in the north. Carranza's allies, Álvaro Obregón, Francisco Villa, and Pablo Gonzales were moving south along a ragged line from the Gulf of Mexico to the Gulf of California, fed by supplies spirited across the United States border in violation of an embargo by the Taft administration. Wilson had already made his views and his tactics clear. He had lifted the weak embargo; he had stationed a considerable fleet of American warships off Tampico and Veracruz—for "watchful waiting." He had refused to recognize Huerta. In doing so, he had abandoned the recognition policy that had been accepted in the United States since the days of Jefferson. The Wilson administration would not extend de facto recognition just because a government was in control of the country concerned; it would extend only de jure recognition, reserving for itself the right to make a moral judgment about whether the government was legal, proper, desirable for the people involved. Recognition under Wilson would be a weapon for imposing America's judgment on her neighbors. Under pressure from American economic interests, Wilson worked out terms by which the situation could be resolved, but they were terms that could never be accepted by Huerta, and terms that would create much resentment in Mexico generally. Constitutional elections must be held; Huerta must refuse to be a candidate; the United States would then intervene to bring the parties together and create a stable government. Then, in October, 1913, the British government recognized Huerta, and almost simultaneously, the Mexican president arrested 110 members of his Chamber of Deputies and emerged publicly as a military dictator.

Wilson blamed the British; he brought relentless pressure upon them until, with European war in the offing, they relented and withdrew their recognition. Then Wilson worked systematically throughout the winter, with all measures short of war, to force the dictator out. But, by March, 1914, Wilson also was in a difficult position. His pressures had resulted in new conservative support for Huerta; the Constitutionalist armies had not moved so rapidly as expected. The nearly inevitable explosion came at Tampico on April 9, when a shore party from one of Admiral Henry T. Mayo's whaleboats was arrested at gun point. Mayo saw it as a violation of American sovereignty, although the boat was in Mexican waters and the crew on Mexican soil. He refused to accept the informal explanation of the local commander, Morelos Zaragoza, and issued a demand that was immediately resented and refused: "I must require that you send me, by suitable members of your staff, a formal disavowal of and an apology for the act, together with your assurance that the officer responsible for it will receive severe punishment. Also that you hoist the American flag in a prominent position on shore and salute it with 21 guns, which salute will be duly returned by this ship." [12] Mayo demanded a reply within 24 hours.

Wilson was out of town when the messages came in. When he did receive word of the incident, he supported Mayo absolutely. Both American civilian officials on the scene and the professionals of the State Department would have objected, but Wilson did not ask. He was certain of his own knowledge, contemptuous of their advice. He distrusted the professionals anyway; he saw the whole matter as a simple moral issue. Now he wired Bryan that the chargé d'affaires in Mexico City should "handle this matter with the utmost earnestness, firmness and frankness, representing to them its extreme seriousness and [the] possibility that unless the guilty persons are promptly punished consequences of [the] gravest sort might ensue.... Lansing can, of course, supply you with the precedents by which to direct our course."[13]

The local incident had become an international affair. Huerta refused to make further apologies. On April 17, Wilson publicly gave him a 24-hour deadline, after which, he threatened, he would go to Congress. Meanwhile, the President ordered the Navy to prevent the expected landing in Veracruz of a German vessel with arms for Huerta. And the fleet prepared for the eventual occupation of Tampico. On April 20, Wilson asked Congress for authority to use armed force; and the Navy was ordered to concentrate on Veracruz, since there were technical difficulties in landing at Tampico. While the congressional resolution bogged down, Wilson went ahead without approval. Before dawn on April 21, upon warning that the German ship was about to dock, he ordered the occupation of the customs house at Veracruz:

And so the line which separates diplomacy from hostilities was crossed in the dark hours of a spring morning with the utterance of a single sentence by the President of the United States.... There would be no firing, no bloodshed. Only Huerta would be harmed, and for this, Mexico would thank the United States. As Wilson's friend and confidant, Colonel Edward House, had told him a few days before: "If a man's house was on fire he should be glad to have his neighbors come in and help him put it out, provided they did not take his property, and it should be the same with nations. If Mexico understood that our motives were unselfish, she should not object to our helping adjust her unruly household." These were Woodrow Wilson's sentiments too.[14]

But there was bloodshed. Robert Quirk has told the story:

As soon as the Mexicans began to realize the import of the landing, ... the atmosphere of festivity changed. The crowds at the waterfront fell back along the adjacent streets and under the Portales to continue watching in silence. Shopkeepers rang down the iron doors that covered and protected their windows. School children were sent home by their teachers. In the market the vendors carefully folded their cloth awnings and gathered up their heaps of fruits and vegetables. Even the vultures seemed to sense the impending trouble. They retired from the streets as though for the night to roost on building ledges or in trees and rudely crowded the arms of the white cross and the tiled cupolas of the parochial church....

The first task of the American forces was to seize the railroad terminal.... As the rail terminal was taken without incident, other marines and bluejackets loped across the plaza toward the post office building and the custom house sheds and down the streets paralleling the railroad tracks to the city's power station. One squad of marines was detailed to take charge of the cable station on Montesinos behind the American consulate.... At 11:45 an armed marine corporal, followed by his men, entered to announce: "I take possession of this office and cable in the name of the United States government." The censor arose from his desk, bowed profoundly to the corporal and said, shrugging his shoulders; "It is useless to resist, señor. I obey." ...

As the largest contingent of marines and sailors moved along Morelos toward their main objective, the custom house, the only sounds to be heard in the streets were the dull, rhythmic tread of their boots and the barked orders of their officer. . . . Mexican soldiers quietly trained their rifles on the advancing Americans. At the corner of Independencia and Emparán a group of Contreras' men lay on the rough cobbles, scorning to take cover or to erect a barricade. Liberated prisoners and some venturesome civilians had scaled the rooftops of hotel and office buildings intent on sniping at the invaders. These few Mexicans, scarcely more than a hundred in all, were loyally obeying their commander's decision. At 11:57 the head of the American column reached Emparán and moved into the line of fire of Contreras' men. At that moment an unknown Mexican soldier carefully squeezed his trigger, and the first shot cleaved the silence. In that instant, all hope for a peaceful occupation of Veracruz perished. The shot was followed by a fusillade of fire from various quarters of the city. A navy signalman, flagging a message from the roof of the Terminal Hotel to the ships, fell mortally wounded. He was the first casualty of the invasion.[15]

The resistance went on for two days. Eventually nearly 6,000 marines and sailors were involved. American naval commanders made a desperate attempt to find military or civilian officials who could surrender and reconstitute the local government. They discovered the Mayor cowering in his bathroom. Like others, he refused to act. Mexican law promised the death penalty for traitors who cooperated with an enemy. The Navy set up martial law. The German ship was stopped, held, and then let go with an apology to Germany from the State Department. Eventually, after elaborate evasions, the arms were landed for Huerta, but too late to help him. The United States did not protest; ironically, the arms were later proven to have been shipped from New York, by way of Hamburg.

There were other ironies. The American shellfire had mutilated the statue of Mexico's great liberal, Benito Juárez, with its motto: "Respect for the rights of others is peace." Wilson sought to portray the bloody intervention as a great gesture of friendship for the Mexican people: "We have gone down to Mexico to serve mankind, if we can find out the way." But Mexicans erupted in violent anger. In Mexico City, the headlines spewed venom: in El Imparcial: "The soil of the patria is defiled by foreign invasion! We may die, but let us kill!" —in El Independiente: "While Mexicans were massacring the gringo pigs, the church bells rang out their glory!"—in La Patria: "Vengeance! Vengeance! Vengeance!"[16]

Even Carranza was angry. He would not win, if it meant placing his nation at the mercy of American policy. Only "Pancho" Villa seemed happy with the seizure of the seaports that had kept Huerta alive. Argentina, Brazil, and Chile moved rapidly to offer mediation. Huerta accepted, assuming that the quarrel with the United States was to be mediated. Wilson accepted, refusing mediation affecting the United States and insisting that the mediators limit themselves to Mexico's internal affairs. Carranza's forces stayed away. The mediators met at Niagara Falls, Canada, until late in June, and then gave up. There was no middle ground. And there was no way out for Wilson until the Constitutionalists had destroyed Huerta by force. The army and the marines settled down to the hard, hot, sickening business of military occupation in a fever-ridden, Caribbean town. They cleaned up the garbage, destroyed flies and mosquitoes by the million, made the streets safe from criminals, saved the lives of scores with their health measures, dealt an even-handed justice. Even the vultures fled for lack of the refuse on which they had gorged. And American troops were everywhere resented for their arrogance and superiority, for just being there.

By November, their position was difficult, even dangerous. With the winter storms coming on, their tent city was untenable. Worse yet, the advantage of their staying had disappeared. Huerta had fallen, but Carranza now seemed little better. There was no prospect of elections; the civil war went on, against Villa, against Zapata. On November 23, the troops began to move out, as Carranza's forces marched cautiously into the city by arrangement. It was a dignified, orderly, clean withdrawal, but the United States was unable even to guarantee the safety of Mexicans who had cooperated. For Wilson it was a bankruptcy of policy, but a bankruptcy he himself would not then, or later, admit.

His administration continued to maneuver for a regime in Mexico that would follow "good" advice. For a time it supported Villa. By early October, 1915, the new Secretary of State, Robert Lansing, had persuaded Wilson to give de facto recognition to the dominant Carranza faction. Now it was Villa's turn to raise a crisis. He was anxious to compel American intervention by discrediting Carranza's ability to control the country. His forces murdered sixteen Americans who had been hauled from a Mexican train early in January, 1916. On March 9, Villa crossed the border to burn the town of Columbus, New Mexico, and murder nineteen more Americans. For Wilson there was no longer a question. The fact that this was a national election year made the path even more clear. On March 15, General John J. Pershing was sent across the border to track down Villa.

Carranza soon became alarmed by the 6,600-man force that Pershing led 300 miles into Mexico by April 8. In mid-April, Villa was still free, and Carranza was demanding the withdrawal of the United States Army. Villa struck again, at Glen Springs, Texas, with four more American casualties. By June 21, war seemed inevitable. Preparations had been made on both sides; in the United States, Wilson had called up 100,000 National Guardsmen. And a bloody skirmish had taken place between one of Pershing's troops and a Mexican contingent. Wilson prepared his war message. Then an official report indicating that American troops had started the fateful skirmish was published widely in the United States by a pacifist group. The White House was happily flooded with telegrams and letters opposing action; neither Wilson nor Carranza really wanted war. Wilson withheld his message; Carranza released prisoners and suggested negotiations. Throughout the fall, a Joint High Commission worked to resolve the issue. The Commission broke up without solution in January, 1917. But it had staved off war for a time.

By mid-January Wilson was compelled to order a withdrawal; the European war would no longer allow him the luxury of stubborn resistance in Mexico. Carranza had won; Wilson's stubbornness had been almost monumentally tragic for American foreign policy. But, as Arthur Link has suggested: "Even so, future generations may forget his mistakes and the Mexican people may some day remember that he, almost alone, stood off Europe during the days of the Huertista tyranny, withstood the powerful forces in the United States that sought the undoing of the Revolution, and refused to go to war at a time when it might have ensured his reelection."[17]

NOTES, CHAPTER 9

1. Ray Stannard Baker, **Woodrow Wilson: Life and Letters** (N.Y.: Doubleday, Doran and Company, 1927–39), IV, 55.
2. Woodrow Wilson, **Constitutional Government in the United States** (N.Y.: Columbia University Press, 1908), p. 77.
3. **Atlantic Monthly,** July, 1897.
4. **Atlantic Monthly,** March, 1901.

5. Arthur S. Link, **Wilson: The Road to the White House** (Princeton, N.J.: Princeton University Press, 1947), p. 28.

6. Robert E. Quirk, **An Affair of Honor: Woodrow Wilson and the Occupation of Veracruz** (Lexington, Ky.: University of Kentucky Press, 1962), p. v.

7. Merle Eugene Curti, "Bryan and World Peace," **Smith College Studies in History**, XVI:3–4 (April–July, 1931), 150–51.

8. Richard Hofstadter, **The American Political Tradition and the Men Who Made It** (Vintage Edition; N.Y.: Alfred A. Knopf, Inc., 1948), pp. 199–202.

9. Arthur S. Link, **Woodrow Wilson and the Progressive Era, 1910–1917** (N.Y.: Harper and Brothers, 1954), pp. 81–82.

10. Baker, **op. cit.,** 236.

11. Quirk, **op. cit.,** pp. 1–3.

12. **Ibid.,** p. 26.

13. **Ibid.,** p. 32.

14. **Ibid.,** p. 77.

15. **Ibid.,** pp. 93–95.

16. **Ibid.,** pp. 96, 107, 115.

17. Link, **Progressive Era, op. cit.,** p. 144.

10. THE GREY THREAT OF WAR

As Wilson blundered hopefully with his Mexican policy, Europe had rushed toward a war that would change the face of the entire world. For two decades, tensions had been increasing, as Germany's industrial and military might mounted in gigantic challenge to British supremacy, as Russia and Austria-Hungary fretted dangerously with dreams of expansion in the volatile Balkan states. Through twenty years of devious diplomacy, Germany had become tied firmly to Austria-Hungary; Russia and France and Britain had been bound together. At stake were the commercial supremacy of the world, the balance of power in Europe, the control of the seas, the fate of the old monarchies, and the peace of the world. A careless act by any major power might embroil them all. And carried down with them would be the tiny, and even neutral, nations that might be in the way. Through twenty years of mounting crisis, the American people had lived in a fool's paradise, forgetting that their vaunted isolation depended upon British control of the Atlantic, failing to understand that their far-flung commerce made every event abroad an event of import for New Yorkers, Kansans, and Californians.

Wilson saw the danger, although even he thought it a distant one. It was in a spirit of magnanimous generosity that he sent Colonel House abroad in May and June of 1914 to explore the prospects for disarmament and negotiation that might blunt the terrifying competition of the giants. Wilson saw the danger, but he had other problems, more pressing and some more personally terrifying. The A.B.C. Mediation was winding out its hopeless course. There was work and worry over the faltering domestic program in Congress. The congressional elections loomed in November—prospects looked dim for Democrats. The country seemed to be moving into recession. And Ellen Wilson lay desperately ill in the White House. The President would not give up hope, but, as she wasted away, he knew that this partner of his life and love would soon be gone.

Then, on June 28, 1914, Archduke Franz Ferdinand of Austria and his wife were shot in the Serbian town of Sarajevo. In Washington, it seemed more immediately important that suffragettes were staging a march on the White House, that Huerta was about to be deposed. Wilson still airily believed that Colonel House was making progress in his mission of peace. As Serbia and Austria moved toward war, Wilson made it clear that the United States could do nothing, that America had no role in European affairs. Arriving from Europe on July 1, Louis Brownlow went to the White House: "I told him I thought there was grave danger of civil war in Britain, that the Irish situation might at any moment produce an explosion, and that I was extremely fearful . . . that an outbreak in England might well be the signal for the Germans to strike. The talk lasted for nearly an hour. The President was grave and concerned. . . . The astonishing thing about the interview is how little emphasis was given to the assassination of the Archduke . . . three days earlier. The President referred to it as a type of incident that might well be dangerous to the peace, but he, as well as I, considered civil war in Britain as a more immediate danger."[1]

On July 28, Austria-Hungary declared war on Serbia. On the 30th, Russia mobilized. On August 1, Germany declared war on Russia, and two days later on France.

She was obligated to support Austria, she explained. She must take the initiative rather than await a double attack from Russia and France. That day, Woodrow Wilson called in the Capitol reporters:

> Gentlemen ... I want to say this ... in the present state of affairs ... you should be extremely careful not to add in any way to the excitement. ...
> So far as we are concerned, there is no cause for excitement. ...
> I want to have the pride of feeling that America, if nobody else, has her self-possession and stands ready with calmness of thought and steadiness of purpose to help the rest of the world. And we can do it and reap a great permanent glory out of doing it, provided we all cooperate to see that nobody loses his head.[2]

On August 4, Great Britain declared war on Germany. On August 4, President Wilson issued the inevitable proclamation of neutrality; on the 5th the United States belatedly offered to mediate; on the 6th, a battleship was sent to Europe with five million dollars in gold to help stranded American tourists and businessmen. And, on August 6, Mrs. Woodrow Wilson died:

> Downstairs the chimes of a clock struck softly, five times. The President asked: "Is it all over?" The doctor nodded, and Woodrow Wilson's head fell forward. "When you die, I shall die," he had once written to her. Walking to a window and looking out, he cried: "Oh, my God, what am I to do?"

Mostly he kept his grief in his Scottish innerliness, not daring to give it any escape for fear that it would burst all controls. They heard him say, as he pulled himself together, "I must not give way." He sat in a chair for endless hours, day and night, in lonely vigil beside a sofa on which the lifeless figure lay, its shoulders draped by a white silk shawl that he himself had thrown over them.[3]

Only a little later he would write: "God has stricken me almost beyond what I can bear."[4] Later he described the tough discipline with which he faced the grueling months ahead:

> Immediately after an eight o'clock breakfast ... I dictate my letters and go over the papers on my desk which are waiting to be read. Then, about a quarter before ten, I go over to the office and until one receive visitors.... When lunch is over ... I receive one or two more formal visits, such as from an ambassador; then I hurry into my playing clothes and go off to one or other of the golf courses and play golf till the sun goes down. By the time I get home and have a bath and dress there are only a few minutes ... before dinner in which to go over and sign the papers awaiting my action on the table in the office. After dinner there are generally other consultations necessary on pending business or foreign affairs, or papers to prepare on questions which only I ought to formulate, since I am ultimately responsible; and I fall into bed so tired I cannot think. And it is best so.... Even books have grown meaningless to me. I read detective stories to forget, as a man would get drunk![5]

Already Wilson feared that the nation would be dragged into war. But publicly he insisted on cautious, careful neutrality. Bryan pressed for an active policy of mediation. Wilson resisted for the time. But another Bryan proposal brought his immediate support, as Merle Curti explains:

> He began by informing the President on August 10, 1914, that Morgan and Company had in-

quired whether there would be any objection to a loan for the French government and the Rothschilds, which, presumably, was also intended for the French government. . . . A loan to a Power would be taken as an expression of sympathy, [said Bryan] and if loans were made to all belligerents, our citizens would be divided into groups, each lending to the country it favored. . . . Lansing had contributed a further argument. . . . Our citizens . . . who went abroad and enlisted, lost the protection of their citizenship while so engaged. There was no reason for giving greater protection to American dollars which went abroad and enlisted in the cause of a belligerent. . . . The President approved his proposition not to sanction loans . . . and . . . wrote a sentence stating that position strongly and concisely. Bryan incorporated it in the statement he made on August 15 to the effect that loans by American bankers to any belligerent nation were inconsistent with the true spirit of neutrality.[6]

Meanwhile, Wilson turned aside Bryan's plea for a strategy of complete commercial neutrality:

On August 6, 1914, [Bryan] . . . proposed that the Declaration of London be accepted for the governance of the combatants on the seas. . . . Great Britain, who had refused to accept it in peace time, had no intention of doing so now. . . . since acceptance was regarded in London as tantamount to losing the war. . . . Both Page and Spring-Rice, the British Ambassador in Washington, insisted that war might result if we pushed England too far towards an acceptance of the principles of the Declaration of London; and Wilson and House shared that fear. It was Bryan's pacifism which, ironically, led him to share it too. He did not want a war with England; and he was led to accept . . . concessions. . . . The concessions . . . did not end either

her infractions on our neutral rights, or friction between the two countries. But these concessions did pave the way for German retaliations which even more dramatically encroached on our neutral rights. . . .

As a result of the conciliatory and in a sense unneutral policy to which Bryan assented, the Allies throttled the import trade of Germany and practically monopolized our exports.[7]

But, while Wilson refused to push London too far, he preached at home a total neutrality. To Congress, on August 19, he said: "The effect of the war upon the United States will depend upon what American citizens say and do. Every man who really loves America will act and speak in the true spirit of neutrality. . . . The United States must be neutral in fact as well as in name during these days that are to try men's souls. We must be impartial in thought as well as in action."[8]

It was an impossible demand. The United States was a nation of immigrants with many conflicting ties. For millions, England was homeland. Official culture reinforced a natural sympathy for the land of Shakespeare and Wordsworth, of the English common law and parliamentary democracy. But for other millions, Britain and Russia were symbols of hated oppression. Among the Irish, there was no love for Mother England. Among Jewish refugees from Russian oppression, there was only hatred for the land of the czars. And for millions of German-Americans, there was a deep love of Fatherland. Swedes shared a traditional fear of Russia. Italians were deeply divided by the uncertainty of their own motherland, made irresolute by mingled ambition and fear.

In the coming months, Americans would be assaulted on all sides by gigantically financed and carefully manipulated propaganda campaigns from both sides. English propaganda would eventually win out, because it was so accurately tuned to American culture, because of German blunders, because Germany chose the role of aggressor against neutrals. As Wilson pleaded for neutrality—"We are custodians of the spirit of righteousness."[9] —Americans read in their newspapers the story of the assault on Belgium. Belgium was unhappily on the path from Germany to France. Typical of the news-budget in August of 1914 was the description by a New York Tribune correspondent of the burning of Louvain:

> For two hours on Thursday night I was in what for six hundred years has been the city of Louvain. The Germans were burning it, and to hide their work kept us locked in the railway carriages. But the story was written against the sky, was told to us by German soldiers incoherent with excesses; and we could read it in the faces of women and children being led to concentration camps and of citizens on their way to be shot.
>
> The Germans sentenced Louvain on Wednesday to become a wilderness and with the German system and love of thoroughness they left Louvain an empty and blackened shell. The reason for this appeal to the torch and the execution of noncombatants, as given to me on Thursday morning by General von Lutwitz, military governor of Brussels, was this: on Wednesday, while the German military commander of the troops of Louvain was at the Hôtel de Ville talking to the Burgomaster, a son of the Burgomaster with an automatic pistol shot the chief of staff and German staff surgeons.
>
> Lutwitz claims this was the signal for the civil-guard, in civilian clothes on roofs, to fire upon the German soldiers in the open square below. . . . Fifty Germans were killed and wounded. For that, said Lutwitz, Louvain must be wiped out. So in pantomime with his fist he swept the papers across his table.
>
> "The Hôtel de Ville," he added, "was a beautiful building; it is a pity it must be destroyed." . . .
>
> In other wars I have watched men on one hilltop,

without haste, without heat, fire at men on another hill, and in consequence on both sides good men were wasted. But in those fights there were no women and children, and the shells struck only vacant stretches of veldt or uninhabited mountainsides.

At Louvain it was war upon the defenseless, war upon churches, colleges, shops of milliners and lacemakers; war brought to the bedside and fireside; against women harvesting in fields, against children in wooden shoes at play in the streets. . . .

Outside the station in the public square the people of Louvain passed in an unending procession, women bare-headed, weeping, men carrying the children asleep on their shoulders, all hemmed in by the shadowy army of gray wolves. Once they were halted, and among them marched a line of men. They well knew their fellow townsmen. These were on their way to be shot. . . . You felt it was only a nightmare, cruel and uncivilized. And then you remembered that the German Emperor had told us what it is. It is his Holy War.[10]

Years later, students of propaganda would prove that much of the "news" Americans read was a tissue of lies. And, though it enlisted their deep and lingering emotions, they were at first quite firmly agreed that the war was none of their business. It might be brutal, sad, inexcusable, but it was the duty of Americans, and their interest, to remain aloof. Wilson and his own colleagues were probably less neutral in sentiment than the people they exhorted. As Richard Hofstadter has made clear:

Wilson's Allied sympathies were as vital as his love of peace. He was a thorough Anglophile. He had learned his greatest lessons from English thinkers; he had taken English statesmen as his models of aspiration and the British Constitution as his model of government; his work as President of Princeton had been, in large measure, an effort to introduce the English idea of a university; even his favorite recreation was to bicycle about the villages of the Lake Country with the *Oxford Book of English Verse* in his pocket. He was surrounded by pro-Ally advisers, especially Robert Lansing, Counselor of the State Department and later Secretary of State, and Colonel House.... His Ambassador to England, Walter Hines Page, took it upon himself to represent Britain's cause to America.... "England is fighting our fight," Wilson stated in the presence of Tumulty. "... I will not take any action to embarrass England when she is fighting for her life and the life of the world." ... [And again] "... the Allies are standing with their backs to the wall fighting wild beasts. I will permit nothing to be done by our country to hinder or embarrass them ... unless admitted rights are grossly violated." ... In September, 1915, he admitted to House that "he had never been sure that we ought not to take part in the conflict and, if it seemed evident that Germany and her militaristic ideas were to win, the obligation upon us was greater than ever."[11]

Throughout the later summer and early fall of 1914, Great Britain used her supremacy on the seas to good advantage. She tightened her blockade inexorably about Germany, as British and French armies blunted the great German assault on Paris at the first battle of the Marne. Britain valued American support, but she would not, and could not, accept American definitions of neutral rights on the high seas. As the fall came on, she tightened her list of contraband, stopped American ships for inspection, hauled some under armed escort into British ports. There were no lives lost, but there was immense resentment in the United States. The Wilson administration protested sharply, but the protests were blunted by the judgment in London that

Wilson could not and would not use force, and softened by the forthcoming congressional elections, by the incipient depression, and by Ambassador Page's sympathies with Britain as he delivered the protests with which he did not agree.

Already Wilson was learning that the path of neutrality was difficult to find. A ban on loans to belligerents might seem a neutral act, but in this case it helped Germany and hurt Britain. Similarly, a desperate attempt to gain congressional approval for a United States government purchase and operation of new shipping seemed a wisely neutral plan for keeping American goods off belligerent ships. But it was defeated by congressional fears that government purchase of German ships would enrage the English—that the sinking of government-owned ships would bring war.

The congressional elections went badly. Democrats still controlled both houses, but they had lost strength sharply in the House. It might have been even worse without the war crisis. As he prepared to write an end to his domestic program, Wilson seemed to be struggling for a new objectivity about the European war. In late January, 1915, he sent Colonel House on a new mission to explore the prospects of peace among the warring capitals. But House was still on the high seas when the tension of the struggle deepened in a way that proved fateful for the United States. On February 4, Germany declared a blockade of the British Isles. A week later, the United States sent simultaneous protests, against the German blockade and against the use of the United States flag by British ships. On March 11, the British announced a formal blockade of German ports. On March 30, the United States protested. On April 4, Germany condemned the United States for unneutral conduct, for failure to guard her legitimate commerce with Germany.

The President found it more and more difficult to

maintain his position of strict neutrality, while insisting upon American rights on the seas that actually favored the British cause. But his personal sadness was relieved in a remarkably dramatic fashion:

The President, in this spring of 1915, had fallen suddenly and very deeply in love. Some people blamed him for finding consolation so quickly, not sufficiently considering, perhaps, that his very devotion to his dead wife, combined with the isolation his position imposed on him, had made him intolerably lonely. And few people realized his lifelong need for sympathetic feminine companionship. Mrs. Galt must have appealed strongly to all that was romantic in him. A beautiful and gracious woman, in her early forties, she represented the oldest of old Virginia. . . . But she was no languid Southern beauty, of the kind so often pictured against backgrounds of pillared porticos and magnolia trees. Since her husband's death in 1908 she had had an active part in carrying on his jewelry business in Washington, and had found time to do a good deal of traveling in Europe. She understood the arts of living graciously, entertaining charmingly, and dressing exquisitely. . . .

Mrs. Galt was also cheerful, self-confident, and adaptable. She could throw off cares and enjoy the good things of life in a way the academic and rather ascetic President had never learned to do. She could not only draw him out of his depression and his loneliness, but draw him into pleasures and relaxations of which he had never had enough. Later, they would often be together on bridle paths and golf courses and in theaters. Having had little formal education, Mrs. Galt was more interested in people than in books; but she was not a woman to be satisfied with brightening up the President's leisure hours. She had strong likes and dislikes, and was by no means ready to take Wilson's friends on faith.

She also had decided views; and was so sure that the President was right in almost everything he did that it was her habit to urge him on, not to suggest caution or compromise. Men near the President were to become increasingly conscious of all these things.

... Considering all the difficulties, Wilson's second courtship seems nothing if not impetuous. He first met Mrs. Galt toward the end of March; he asked her to marry him during the first week in May. . . . it was not until September that their engagement became a fact. Wilson seemed rejuvenated by his love affair. Mrs. Galt was showered with flowers and letters and telephone calls on a private wire. There must have been a small boom in the production of purple orchids for the Washington market. If one may believe "Ike" Hoover, even official business suffered; and the President's friends became anxious. It was apparently a relief when the announcement came that the wedding was to take place a week before Christmas. Thanks, apparently, to Wilson's taste for simplicity, it was to be an evening wedding in Mrs. Galt's small house. . . .

In January, Mrs. Wilson settled into the White House, assumed the task of arranging documents for the President's signature, and shared with the famous typewriter the privilege of bearing him company in his most secluded hours. . . . she rapidly became the closest of all his confidants, closer than Tumulty, closer even than Colonel House.[12]

Woodrow Wilson would need the comfort of his new companion. Long before Edith Bolling Galt had decided to marry the President of the United States, the war had taken a turn that would destroy completely his policy of neutrality. Early in 1915, Germany had resorted to submarine warfare, her only effective answer to the British naval blockade On May 1, it became suddenly and tragically clear that German submarines would not distinguish between neutral and allied shipping. On that day, the American tanker Gulflight was sunk in the Irish Sea, with a loss of three men. That same day a web was being spun that would entangle the American people in the affairs of the great world abroad. As Oscar Handlin tells the story:

Envy and regret were the dominant emotions on May 1, 1915, as the Cunarder *Lusitania* set sail from New York. A new summer season was about to begin. . . . There were no forebodings. Those who had found time to glance through the morning's newspapers may have noticed an official German advertisement: Americans were warned that a war zone existed around the British Isles and that they sailed on Allied vessels at their own risk. But the grim announcement attracted little attention. . . .

The *Lusitania* never reached port. . . .

The trip was uneventful. Shipboard life ran its usual carefree course. . . . The war news hardly intruded, and the crew was studiously determined to carry on imperturbably as if nothing mattered but the self-contained life of the ship. . . . Captain [W. H.] Turner . . . had no illusions about the seriousness of the fighting. . . . Indeed, as he watched more than four thousand cases of ammunition come aboard in New York, he might have reflected that the ship was already doing its part. More than half his cargo was involved in the war effort.

Captain Turner knew also that the war was . . . capable of washing up against the sides of his own vessel. . . . He was directed to shun the usual route, to take a zigzag course, to be constantly alert, and to ram enemy submarines if he saw them.

The captain felt uneasy in the face of these directions. Orders were orders. But then, he had other obligations as well. He could envisage the subtle spread of panic among the passengers if the change of course became known. . . . Perhaps . . . he thought back to another incident three months earlier, when a sudden alarm had induced him to lower his own flag and to come into Liverpool flying the American colors. He had not liked that. . . . One way or another, the decision was made: the vessel followed its usual route and ignored Admiralty instructions.

On the morning of May 7, the Irish coast loomed on the horizon. . . .

Another captain approached a rendezvous at the same spot that day. Lieutenant Commander Schweiger of the Imperial German Navy had left his base at Emden in the middle of March. His instructions were to lurk unobserved in the Irish Sea and its channels and to attack British shipping plying in and out of Liverpool. So far he had not had much luck in his two-month cruise. . . . The men were tired, supplies were running low, and further continuation of the cruise seemed pointless.

Most of all the submarine's crew worried about its vulnerability. . . . It was painfully slow; fortunate indeed, if it could get up to twelve knots. Its armor was paper thin. Attacked, it could not even withdraw to the safety of submersion, for it could operate only close to the surface of the water. A single hit from even a small gun was likely to be fatal; and a vessel of moderate size used as a ram could crush the submarine like an eggshell. . . .

On May 7 the silhouette of a large ship loomed up suddenly before him in the lens. . . . Captain Schweiger watched the ship speed across his periscope. Its name was unclear. But it was certainly British and large. A fair prize. . . . The time was short. The tube was ready. He ordered a torpedo released.

As he watched the course of the speeding missile, Schweiger's heart sank in disappointment. The torpedo was obviously wide of its mark.

He had not time, however, to move back from the eyepiece when he noticed the target unaccountably veer and head directly into the path of the approaching torpedo. The torpedo struck home, and the ship quivered from the impact. Slowly she began to sink.

The U-20 stood back to watch its victim's boats being lowered and to see the passengers taken off. . . . the work went slowly. Eighteen minutes later a sharp explosion tore the vessel apart. She went down stern foremost. Just before the waters closed over her proud bow, the U-boat commander could at last make out her name. His prize had been the *Lusitania*.

. . . Along with the 600 crewmen almost 1,200 passengers had perished. A shock of revulsion passed through neutral America. Civilians, it had believed, ought not to be spattered with the blood of the battlefields. Now all the faith in the gallantry of war began to fade; those battles were not limited to the men in arms, but reached out to embrace everyone. And the Germans had been responsible.

Now the stories of the rape of Belgium became all at once credible. . . . Among those who went down with the *Lusitania* were more than one hundred Americans. Their death was a direct challenge to the President who had said that he would hold the Germans strictly accountable for such loss of lives. . . .

For Wilson, who moved reluctantly toward it, and for many Americans who welcomed their involvement innocently, almost gaily, the destruction of the *Lusitania* had been a turning point.[13]

NOTES, CHAPTER 10

1. Louis Brownlow, **A Passion for Politics** (Chicago: University of Chicago Press, 1955), p. 592.
2. Ray Stannard Baker, **Woodrow Wilson: Life and Letters** (N.Y.: Doubleday, Doran and Company, 1927–39), V, 2–3.

3. Arthur Walworth, **Woodrow Wilson** (London: Longmans, Green and Company, 1958), I, 400.
4. Baker, **op. cit.**, IV, 479–80.
5. **Ibid.**, V, 139–41.
6. Merle Eugene Curti, "Bryan and World Peace," **Smith College Studies in History**, XVI: 3–4 (April–July, 1931), 191–93.
7. **Ibid.**, pp. 193–95.
8. U. S. 63rd Congress, 2nd Session, **Senate Documents** (Washington, D. C.: 1914), No. 566, pp. 3–4.
9. Baker, **op. cit.**, V, 151.
10. **New York Tribune**, August 31, 1914.
11. Richard Hofstadter, **The American Political Tradition and the Men Who Made It** (Vintage Edition; N.Y.: Alfred A. Knopf, Inc., 1948), pp. 261–63.
12. H. C. F. Bell, **Woodrow Wilson and the People** (N.Y.: Doubleday, Doran and Company, 1945), pp. 182–84.
13. Oscar Handlin, **Chance or Destiny** (Boston: Little, Brown and Company, 1955), pp. 143–44, 147–51, 160–62, 165.

11. "TOO PROUD TO FIGHT"

At the close of a busy cabinet meeting, about one o'clock on May 7, 1915, a secretary hurried into the President's room with a cablegram in his hand. It contained the startling news that the great ship *Lusitania* had been sunk by a German submarine.... It was not until late in the evening that the President knew the worst....

The President's response was one of deep emotion. "Tears stood in his eyes," as the heart-rending reports came in. Nevertheless, he met the flood of passionate comment that filled the press, the demands for immediate and drastic action, pouring in upon him in hundreds of telegrams and letters, with the self-mastery and the calmness of judgment he had been so earnestly commending to the nation.

"If I pondered over those tragic items ... I should see red in everything and I am afraid that when I am called upon to act ... I could not be just to anyone."[1]

On May 10, he went to Philadelphia to make his appeal to the nation:

There is such a thing as a man being too proud to fight. There is such a thing as a nation being so right that it does not need to convince others by force that it is right.[2]

Privately, he was not so certain. By mid-July, Lansing would be concluding: "Germany must not be permitted to win this war, or to break even, though, to prevent it, this country is forced to take an active part." A week later, Wilson was writing to an old friend: "The opinion of the country seems to demand two inconsistent things, firmness and the avoidance of war, but I am hoping that perhaps they are not in necessary contradiction and that firmness may bring peace."[3] About the same time he would explain:

> Two things are plain to me:
> 1. The people of this country count on me to keep them out of the war.
> 2. It would be a calamity to the world at large if we should be drawn actively into the conflict and so deprived of all disinterested influence over the settlement.[4]

And late in September, he would confess to House: "My chief puzzle is to determine where patience ceases to be a virtue."[5] His patience would be much tried during that difficult summer of tedious negotiations. On May 13, he sent the first "Lusitania Note" to Germany, as Robert Lansing has explained:

> The instruction in substance called upon the German Government to cease submarine attacks against merchant ships since they could not be made according to the accepted rules of humane naval warfare.

On May twenty-eighth the German Minister of Foreign Affairs made a long and detailed reply to the American note, which he supplemented with another on June first concerning the case of the American vessel *Gulflight*. These notes contained excuses for the method employed by German submarine commanders and sought to cast the blame upon the British and American shipowners in subjecting their vessels to the risk of being attacked by passing through the sea war-zone, which had been proclaimed by Germany without color of legal right and which covered a great ocean area embracing the waters about the British Isles. There was, however, in the German reply no intimation that the existing practice would cease.

It was the note in answer to these two unsatisfactory communications to which Mr. Bryan objected. Rather than sign it he resigned from the Cabinet, believing that, if the American note as drafted were delivered to the German Government, it would result in war. . . .

To the American note . . . the German Government sent a reply dated July 8, 1915. It contained the assurance "that American ships will not be hindered in the prosecution of *legitimate* shipping and the lives of American citizens on *neutral* vessels shall not be placed in jeopardy." The italics are mine, and indicate the two words which made the assurance worthless. . . .

The assurance in no way met the demands of the United States or insured against a repetition of the *Lusitania* horror. The United States had insisted that the international rules requiring a belligerent to "visit and search" a merchant ship should be complied with. As to that, the German Government replied that to have done so in the case of the *Lusitania* would have been to expose the submarine to almost certain destruction by being rammed.[6]

Lansing became Secretary of State, on Bryan's resignation, but he faced a muddled confusion of problems and policies. As Baker has described it:

It was a period of interminable note-writing, protests, secret negotiations—with gradually increasing asperity on all sides. American policy was reduced to futility. Lansing sought vainly to strait-jacket the controversies into the neat traditions of an outworn international legalism—while Europe was dealing terribly with instrumentalities, submarines, aeroplanes, poison gas, and the like, which were beyond the law.... Yet we continued to make demands upon both combatants, complied with by neither. There was no way ... to remain truly neutral.[7]

But the yearning for peace was only one dimension of the problem with which Wilson wrestled throughout the winter of 1915–16. Another side of it was the impact of war on the American economy. In 1914, there had been signs of incipient depression. By the summer of 1915, Allied war orders had offset the downward trend; but Allied funds in the United States were nearly exhausted. Loans were needed, and the President faced a mounting pressure to reverse the neutral, anti-loan policy that he and Bryan had worked out. In his own family, both Lansing and McAdoo pushed hard. As Lansing posed the question:

We are face to face with what appears to be a critical economic situation, which can only be relieved apparently by the investment of American capital in foreign loans to be used in liquidating the enormous balance of trade in favor of the United States.

Can we afford to let a declaration as to our conception of the "true spirit of neutrality" made in the first days of the war stand in the way of our national interests which seem to be seriously threatened?[8]

Wilson relented. And so the flow of goods to Britain that had first inspired the German submarine campaign was reinforced by credits from neutral America, at the very moment she demanded that Germany abandon her chief defense against this aid to her enemy. The Kaiser put it bluntly as he commented upon a report that Americans wanted only peace: "Then stop the ammunition!"[9]

As the summer and fall wore on, incident after incident piled up to deepen the feeling against Germany. On July 24, a German propaganda agent carelessly left his briefcase on a New York subway. A Secret Service man picked it up, and three weeks later the newspapers began to publish the spine-chilling revelations its documents contained. On July 25, an American ship was sunk off Scotland. On August 19, the British ship Arabic went down with the loss of two Americans. On protest from the United States, the German government announced that liners would "not be sunk . . . without warning and without safety in the lives of noncombatants, provided that the liners do not try to escape or offer resistance."[10] But the Lusitania issue was still unresolved, despite a third American protest, and early in November, an Italian liner was sunk by an Austrian submarine, with a loss of 27 Americans. On November 30, a gigantic explosion tore the DuPont powder works; it was assumed at once that German agents had done the dirty work. The next day, the United States demanded the recall of German diplomats who had been implicated in the espionage exposures.

Throughout the waning autumn, the President faced urgent demands for preparedness, and the lowering threat of defeat in the 1916 election. The election would have been difficult in any case; now a misstep in the grave international crisis would certainly seal his fate. But there was more than personal ambition and party pride riding on the November vote. A defeat, in Wilson's eyes, would place the country at the mercy of the strident interventionists among Republican leaders, at the mercy of men like Henry Cabot Lodge and Theodore Roosevelt.

Tortured with indecision, Wilson gave in to the demands for preparedness. He told the Navy to go ahead with the expansion plans for which young Franklin Roosevelt, as well as Republicans, had been arguing for many months. On December 7, he went to Congress to request an army of 142,000 men, a reserve of 400,000. Congress moved slowly—there was immense opposition from Southern and Western Democrats. But on June 3, Wilson would sign the National Defense Act, providing a standing army of 175,000 men and a National Guard of 450,000. And on August 29, he would have a Naval Appropriation of $313 million dollars. He had been compelled to seek Republican aid. And, late in January, he had taken this new crusade to the country, with a far-flung tour of speeches arguing for preparedness, warning the nation that peace could not be guaranteed, that national honor might someday demand war. And, while he talked preparedness, the negotiations with both Britain and Germany continued, with warning after warning to both, and by both largely ignored. Early in February, 1916, Germany announced the resumption again of unrestricted submarine warfare against armed merchantmen But almost simultaneously, the German ambassador in Washington admitted his government's liability for the death of Americans aboard the Lusitania. And then, on March 24, an unarmed French liner, the Sussex, was sunk with the loss of three American lives.

There was a sharp protest from Wilson: "...unless the Imperial German Government should now immediately declare and effect an abandonment of its present methods of warfare against passenger and freight carrying vessels, this Government can have no choice but to sever diplomatic relations with the Government of the German Empire altogether."[11] Finally, on May 4, Germany replied with its "Sussex pledge" that it would not sink merchantmen without warning.

Yet, while he talked preparedness, the President continued also to talk peace. On December 28, 1915, Colonel House had sailed for Europe in a last attempt to bring the warring powers together. His plan was to press for mutual agreement to mediation by the United States, and, if this failed, to move toward American intervention on the side of Britain. He hoped for agreement to an armistice based upon disarmament and a League of Nations to preserve the peace. The devious diplomacy of the spring and summer was largely secret from the American people, and it was filled with confusion. A part of the confusion lay in House's use of the term "intervention." The British assumed that he meant military intervention. House was talking only of diplomatic pressure.

Another difficulty lay in the early and apparent German agreement to House's proposition. But a study of their views made it clear that they would not tolerate actual American participation in the peace arrangements, and that they intended disarmament and a League of Nations only after this war had been settled. But the greatest confusion lay between the State Department and Colonel House. While House, with the President's blessings, sought a rapprochement among the belligerents, Lansing, also with the President's blessing, sought to bring Germany to terms on the submarine issue and to avoid future crisis.

The controversy came to a head when the allies began to arm their merchantmen, and Lansing took to the President the apparently reasonable proposition that armed merchantmen must be dealt with as vessels of war. Lansing warned both Britain and Germany that the United States was thinking of treating armed merchantmen as auxiliary cruisers and suggested to the British that they resolve the crisis by disarming their merchant ships again. Lansing saw clearly that, vulnerable as the submarines were, Germany would never agree to treat gun-carrying freighters and liners as anything but ships of war to be attacked without warning. The German government was delighted. And Lansing's diplomacy at that moment played a strong role in encouraging it to announce a resumption of unrestricted submarine warfare. Lansing's diplomacy had also come near to wrecking House's attempts to make Wilson a mediator, for the British protested at once that the new American policy would mean the sinking of merchantmen as "the rule and not the exception."[12]

Wilson now had to choose between his two policies. He chose House's, and Lansing informed the German government that the United States would not accept the latest Lusitania note or the resumption of submarine warfare, and that it would not insist on the disarming of merchantmen. Unable to explain his reasons, Wilson had to use every political weapon to beat down the resentment and disillusionment of congressmen who insisted that the new state of affairs would bring war, and who fought to push through resolutions advising American citizens to stay off belligerent merchant ships. The Sussex crisis and the "Sussex Pledge" resolved the issue for the moment. But it remained a dangerous thread upon which the fate of Wilson's policy hung. For the Sussex Pledge had been made conditional on British behavior consistent with international law. Wilson had refused to accept the conditions, had blandly assumed that Germany must honor her pledge without the conditions upon which it had been based.

In the United States, public opinion wavered uncertainly with the uncertainty of the administration's policy. Even as he asked for a large army, Wilson asked: "What is America expected to do? She is expected to do nothing less than keep law alive while the rest of the world burns."[13]

There were tokens of his uncertainty in the very preparedness he requested. As Herbert Bell has pointed out:

The best that can be said for Wilson's attitude is that it corresponded with the general sentiment, both of the people and of Congress. But Wilson helped to create the sentiment. . . . He had his way. As a result, we entered the war almost totally unprepared in so far as the Army was concerned; were consequently responsible for some prolongation of its miseries; and might well have been involved in an Allied defeat. . . . his scheme for preparedness was no more than a gesture. He offered an increase in the regular Army too small to be significant, and the creation of a "continental army" of 400,000 men. The figure looked imposing; but it was the quality of the new army that would count. It would need good organization; and it would need considerable expert training, if it was to function as anything but a home guard, recruited to meet invaders who were as likely to come from Europe, as from Mars. The kind of warfare that was going on in Europe was new and, for those days, very technical. Moreover, military men agreed that infantry must be so disciplined by continuous training as to give automatic obedience to commands. Only this would take all the men of a unit "over the top."

But what was the President's "continental army" to be like? It was to consist of volunteers. It was to reach full recruitment in about three years. It was not to be "organized." It was to receive training for "very brief" periods each year; and it was to get its training largely from the National Guard. Yet the National Guard, as events would amply prove, varied in quality from State to State, knew nothing whatever of current methods of warfare, and had never had opportunity to learn automatic obedience. . . .

Yet Wilson stood as firmly on his insistence that the American people's rights should be respected as though the nation had been ready to go into action at any time.[14]

Wilson's inadequate plans for preparedness deepened the hostility of the interventionists. His Assistant Sec-

retary of the Navy, Franklin Roosevelt, complained publicly that "half a Navy is worthless." Secretary of War Lindley K. Garrison resigned in protest against Wilson's refusal to nationalize the state-controlled National Guard. The widely-respected Elihu Root put bluntly the crux of the Republican protest against the President's tactics: "No man should draw a pistol who dares not shoot. The government that shakes its fist first and its finger afterward falls into contempt. Our diplomacy has lost its authority and influence because we have been brave in words and irresolute in action."[15]

In the process, the people were distracted—by the politics of an election year, by the fruitless chase of "Pancho" Villa, by the continued debate over Wilson's domestic policies. As they watched the grim death struggle of Europe on the battlefields of Verdun, they were alternately encouraged by Wilson's bids for peace and alarmed by his preparations for war. Now, in May, 1916, Wilson turned his attention to the British. On the sixteenth, he wrote to Colonel House in Europe:

I have been giving some very careful thought to your question how we should deal with Sir Edward [Grey] and his Government at this turning point,—for it really is that.

It seems to me that we should really get down to hard pan. . . . We are plainly face to face with this alternative. . . . The United States must either make a decided move for peace . . . or, if she postpones that, must insist to the limit upon her rights of trade and upon such freedom of the seas as international law already justifies her in insisting on against Great Britain, with the same plain speaking and firmness that she has used against Germany. And the choice must be made immediately. Which does Great Britain prefer? She cannot escape both. To do nothing is now, for us, impossible.[16]

Yet Wilson could never really "get down to hard pan" with the British. The Ambassador to London warned of the blockade: "They won't relax it; they can't. Public opinion wouldn't stand it an hour. As things are now, an Admiral has said in a public speech that it is necessary to hang Grey if they're going to win the war."[17] British interference with neutral trade always seemed little more than a petty irritation, as compared with the sunken vessels and civilian deaths the German submarines produced. Wilson threatened to ask Congress for authority to prohibit loans and exports to the allies. In September, Congress gave him the power he wished. Yet he held up action until after the election, and then again renewed submarine warfare took the pressure from the British.

Meanwhile, the Republican National Convention had nominated Charles Evans Hughes, Supreme Court Justice, only recently the popular and progressive Governor of New York. Hughes was dignified, but Hughes was also a great campaign orator. He would be hard to beat under the best of circumstances. A week later, Democrats met in St. Louis for the ritual of renominating Wilson. House and Wilson had designed a campaign that relied on the urban machines. They hoped to undo the bitter damage that had been wrought in 1912. It was the New York "regular" Governor Martin Glynn who was chosen to make the keynote address. New York "progressives" like Franklin Roosevelt were pushed into the background. William Jennings Bryan, denied even a delegate's seat, was forced to find a place in the press gallery.

Out of this convention came the slogan and the issue that would save the election for Wilson—a slogan he mistrusted, an issue he doubted: "He kept us out of war." As Herbert Bell notes, the sentiment was strong in the convention itself:

... the keynote speech of Governor Glynn of New York:

"[The President's] policy may not satisfy those who revel in destruction and find pleasure in despair ... but it does satisfy ... the mothers of the land at whose hearth and fireside no jingoistic war has placed an empty chair. It does satisfy the daughters of the land. ..."

... the words of the ... permanent chairman:

"Without orphaning a single American child, without widowing a single American mother, without firing a single gun, without shedding a single drop of blood [the President] has wrung from the most militant spirit that ever brooded above a battlefield an acknowledgement of American rights and an agreement to American demands."

And then, of course, Mr. Bryan was forced to speak:

"I join the rest of the nation in gratitude that at a time like this we have a President who is trying to keep us out of war."[18]

Wilson protested quietly: "I can't keep the country out of war. They talk of me as though I were a god. Any little German lieutenant can put us into the war at any time by some calculated outrage."[19]

Yet the promise of peace became the essence of the campaign. Wilson himself was often frank. In October, he told a Cincinnati audience: "I believe that the business of neutrality is over. The nature of modern war leaves no state untouched."[20] And, as the campaign progressed, there were headlines to reinforce his warning. On July 30, the submarine Deutschland arrived in the United States on a trading mission, which incidentally dramatized the breakdown of the sea as a protective barrier for America. On July 30, the Black Tom explosion in a munitions plant was almost immediately assumed to be the work of saboteurs. On October 7, the U-53 appeared at Newport, Rhode Island. In the next two days, she sank nine British ships off the shores of Nantucket Island.

But, while the events of the summer promised only a grim prospect, the mammoth party propaganda campaign spoke of peace. Typical was the paid advertising run on the eve of election day:

> YOU ARE WORKING;
> —NOT FIGHTING!
> ALIVE AND HAPPY;
> —NOT CANNON FODDER!
> WILSON AND PEACE WITH HONOR?
> HUGHES WITH ROOSEVELT
> AND WAR?[21]

But the campaign was not all foreign policy. Throughout the spring, Wilson suddenly renewed his progressive vigor as he virtually forced Congress to pass a series of domestic reforms that went well beyond his own New Freedom and implemented broadly the very progressive nationalism he had attacked so sharply in 1912. Some of that summer's harvest was the inevitable product of war conditions; other items represented Wilson's belated adoption of ancient reform crusades of the progressive movement. But the total effect was to bring firmly into his camp much of the reform support that otherwise might have gone to Hughes. It was an amazing legislative achievement. On July 11, a program of federal appropriations for highways; on the seventeenth, a Federal Farm Loan Act; on August 29, a measure of limited self-government for the Philippines; on September 1, the Keating-Owen Child Labor Act, which Wilson himself had strongly opposed four years earlier; on September 3, the eight-hour day for railroad workers; on

September 7, a United States Shipping Board, to build and operate ships and coordinate that strategic industry; and, on the same day, a Federal Workmen's Compensation Act; and on the next day the Emergency Revenue Act, which pointed the new trend toward steeply progressive taxation.

While Wilson hammered through this progressive program, Hughes became bogged down in the party vendetta that Theodore Roosevelt had started. Conservatives resented his welcoming back T. R. and his Bull Moose secessionists. And Hughes had further trouble with the campaign. He failed to show concretely how he would have managed foreign policy differently from Wilson. In the process, he became inadvertently identified with the warlike rumblings of the belligerent Teddy. And he was equally embarrassed by the Anglophobe support of German-Americans. Wilson sank the barb deeply as he wrote to an Irish nationalist his own repudiation of the "hypenate" vote: "I would feel deeply mortified to have you or anybody like you vote for me. Since you have access to many disloyal Americans and I have not, I will ask you to convey this message to them."[22]

Wilson more than half expected defeat. On November 5, he sent to his Secretary of State a revolutionary plan for easing the transition, if Hughes were elected:

> The course I have in mind is dependent upon the consent and cooperation of the Vice-President; but, if I could gain his consent to the plan, I would ask your permission to invite Mr. Hughes to become Secretary of State and would then join the Vice-President in resigning and thus open to Mr. Hughes the immediate succession to the presidency. . . . I would have no right to risk the peace of the nation by remaining in office after I had lost my authority.[23]

On election night he seemed to look forward to defeat. He told his doctor:

Grayson, I'm something like the Confederate soldier who returned to his home after Lee's surrender. He looked over his farm. The buildings had been burned, the stock run off and the fences demolished. Then he looked at his bleeding feet and at his wounded arm, and said:

"I'm glad I fought. I'm proud of the part I played. I have no regrets, but—I'll be damned if I ever love another country!"[24]

Wilson went to bed early that night. He was content. In a New York hotel, Charles Evans Hughes retired comfortably with the certain prospect of victory. But, during the night the returns from the West Coast drifted slowly in. California, New Mexico and North Dakota had gone for Wilson by narrow margins, and with them, Wilson had won.*

Wilson had been helped by a fair number of Socialist votes, by many from labor, and by the apparent dissolution of the German-American bloc. But, as Arthur Link has noted, the significance of the election was clear and stunning:

It was . . . the South and West united again in an emphatic mandate for progressivism and peace. In short, Wilson had consummated the union of most of the agricultural states, which Bryan had narrowly failed to do in 1896, and had added to the Democratic column two Eastern states and a large portion of the social justice element, who had heretofore followed Roosevelt.[25]

*1916 Electoral College Vote: 277–254.
Popular Vote: Wilson: 9,129,606.
            Hughes: 8,538,221.
            Benson (Socialist): 585,113.
            Hanly (Prohibition): 220,506.
            Reimer (Socialist-Labor): 13,403.

For the moment, Wilson stood on the threshold of a new structure for the Democratic Party. That he proved unable to make it a permanent structure became a major party tragedy.

As the President turned to the problems of another four years, he seemed more sure than ever that peace could be attained. The submarine threat was momentarily over. It was no longer necessary to conduct negotiations and to win a campaign at the same time. He would press strongly for peace. But he moved too slowly. Before he could send his formal appeals to the warring powers on December 18, the German government had beaten him to the headlines with its own statement that it was willing to enter peace negotiations—under certain conditions. Worse yet, there had been a shift of power in Germany. The militarists were firmly in control; the decision had already been secretly taken to resume submarine warfare if the December peace bid did not work. But the decision was secret, and Wilson's peace appeals would be pressed for nearly two months before it became known. Charles Seymour has explained:

In the circumstances the effort was bound to fail. . . . The Allies were quite unwilling to negotiate with an unbeaten Germany. The Germans were determined to insist upon terms which the Allies would not have accepted until all hope of victory had faded. Neither side wished the mediation of Wilson. The British . . . felt that Wilson merely talked about ideals for which the Allies were dying. "We entertain but little hope," von Jagow had written to Bernstorff, "for the result of the exercises of good offices by one whose instincts are all in favor of the English point of view, and who in addition to this, is so naive a statesman as President Wilson." . . .

Wilson was not discouraged by the failure of the

December peace notes.... He was determined to save American neutrality. On January 4, 1917, in reply to House's suggestion of the need of military preparation "in the event of war," the President insisted: "There will be no war...." On January 22 he delivered before the Senate the address which he hoped would serve as a general basis for a negotiated peace, a settlement that would leave neither the one side nor the other crushed and revengeful, "a peace without victory." ...

But the decision had already been taken in Germany. On January 9 Hindenburg and Hotzendorf insisted that all chance of peace had disappeared and forced approval of the intensive submarine campaign. On January 31 Bernstorff gave notice that from the following day the engagements of the pledge given after the sinking of the Sussex would no longer be observed.[26]

"In one instant," said Richard Hofstadter, "Wilson reaped the whirlwind of unneutrality that he had sown in the first two years of the war. For the Germans, realizing that the United States was already heavily engaged against them with its productive capacity, and assuming that she could not otherwise intervene effectively before a fatal blow could be struck against the Allies, were calculating on American entrance into the war."[27]

In a sense it had always been too late. Whatever the merits or demerits of Wilson's shifting policies, the poignant and compelling fact was a simple one. Americans were not willing to pay the price of neutrality. Savoring the profits of war—in jobs as well as business income—they had insisted that they be protected from the horrors of war. Insisting upon neutral rights, which neither Germany nor Great Britain could possibly honor, they had placed their future firmly in the hands of these hard-pressed belligerents. Jefferson had known over a hundred years earlier that the only guarantee of neutrality was complete isolation. To be safe, American lives and American dollars must stay home.

And there was another compelling fact upon which Americans acted, even though they could not or would not articulate it. For over a hundred years, American security and American prosperity had grown comfortably behind the protective screen of British control of the Atlantic Ocean. As Walter Lippmann later would point out, once this screen had been shattered by a potentially hostile German navy, the United States could never again be isolated in a comfortable dream world of opportunity without danger.

NOTES, CHAPTER 11

1. Ray Stannard Baker, **Woodrow Wilson: Life and Letters** (N.Y.: Doubleday, Doran and Company, 1927–39), V, 330–31.
2. Ray Stannard Baker and William E. Dodd (eds.), **The Public Papers of Woodrow Wilson** (N.Y.: Harper and Brothers, 1925–27), III, 321.
3. Robert Lansing, **War Memoirs** (Indianapolis, Ind.: The Bobbs-Merrill Company, 1935), p. 21; Baker, **op. cit.**, V, 364.
4. Baker, **op. cit.**, V, 373.
5. **Ibid.**, V, 361.
6. Lansing, **op. cit.**, pp. 29–32.
7. Baker, **op. cit.**, V, 362.
8. **Lansing Papers, 1914–1920** ("Papers Relating to the Foreign Relations of the United States") (Washington, D. C.: Government Printing Office, 1939), I, 146.
9. Arthur S. Link, **Wilson: The Struggle for Neutrality, 1914–1915** (Princeton, N.J.: Princeton University Press, 1960), p. 357.
10. **New York Times**, September 2, 1915.
11. U. S. 64th Congress, 1st Session, **Congressional Record** (Washington, D. C.: 1916), p. 6449.
12. Arthur S. Link, **Woodrow Wilson and the Progressive Era, 1910–1917** (N.Y.: Harper and Brothers, 1954), p. 208.
13. Baker, **op. cit.**, VI, 1.
14. H. C. F. Bell, **Woodrow Wilson and the People** (N.Y.: Doubleday, Doran and Company, 1945), pp. 190, 192–93.
15. Baker, **op. cit.**, VI, 3.

16. **Ibid**, pp. 212–13.
17. Charles Seymour, **American Diplomacy During the World War** (2nd edition; Baltimore, Md.: The Johns Hopkins Press, 1942), p. 75.
18. Bell, **op. cit.**, p. 199.
19. Baker, **op cit.**, VI, 258.
20. Baker and Dodd, **op. cit.**, IV, 381.
21. **New York Times**, November 4, 1916.
22. Baker, **op. cit.**, VI, 290.
23. **Ibid.**, p. 292–93.
24. **Ibid.**, p. 296.
25. Link, **op. cit.**, pp. 250–51.
26. Charles Seymour, **American Neutrality, 1914–1917** (New Haven, Conn.: Yale University Press, 1935), pp. 19–22.
27. Richard Hofstadter, **The American Political Tradition and the Men Who Made It** (Vintage Edition; N.Y.: Alfred A. Knopf, Inc., 1948), p. 269.

12. TOO PROUD TO RETREAT

After February 1, the nation was caught up in an inexorable pattern of fate. War was inevitable, unless Wilson and the United States made concessions that neither pride, honor, nor interest would allow.

On February 3, the President broke off diplomatic relations with Germany. Theodore Roosevelt protested bitterly: "I do not believe Wilson will go to war unless Germany literally kicks him into it."[1] Yet, when the President asked Congress on February 26 for authority to arm American merchant ships, a filibuster developed at once. Always impatient of opposition, Wilson raged: "... a little group of willful men, representing no opinion but their own, have rendered the great Government of the United States helpless and contemptible."[2] The peace sentiments that the President himself had so assiduously cultivated were a nuisance now. Then, on March 1, the Zimmerman note was published. A secret instruction to the German Ambassador at Mexico City, it had been intercepted and decoded by the British. It was a natural maneuver for a warring power, but to the American people it seemed the depth of infamy:

> ... it is our intention to keep neutral the United States of America.

If this attempt is not successful we propose an alliance on the following basis with Mexico: That we shall make war together and together make peace. We shall give general financial support, and it is understood that

Mexico is to reconquer the lost territory in New Mexico, Texas, and Arizona.[3]

On March 12, Wilson ordered American merchantmen armed, without congressional authorization. Three days later, the news of the Russian Revolution reached the United States, removing for the moment the objections of many Americans to support of an alliance that included the reactionary Czarist regime. It would be easier now to believe that this was a war for democracy. On the eighteenth, three more American ships went down. On the twentieth, the Cabinet agreed quietly that war was inevitable. The next day, Wilson recalled Congress. On the twenty-second, the United States became the first government to recognize the new regime in Russia. By April 1, Wilson was ready to act, but still deeply disturbed. He sent for his old friend Frank Cobb, who later wrote:

> I'd never seen him so worn down. . . . He said he probably was going before Congress the next day to ask a declaration of war, and he'd never been so uncertain about anything in his life as about that decision. . . . He said war would overturn the world we had known. . . . It would mean that we should lose our heads along with the rest and stop weighing right and wrong. . . . "To fight, you must be brutal and ruthless, and the spirit of ruthless brutality will enter into the very fibre of our national life. . . ."
>
> He thought the Constitution would not survive it; that free speech and the right of assembly would go. . . .
>
> "If there is any alternative, for God's sake, let's take it!" he exclaimed.[4]

The next day, Woodrow Wilson drove down Pennsylvania Avenue to the Capitol Building to ask the Congress and the nation for war. A newsman watched

as the President walked toward a large mirror. . . .
The features were twisted in spiritual agony, the chin
awry, the flesh deeply drawn and flushed. The President
placed his left elbow on the mantel and looked stead-
fastly at his distorted countenance. "A stroke!" the
editor whispered to himself. But no; the tortured figure
put his left hand to his brow to smooth the corruga-
tions, the right to his chin to set it straight and firm;
and gradually the features fell into a physiognomy as
rigid as Calvin's. His "make-up" completed, Woodrow
Wilson was resolved to play out the tragedy that had
been forced upon him.[5]

He spoke in terms that gave to disaster the aura of
a grand crusade. A war spawned in a faltering diplomacy
and a grim conflict of interests became, in an hour, a
glorious quest for unassailable ideals:

Neutrality is no longer feasible or desirable
where the peace of the world is involved and the freedom of its peoples, and the menace to that peace and
freedom lies in the existence of autocratic Governments,
backed by organized force which is controlled wholly by
their will, not by the will of their people. We have seen
the last of neutrality in such circumstances. . . .

We have no quarrel with the German people. . . . Self-
governed nations do not fill their neighbor States with
spies or set the course of intrigue to bring about some
critical posture of affairs which will give them an opportunity to strike and make conquest. . . .

A steadfast concern for peace can never be maintained
except by a partnership of democratic nations. . . . The
world must be made safe for democracy. Its peace must
be planted upon the tested foundations of political liberty.

We have no selfish ends to serve. We desire no conquest, no dominion. . . . We are but one of the champions of the rights of mankind. . . .

. . . It is a fearful thing to lead this great, peaceful people into war, into the most terrible and disastrous of all wars, civilization itself seeming to be in the balance. But the right is more precious than the peace, and we shall fight for the things which we have always carried nearest our hearts—for democracy, for the right of those who submit to authority to have a voice in their own Governments, for the rights and liberties of small nations, for a universal dominion of right by such a concert of free peoples as shall bring peace and safety to all nations and make the world itself at last free.[6]

As the President returned to the White House, he was impressed with the enormity and tragedy of the situation. "Think what it was they were applauding," he said to Tumulty. ". . . My message to-day was a message of death for our young men. How strange it seems to applaud that."[7] But the applause was not unanimous. The debate in the Congress went on for four days. Senator George Norris among others protested bitterly:

We have loaned many hundreds of millions of dollars to the allies in this controversy. . . . Through this instrumentality and also through the instrumentality of others who have not only made millions out of the war in the manufacture of munitions, etc., and who would expect to make millions more if our country can be drawn into the catastrophe, a large number of the great newspapers and news agencies of the country have been controlled and enlisted in the greatest propaganda that the world has ever known, to manufacture sentiment in favor of war. It is now demanded that the American citizens shall be used as insurance policies to guarantee the safe delivery of munitions of war to belligerent nations.[8]

There were six votes against war in the Senate, 50 in the House. But the bulk of the country supported the heavy congressional majorities. There was that strange, almost suicidal, sense of relief that comes when years of tension have been resolved, even tragically. And Wilson's speech had played magnificently to the emotions and ideals, to the pride of his people. But few of them, least of all Wilson himself, understood the deep significance of that moment. As Henry May has written:

> Theodore Roosevelt called the speech a great state paper.
>
> It was more; it was an enduring monument to a whole passing period of American civilization. Its assumptions and its purposes embodied the country's conception of itself and of the world. Unfortunately they had little to do with the particular war. . . . The most famous phrase, for instance, asserted that the world must be made safe for democracy. For a long time, a great many different people had demonstrated that the world was not and never could be safe for anything, let alone that precarious product of hard work and good fortune, democracy.[9]

But, for the moment, there was a war to be fought:

> People who had deplored Wilson's cautious hesitancy and the lack of consistency and realism in some of his policies as long as we remained neutral, were pleasantly surprised when he turned out to be a very good war President. Almost overnight he appeared his confident, clear-headed, hard-driving old self again. . . .
>
> In the war fervor that took hold of the nation, the President seemed more than ever The Leader, the "common voice." . . . Lincoln's wartime government had been a sort of temporary dictatorship, based mainly on his "Commander-in-Chief" powers. Wilson made use of

those powers too, not only in such matters as deciding
that an expeditionary force should go to France, but in
creating a Committee on Public Information, with
authority over censorship, and a War Industries Board,
with the duty of "co-ordinating" private industry. In general, however, he relied as usual on his legislative leadership in Congress. . . . In view of possible emergencies,
the powers given to the President had sometimes to be
very broad. Witness the fact that he had only to sign a
paper, in order to make himself, in December 1917, the
tsar of all the railroads. . . . he made his work even heav-
ier than it need have been. In almost everything but
military and naval matters he reserved all important
decisions for himself. What is more, he resisted every
effort made by Congress to diminish his responsibility
and authority. . . . He would not have liked being called
a "war lord," but he wielded all the powers of one.[10]

Wilson could not, in fact, as he once protested, "run
the country." Yet there must be rapid coordination of
the nation's economy, if America's industrial strength
were to weigh in the balance against Germany. And the
job was practically unprecedented for Americans. There
was a strong national tradition against centralization,
against economic interference by government. And there
was no modern experience in national planning or management. Even the military services themselves faced
the gigantic problems of procurement with fuzzy plans,
competitive, stuffy and confused procedures. As Joseph
Dorfman has explained:

Even after the declaration of war . . . there
was no effective co-ordination among the numerous
supply divisions of the Army and Navy. In the Army
alone ten separate procurement agencies were bidding
against each other for supplies. And purchases by the
Allies increased the confusion. Bernard Baruch, chairman of the reconstituted War Industries Board,

recalled later that the various Army contracting agencies "fought each other as bad as they fought the Germans, and then they fought me just as hard, and fought the Navy just as hard." In fact, it took more than a year to achieve some sort of effective co-ordination.

The problem of essential industries became very perplexing. Every business considered itself essential, and so many priorities were issued that by 1918 there was danger of breakdown. In general, the business community wanted changes in the economy to be gradual. . . .

For some time after the United States entered the war the railroads were left to their own devices. They attempted to meet the need for unified action by a voluntary organization, called the Railroad War Board, composed of five railroad executives. This proved ineffective, and in December, 1917, President Wilson commandeered the roads. In July, 1918, the Government took over the telephone and telegraph lines; later the cables, and just a few days before the Armistice, the express business was placed under government operation. . . . In an attempt to bring about unity, more and more boards were created. The quality of many of these boards gave rise to the bon mot, "A board is long and narrow and wooden."

In recalling this period, Baruch stated that "the greatest deterrent to effective action" during the war was the lack of facts.[11]

But more difficult even than arranging the machinery to collect the facts was the task of commanding public support for this revolutionary change in economic arrangements. In November, 1918, the War Industries Board itself sought to make clear to the American people the monumental dimensions of the job: "It is not enough to mobilize the nation's military strength. There must be a mobilization of her full economic resources—industrial, agricultural, and financial. These must be organized, coordinated, and directed with the same strategy that governs the operations of the purely military arms of service."[12]

The War Industries Board had power. But years later Baruch would explain that this power must be used subtly:

There is something in public sentiment in a community that is imponderable and is of greater value and force perhaps than anything else. Many times in the war powerful men asserted that they were not going to do this and were not going to do that, and we said to them . . . : "All right; if you don't want to do it, don't do it; but when you get back home there will not be any coal in your factory and not a wheel turning. Doubtless your friends and neighbors will want to know why you are not on the job. You will have to explain that to people whose sons are on the other side, and say that you got into a heated discussion as to how much you wanted to get paid for what you were doing."[13]

Joseph Dorfman has concluded:

The price-control program did, to some extent, prevent runaway prices. An index number of 573 commodities brought under price control at various dates from midsummer, 1917, to the Armistice dropped from 209 in July, 1917, to 189 in June, 1918. Thereafter, with moderate advances permitted, the index rose again, but it did not rise to the pre-price-fixing point. . . .

As for war financing, there was a danger at the start that the government would to an overwhelming degree have recourse to loans rather than taxes; and taxes of a character primarily in the nature of excises and custom duties rather than income and excess profits taxes. . . . Each successive revenue measure raised the tax rates, with special emphasis on personal income taxes and excess profits taxes. Thus in 1916 the normal income tax rate was 2 per cent, with a surtax on incomes exceeding $20,000 ranging from 1 per cent to 13 per cent on incomes in excess of $2,000,000. By 1918 the normal rate was 6 per cent on net incomes up to $4,000 and 12 per cent on higher incomes, with a surtax ranging from 1 per cent on incomes exceeding $5,000 to 65 per cent on incomes over $1,000,000. The business and financial community did not let this "dangerous tendency" toward "excessive taxation" go unchallenged.... But in spite of the heavy increases in taxation and of numerous pronouncements from President Wilson on down, that there should be no profits from the war, substantial profits were reaped....

Control of labor was even more gropingly applied. The need for unified administration of the labor supply and for centralized treatment of labor questions was belatedly recognized.... In general, ... the government was not hostile to labor unions, and they flourished. There was a proliferation of boards—for mediation, policy, and labor standards—but only toward the end of the war was the machinery becoming comprehensive and fully effective.[14]

Wilson himself was sharply torn on the labor issues. He would resist the setting up of a labor czar. He would write strongly to the Governor of Pennsylvania: ". . . I think it would be most unfortunate for any of the states to relax the laws by which safeguards have been thrown about labor."[15] *He would maintain the most cordial relations with Samuel Gompers, the moderate, comfortable chief of the AFL.*

But the Industrial Workers of the World (the IWW), Wilson, like most middle-class Americans, feared and resented. The IWW abhorred moderation and laid challenge to the whole economic and social system. Organizing rapidly among the unskilled workers whom Gompers's AFL had ignored, it announced: "The work-

ing class and the employing class have nothing in common. . . . Between these two classes a struggle must go on until the workers of the world organize as a class, take possession of the earth and the machinery of production and abolish the wage system."[16]

Jack London's widely-circulated blast at strikebreakers illustrates the spirit of the movement:

> After God had finished the rattlesnake, the toad and the vampire, he had some awful substance left with which He made a SCAB. A SCAB is a two-legged animal with a corkscrew soul, a water-logged brain and a combination backbone made of jelly and glue. Where others have hearts he carries a tumor of rotten principles.
>
> When a SCAB comes down the street men turn their backs and angels weep in heaven, and the devil shuts the gates of hell to keep him out. . . .
>
> A STRIKEBREAKER IS A TRAITOR TO HIS GOD, HIS COUNTRY, HIS FAMILY, AND HIS CLASS![17]

IWW strikes seemed treason to white-collar workers, as they loyally bought Liberty Bonds and sang "The Yanks Are Coming." IWW propaganda was soon associated in the public mind with the violence of a Russian revolution turned Bolshevist. Typical of the reaction was the incident at Butte described by Marc Karson:

> The strike dragged on throughout the summer of 1917 and spread until it reached the proportions of a general mine strike in Butte. Assisting the IWW local was Frank Little, veteran IWW organizer and chairman of the IWW general executive board. Late in the night of July 31, 1917, he was seized in his room at the Finn Hotel by six armed men who beat him, tied him behind their automobile with a rope, and drove to the outskirts of Butte. He was then murdered by hanging

on the Milwaukee Railroad trestle, and a card was pinned on his coat reading: "First and last warning" followed by the numbers 3 plus 7 minus 77, the sign of the old Vigilantes.... Deciding that tolerance was a virtue too expensive for a war, the government planned to wipe out the IWW through a campaign of mass arrests of its leaders. About one hundred special agents of the Department of Justice trailed and spied on IWW leaders during 1916 and 1917. On September 5, 1917, federal officers acting in unison throughout the country raided various IWW headquarters and union offices and seized all available records, documents, correspondence, and literature. In another mass raid on September 28, 166 IWW leaders were arrested and indicted in Chicago for violation of the Espionage Act of June, 1917. For several months thereafter raids and arrests continued.... until practically every important leader connected with the IWW was rounded up. So thoroughgoing were the results of the government's campaign of mass arrests that the IWW lacked the leadership by the end of 1917 to maintain itself.[18]

But it was freedom of speech and press that were most dramatically endangered by the first brief American excursion into total war. For Wilson personally this was a more crucial challenge than the problems of the economic front. At stake was his own and his nation's deep faith in democracy, individualism, and freedom. Yet there were problems to be solved, the security of military secrets, the need to promote the war effort, the draft, a high level of production, the sale of liberty bonds, and the maintenance of a spirit that would support the "doughboys" overseas.

There were few precedents. The treason clause of the Constitution was virtually unenforceable. The Civil War experience had taught the country the dangers of martial law. And there were problems of public opinion.

The country and the Congress were ready for an hysteria that would have wiped out the entire Bill of Rights and substituted the justice of the mob. The extremes to which false patriotism could be carried were silly, but hardly funny. German language instruction was dropped from the schools; sauerkraut was relabeled "liberty cabbage"; a clergyman was tarred and feathered for having prayed in German at the deathbed of a non-English speaking immigrant. Overnight the German had become the Hun, the honest pacifist a traitor. George Creel, Chairman of the administration's Committee on Public Information, has described this virus of unreasoning hate:

> . . . "patriotic" bodies . . . sprang up all over the land. . . . As they were outside the regular war machinery, and especially as they were not organized for fixed service, it was inevitable that these "societies" and "leagues" should turn to the emotions as a field of activity, and try to create an effect by noise, attack, and hysteria. . . .
>
> Not the least of their complaints was our refusal to preach a gospel of hate. From the first we held that undocumented "atrocity stories" were bound to have bad reactions, for if the Germans could manage to refute one single charge, they would use it to discredit our entire indictment. . . . The chauvinists, however, managed to figure largely in the Liberty Loan drives, over which the Committee had no control, and flooded the country with posters showing "bloody boots," trampled children, and mutilated women. . . .
>
> The sweep of mean intolerance, of course, developed a mob spirit. . . . The press, from which we had the right to expect help, failed us miserably. One alien speaking disrespectfully of the flag could be sure of front-page notice, but ten thousand aliens could gather in a great patriotic demonstration without earning an agate line.

... The chauvinists had the field to themselves, singing their hymns of hate and damning officials for inefficiency and spinelessness when they failed to produce traitors to be put before a firing squad.[19]

Frederic L. Paxson wrote:

And in a mining town in Illinois, one Robert Prager was done to death. Robert Prager ... had lived in the United States since 1905, and worked in a zinc smelter at Collinsville. He was by birth a German, by preference a union worker, and by conviction a Socialist. He was unpopular among his fellows before he was arrested, and on Thursday, April 4, he was in a local jail where he and others had been gathered on suspicion of disloyalty. ...

A dismissal of suspects had occurred in Collinsville at the end of March. Prager, unfortunately, was still in jail when a mob of miners succumbed to enthusiasm and alcohol and took him from his cell. No violence was needed. An officer at the jail testified at the inquest that he had refrained from drawing his revolver on the mob because the telephone rang and he had to answer it. Other officers averred that they would have shot had the mob tried to hang its victim within the city limits. Outside these, they disclaimed jurisdiction. The mob gave its victim time to write a pathetic letter to his parents in Dresden, then killed him.[20]

No President since Jefferson himself had been so ardent an advocate of freedom as had Wilson. He put the matter simply: "If there is one thing we love more than another in the United States it is that every man should have the privilege, unmolested and uncriticized, to utter the real convictions of his mind."[21] Even after the war, he could say, "I have always been among those who believe that the greatest freedom of speech is the greatest safety."[22] On occasion, even when sharply harrassed, he sensed that toleration could be wise policy, as well as just principle. When Theodore Roosevelt lashed out endlessly against the administration's war management and peace aims, Wilson said quietly: "I really think the best way to treat Mr. Roosevelt is to take no notice of him. That breaks his heart and is the best punishment that can be administered."[23]

But the problems were too steep for faith to surmount, and war had hardly been declared before Wilson was requesting the tools for limiting freedom of speech and press. He spoke for censorship: ". . . it is absolutely necessary for the public safety. . . ."[24] He concluded very early that "a time of war must be regarded as wholly exceptional," and that it was "legitimate to regard things which would in ordinary circumstances be innocent as very dangerous to the public welfare."[25] Like many another strong leader, he thought power would be safe in his own hands. He seemed certain he could control his administration: "I shall not expect or permit any part of this law to be used as a shield against criticism. . . . I can imagine no greater disservice to the country than to establish a system of censorship that would deny to the people . . . their indisputable right to criticize their own public officials."[26] From the interaction of President and Congress there came a spate of laws loose enough and broad enough to crush the basic freedoms of the Bill of Rights. That the war was short, that the President himself was cautious of authority were fortunate accidents for the future of American democracy.

Enemy aliens could be handled under existing laws, and on the first day of the war, the President issued a proclamation prohibiting them from possessing firearms or visiting military installations, and providing for arrest of suspects. Throughout the war such arrests were made, quietly and often without trials or other judicial procedure. A system of voluntary self-censorship by the press was arranged, when Congress refused to violate the

First Amendment directly with a censorship law.

Congress did pass two laws: the Espionage Act and the Trading with the Enemy Act, which provided direct censorship over radio, telephone and telegraph connections overseas. The Espionage Act made it illegal to obstruct the enlistment of troops, to cause "insubordination" in the armed forces, or to make false statements with the intention of interfering with the work of the army or navy, or of "promoting success" for the enemy. The actual wording was mild, but vague. In the hands of lower courts sensitive to public opinion, it became a catchall for the prevention of opposition to government policy. As Zechariah Chafee was soon to explain: ". . . the teeth which the government wanted were never there until . . . judges in an excess of patriotism put false ones in."[27]

But the most debated section of the Espionage Law gave to the Postmaster General the duty of excluding from the fourth-class mails all matter "urging treason, insurrection, or forcible resistance to any law of the United States. . . ."[28] For most periodicals, their removal from the mails was a death sentence. And Burleson soon proved himself more sensitive to criticism than to the need for free discussion. He moved especially sharply against the foreign-language press. There was little chance for appeal, and the judicial procedures could be of little help, in any case, when the periodical had already expired from lack of circulation. But it was the blanket of general fear created throughout the press that carried import for the country. It was not what was censored, but what was left unsaid for fear of censorship that counted.

The publisher could not usually discover what it was that had aroused the Department's anger. Sometimes, when the cause was pinned down, it smacked more of political criticism than of sedition. In one case the censors had objected to the expression of a "suspicion that the administration has turned the 'labor element' over to the tender mercies of the National Civic Federation...."[29]

Wilson tried, as he had promised, to curb the restrictive enthusiasm of his subordinates. He protested the barring of the Socialist paper, the Milwaukee Leader: "I am afraid you will be shocked, but I must say that I do not find this hearing very convincing.... there is a wide margin of judgment here and I think that doubt ought always to be resolved in favor of the utmost freedom of speech."[30]

But the ban stood. In the case of The Masses, he tried persuasion: "Now, Burleson, these are well-intentioned people. Let them blow off steam!" But when Burleson threatened to resign, he relented: "Well, go ahead and do your duty."[31]

Yet the administration continued to press for more stringent laws, and in 1918 the Congress passed a broad and dangerously fuzzy Sedition Act:

> Whoever, when the United States is at war, shall wilfully make or convey false reports or false statements with intent to interfere with the operation or success of the military or naval forces of the United States ... or ... obstruct the sale by the United States of bonds ... or incite ... insubordination, disloyalty, mutiny, or refusal of duty in the military or naval forces of the United States, or shall wilfully obstruct ... the recruiting or enlistment service ... wilfully utter, print, write, or publish any disloyal, profane, scurrilous, or abusive language about the form of government of the United States, or the Constitution of the United States, or the military or naval forces of the United States, or the flag ... or the uniform ... or shall wilfully ... urge, incite, or advocate any curtailment of production in this country of any thing or things ... necessary or essential to the prosecution of the war ... and whoever shall

wilfully advocate, teach, defend, or suggest the doing of any of the acts or things ... enumerated ... shall be punished by a fine of not more than $10,000 or imprisonment for not more than twenty years, or both.[32]

What was false or true might be a matter of judgment. Words like "insubordination," "disloyalty," "abusive" were open to wide interpretation. And, by the most restrictive definition, the law presented a stark prohibition to labor's major bargaining weapon, the strike, made advocacy of pacifism a crime. And, would not criticism of any administration's war policy "interfere with" the success of the armed forces?

In the hands of frightened and eager prosecutors, the definitions of the Espionage and Sedition Acts became vague in the extreme, and the government was soon open to the charge of dignifying "Barroom brawls" and pacifist tea parties. One man was arrested for claiming, in a saloon argument, that "President Wilson was fooling the people and the American soldiers in Europe were only boys."[33] Indictments based on similar statements were frequent: "There is no security behind the Liberty bonds." "The first thing we ought to do right after congress meets is impeach Wilson." "The Attorney General of the United States is so busy sending to prison men who do not stand up when the Star Spangled Banner is played that he has no time to protect the food supply from gamblers."[34] By June 6, 1918, there had been 184 convictions and 56 acquittals under the Espionage Act, and there were 858 cases pending in the courts. The stifling effect of the law grew partly from the variations in lower court decisions. Rose Pastor Stokes was sent to jail for having said to a group of women: "I am for the people and the government is for the profiteers."[35] But another judge freed a defendant who had been indicted for having said: "So your boy Edwin has gone to war with the rest of them. He will never come back.

Most of them that go . . . will never get there, and if they do get there they will all be killed. . . . America can never whip Germany."[36]

Only when the war had long been over did the Supreme Court finally deal with the basic issues and lay down principles for the future. The majority of the court moved gradually to a position that placed stringent restrictions on liberty in wartime. They approved, for example, the postal censorship, insisting that the use of the mails was a privilege, not a right, and thus not subject to the protection of the freedom of speech clause. And they approved the conviction of a person who had advocated resistance to American interference with the Russian revolution. In the process, they created the "dangerous tendency" doctrine, that speech might be punished if it tended in the direction of producing an illegal action.

But, as the majority of the court hammered out a doctrine to justify restriction of free speech, Justices Oliver Wendell Holmes and Louis D. Brandeis pioneered a path that could lead to a more liberal definition of freedom. The government, they insisted, must prove the evil intention of the suspect, rather than assume it and cast upon him the impossible burden of disproof. More important, speech must be restricted only when there was a "clear and present danger" that some illegal action would take place.

Holmes made the classic defense of free speech in a crisis-ridden democracy:

Persecution for the expression of opinions seems to me perfectly logical. If you have no doubt of your premises or your power and want a certain result with all your heart you naturally express your wishes in law and sweep away all opposition. To allow opposition by speech seems to indicate that you think the speech impotent . . . or that you do not care wholeheartedly for the result, or that you doubt either your power or your premises. But when men have realized that time has upset many fighting faiths, they may come to believe even more than they believe the very foundations of their own conduct, that the ultimate good desired is better reached by free trade in ideas—that the best test of truth is the power of the thought to get itself accepted in the competition of the market, and that truth is the only ground upon which their wishes safely can be carried out. That at any rate is the theory of our Constitution. It is an experiment as all life is an experiment. Every year if not every day we have to wager our salvation upon some prophecy based upon imperfect knowledge.[37]

Yet, in his own time, Holmes's was a voice crying in the wilderness. For the war unleashed the worst prejudices of the very isolationist, defensive, substantial middle class that had sparked the crusade for progressive reform. As the temper of intolerance grew, there grew with it a race hatred that would lead to immigration restriction, a fear of radicalism that would bring the orgy of the Great Red Scare, and would make the Twenties the dark decade for American labor. The dislocations of war would bring race riots. The conformity of war would breed intolerance for new and strange ideals. The fatigue and disillusionment of war, the High Cost of Living, the rebellion against discipline would spawn a strange revulsion against idealism. Wilson would move hurriedly to abandon government controls and planning as soon as the war ended. But the net effect of war would be to make worse the problems of concentration against which the progressives had fought, and at the same time to discredit the government regulation that might offer solution. And the net effect of war would be to discredit the very idealism it had featured. The people who had cried both to "Hang the Kaiser" and to "Save the World for Democracy" would find that they had accomplished neither.

NOTES, CHAPTER 12

1. Thomas A. Bailey, **Woodrow Wilson and the Lost Peace** (N.Y.: The Macmillan Company, 1944), pp. 6–7.
2. Ibid., p. 8.
3. J. B. Scott (ed.), **Diplomatic Correspondence Between the United States and Germany, August 1, 1914–April 6, 1917.** (N.Y.: Oxford University Press, 1918), p. 338.
4. John L. Heaton, **Cobb of "The World,"** (N.Y.: E. P. Dutton and Company, 1924), pp. 268–70.
5. Arthur Walworth, **Woodrow Wilson** (London: Longmans, Green and Company, 1958), II, 98.
6. U. S. 65th Congress, 1st Session, **Congressional Record** (Washington, D. C. 1918), pp. 102–04.
7. Joseph P. Tumulty, **Woodrow Wilson as I Know Him** (N.Y.: Doubleday, Page and Company, 1921), p. 256.
8. U. S. 65th Congress, op. cit., p. 213.
9. Henry F. May, **The End of American Innocence** (N.Y.: Alfred A. Knopf, Inc., 1959), p. 386.
10. H. C. F. Bell, **Woodrow Wilson and the People** (N.Y.: Doubleday, Doran and Company, 1945), pp. 218–20.
11. Joseph Dorfman, **The Economic Mind in American Civilization: 1865–1918** (N.Y.: The Viking Press, 1949), pp. 476–77.
12. B. M. Baruch, **American Industry in the War** (N.Y.: Prentice-Hall, Inc., 1941), p. 4.
13. U. S. 74th Congress, 1st Session, **Hearings Before the House Committee on Military Affairs** (Washington, D. C.: 1935), p. 557.
14. Dorfman, **op. cit.**, pp. 480–81, 483.
15. Ray Stannard Baker, **Woodrow Wilson: Life and Letters** (N.Y.: Doubleday, Doran and Company, 1927–39), VII, 100.
16. "Preamble of the Industrial Workers of the World," (Chicago, 1919).
17. Philip S. Foner (ed.), **Jack London: American Rebel** (N.Y.: The Citadel Press, 1947), pp. 57–59.
18. Marc Karson, **American Labor Unions and Politics—1900–1918.** (Carbondale, Ill.: Southern Illinois University Press, 1958), pp. 206–07.
19. George Creel, **Rebel at Large** (N.Y.: G. P. Putnam's Sons, 1947), pp. 195–99.

20. Frederic L. Paxson, **America at War, 1917–1918 (American Democracy and the World War,** Boston: Houghton Mifflin Company, 1939, Vol. II) pp. 273–74.
21. **New Republic,** XIX (May 10 ,1919), 42.
22. **New Republic,** XIX (May 24, 1919), 99.
23. Baker, **op. cit.,** VII, 424.
24. **Ibid.,** pp. 81–82.
25. **Ibid.,** p. 273.
26. **Ibid.,** p. 36.
27. **Harvard Law Review,** XXXII (June, 1919), 962.
28. **Statutes at Large** (Washington, D. C.: Government Printing Office), Volume 40, Title XII, Section 2, p. 217.
29. **New Republic,** XIX (May 17, 1919), p. 76.
30. Baker, **op. cit.,** pp. 312–13.
31. **Ibid.,** p. 165.
32. **U. S. Statutes at Large, op. cit.,** pp. 553 ff.
33. James R. Mock, **Censorship, 1917** (Princeton, N.J.: Princeton University Press, 1941), p. 194.
34. Walter Nelles, **Espionage Act Cases** (New York: National Civil Liberties Bureau, 1918), pp. 43, 59.
35. Zachariah Chafee, **Free Speech in the United States** (Cambridge, Mass.: Harvard University Press, 1941), p. 52.
36. Grubl. **vs.** U. S., 264 Fd. 44 (1920).
37. Abrams **vs.** U. S., 250 U. S. 616 (1919).

13. SEAR OF THE HOT IRON

Americans had feared war. Yet, for the first few months, the deep horror did not grip them. 1917 was a year of preparation. They were caught up in the heady discipline of crisis, which crushes narrow concerns. And they were mastered by the romance and enthusiasm of the crusade, blinded by their own propaganda, made naive by inexperience. For one thing, few Americans expected that major armies would be sent overseas; many assumed it would be a naval war, with perhaps a few token contingents to fight with the French and British.

There was no army to send; the new naval construction was still on the way. Both Army and Navy procedures and staff were tormented with the torpors of tradition. The Navy was beginning to make headway under the pushing and hauling of its two chief executives: Secretary Josephus Daniels, cautious, deliberate, suspicious of the professionals—Assistant Secretary Franklin D. Roosevelt, a dynamic admirer of the activist admirals. At the War Department, the new Secretary, Newton D. Baker, was only beginning to master the complicated routines of his ancient establishment. But both government and people were soon shocked to a remarkable pace of mobilization they could never have imagined when the President had sought war in early April.

Late in the month, Lord Balfour and Marshal Joffre arrived in Washington with military missions from the Allies. Their demands were blunt; their needs were pressing and great. Within days, after a bitter struggle within the Navy Department, the American battle fleets had been stripped of destroyers to provide desperately needed reinforcements for the British anti-submarine command. They reached Queenstown on May 4. By May 18, the administration had fought through Congress the first National Selective Service Act, and Wilson had ordered the first contingents of the American Expeditionary Force to France. On June 5, the nation began to recognize the face of war as 9,586,508 American young men registered for the "draft." On June 13, the regular Army's First Division embarked for France; on July 4, General John J. Pershing would lead 14,500 American soldiers in a parade through war-worn Paris. For France it was a great moment. Everywhere men quoted "Blackjack" Pershing's inspired salute: "Lafayette, we are here!" And Pershing himself, with his tough, stern air of competence and dignity, became the very symbol of French hopes. Two days later, Pershing told the world, and the American people, that he must have a million American troops within ten months! It was all but unbelievable; but it must be done. For the United States had entered the war at a moment of travail and disaster for the Allies. Thomas Bailey has summarized bluntly the challenge of 1917:

In the last two weeks of April, 1917, and the first week of May, 1917, the U-boat took a terrifying toll of Allied shipping. Brought face to face with the gaunt specter of starvation, England passed through her darkest hour from Napoleon to Hitler.

Late in 1917, the Italian front crumbled and was reestablished with enormous difficulty. Shortly thereafter Russia withdrew from the war, thus releasing approximately one million German veterans for the Western Front, and insuring preponderant man power to Germany for the first time in the war. In March, and again in May, 1918, the gray German flood came within a hairbreadth of breaking through to Paris and knocking France out of the war.[1]

And Preston Slosson has outlined the danger in more detail:

The whole German war plan from February, 1917, onward was a huge gamble that the war could be won before American troops arrived in sufficient numbers to give the Entente Allies a distinct advantage in man power. Germany had at least five chances in her favor in this hazard.... her object would have been equally obtained; if the submarine campaign had starved out England; if it had halted the movement of men or goods from the United States; if the transportation of the American army should interfere with the export of war material to France or Britain; if the United States failed to organize an adequate force; or if the American soldiers, nearly all of them wholly inexperienced in modern warfare, proved incompetent at the front....

In April, 1917, Germany sank 875,000 tons of shipping. Ships were being destroyed several times as fast as they were being built, and submarines built several times as fast as they were being sunk.... The arming of merchant ships proved ineffective, and a convoy system was adopted instead.... The course followed was irregular, the time of sailing rigidly concealed and all lights darkened. By autumn the monthly tonnage losses had been cut to half the April figure.... The hunting of the submarines was carried out in various ways, in cooperation with the Allied fleets, chiefly by depth charges from destroyers or patrol boats or by the use of contact mines. Some were also destroyed by machine gun fire, caught in mine nets, bombed by airplanes, rammed by warships, or lured to doom by "mystery" decoy ships, destroyers camouflaged to resemble merchant vessels.[2]

Every bit of good news was featured strongly; the arrival of the first Americans in the trenches at Sommerville on October 21—the first shots from American soldiers at the front, on October 27. But Pershing's forces could be only a token for the moment. Most regular army men must be kept home to provide hasty, intensive training for millions of civilian soldiers. It would take many months to hammer out combat divisions from the masses of raw recruits. And, while the Allies faced disaster in the fall of 1917, the Americans were only beginning to trickle into the mushroom tent and barracks cities where they would be trained.

And American aid would be slowed somewhat by the President's basic strategic decision. The Americans must eventually fight as a distinct army; they must not be used up anonymously or recklessly to fill the thinning ranks of the French and British. Partly this was a matter of pride, partly of concern; Wilson had no wish to see his people thrown as untrained cannon fodder into every desperate emergency. But partly it was design for the future; American aid must be dramatic and clear, so that America's prestige in the peace negotiations would be unquestioned.

In Pershing, Wilson had chosen the ideal vehicle for his policy. The man had an air of command and certainty; he was a fighter; he was thorough, but he was impatient of red tape; he was ambitious to command, not likely to squander his men easily as stopgap replacements. He had proved his ability to follow the policies of his commander-in-chief.

Wilson had given Pershing few orders. He was commanded only to win and to return. He was cut free of responsibility to the General Staff in Washington, and he made the most of it. In France he commanded absolutely the total process. There was constant nagging friction with the War Department. Pershing always demanded more than they could give, and more quickly.

They resented his presumption of total authority. Secretary Baker found himself endlessly mediating between the Chief of Staff, General Peyton March, and the Commander in Europe.

In France, Pershing was universally respected, almost worshipped. War correspondent Frederick Palmer described the popular picture of the man's method:

> Subordinate chiefs might explain difficulties to him, but they learned to beware of saying that a thing "can't be done." . . . They learned, too, that they must not bring any air of pessimism into his office, where his own supply of vitality for communication to others seemed inexhaustible.
>
> Who at headquarters and among the chiefs in the field has not seen his penciled notes with the bold initials "J.J.P." attached to papers?" . . . He practiced his own text of "Make it brief. . . ."

"Cut this down and we'll make it an order."—"A good idea! Have X make a memorandum of it."—"Wait a while!"—"This reads well in theory, but it will not work out in practice."—"Go ahead!"—"Tell H. I want to see him to-morrow about this!"—"That will carry us on for the present."—"Use your judgment and plenty of it, quick!" "J.J.P." under the legible script, never hurried, never careless, was no less an order than "By Command of General Pershing," in full, official form. . . . Subordinate chiefs found, too, that he was not afraid to recognize his own mistakes which possibly was one of the reasons why he kept growing with the growth of his task. . . . The French spoke of the "Pershing mentality," which meant coming direct to the essentials of the subject in hand.[3]

Later, Frederick Paxson would describe some of the limits within which Pershing had to operate:

By elimination, the American front was pushed to the east of Verdun, where war was expected to be quiescent, where an army as incompetent as the A.E.F. was expected to be, if it should be at all, could do no damage too bad to be repaired before it wrecked the enterprise. . . . Here Pershing was permitted to aspire to independent operations.

Acting relentlessly on his own judgment, Pershing accepted cheerfully what was offered with reluctance, and published in July the basic orders for the concentration and training of any army east of Verdun, and for its continuous supply. . . . Europe was short of goods. . . . It was accepted in the undertaking that the A.E.F. must fetch its own supplies. The railroads north of Paris were too vital to the French war to be clogged by these, or by the troops to use them. Both must find entry into France by lines running to the south of Paris and through ports not already working to a full capacity with English business. . . .

There did not exist any main lines of railroad running where the Americans and their supplies must travel. There were local and branch lines . . . . but none was equipped for heavy through service, none could carry the locomotives and rolling stock that the A.E.F. must bring to France to move its goods. . . . The Toul sector was nearly as remote from the seacoast as Louisville is from Washington, and to bring reality to Pershing's dream . . . there was work to be done along every mile of the intervening country. The call went home for engineer regiments, railroad regiments, forestry regiments: not as yet for men to fight, but for technicians to get ready for men to fight. . . . There were many miles of land travel before any American could be floated; the first contingent averaged 2,392 miles per man. There were three thousand miles of ocean and after this a journey.[4]

In Europe, the trickle of American troops seemed disastrously slow. But the miracle was, perhaps, that they got there at all. Only one transport was sunk in the sub-infested waters, and only ten percent of her 2,000 troops were lost. Yet, despite gigantic American efforts, the arrival of spring seemed a harbinger of sheer disaster. On March 3, the Treaty of Brest-Litovsk took Russia permanently out of the war. On the 26th, the uneasy Allies at last agreed to the choice of a Supreme Commander—Marshal Ferdinand Foch of France. A Supreme War Council had already been organized. And in March, the Germans used their rested, experienced troops from the Eastern Front to smash deep through the French and British lines at the Somme. In April, they would strike again through Flanders. And, at the end of March, Lord Reading would present clearly to the President through Colonel House the enormous dimensions of the moment:

Our losses so far have reached about 120,000 men. We can barely make good these losses by bringing in our whole resources of partially and fully trained men. ... We think that in all it is possible to embark 120,000 men from the United States during April, a number which could be somewhat increased in the following months. ... If the struggle should be decided against us without these troops. ... it is quite possible that the war may be terminated and the cause lost.[5]

At the beginning of March, there had been less than 300,000 American troops in France. But somehow, Britain found the transports. Men moved in relentless stream from the ramshackle training camps to Boston, Hoboken, and Philadelphia. By July, Pershing's million-man army was a fact.

While the great build-up went on, the war came

home to Americans in innumerable little ways. Hysteria grew in the country until Leopold Stokowski sought the President's guidance on whether to ban Bach and Beethoven from the concert hall. "Suspected slackers" were rounded up on Sunday afternoons on Fifth Avenue to be carted to jail at gunpoint on Army trucks. But there were more positive products of the war spirit. Americans invested millions in Liberty Loans. In the spring of 1918, tens of thousands of "Liberty Gardens" were planted in vacant lots and urban backyards. Red Cross and Y.M.C.A. enlisted hundreds of girls for war work at home, for ambulance driving and staffing canteens in France. And thousands of women learned what it was like to do "men's work" in factories. One newspaper pathetically protested that something must be done to show young ladies that being a good dishwasher was more patriotic than being a bad ambulance driver.

For Wilson himself, the war was a deadly race between responsibility and sheer fatigue. Sometimes he confessed the confusion and the desperation of it all: "I every day use up all there is in my brain in performing the tasks from which I cannot in duty escape. . . ."[6] Both personal necessity and profound matters of principle dictated that he limit his role as commander-in-chief. He could not do everything. He knew that the limits of his own military knowledge were serious. But he shared also the deep-grained American fear of military domination. When a cartoonist portrayed him in uniform, he protested sharply. As Ernest May explains:

> . . . he . . . asserted, "the armed forces of the country must be the instruments of the authority by which policy [is] determined . . . I do not think this is a mere formal scruple on my part. I believe it goes to the root of things." . . . He did not think of himself in Hamilton's *Federalist* phrase, as the "first general and admiral of the Confederacy." On the contrary, viewing

the armed forces as something separate from, almost alien to, civil authority, he tried not to mix himself in their affairs. He believed that the president should control but not command . . . . he thought it . . . clear that if military men should not involve themselves in policy, neither should policy-makers meddle in military affairs. . . . During the whole year and a half that the United States was at war, Wilson endeavored to avoid acting as commander in chief. . . . By abstaining from interference with the generals in France, by pushing off responsibility, Wilson minimized American involvement in and commitment to the alliance. . . . From the first day of the war to the last, all that Wilson sought was a peace that could be secured by a League of Nations, a peace that would make the world safe for democracy.

He refused to act as commander in chief because to do so would have jeopardized this aim. Any attempt to steer Allied strategy would almost certainly have led to political complications. . . . By allowing such questions to be dealt with almost entirely by generals possessing his delegated powers, he evaded requests for such political commitments. In the meantime, as he foresaw, the potential influence of the United States grew. When the armistice was negotiated, he could and did demand acceptance of his principles, his conditions for peace, not only by the enemy but by the Allies as well. He evaded duty as commander in chief in order to do his larger duty as president of the United States.[7]

Yet Wilson could not always separate himself from the military. In fact, his hand was to be seen constantly, in both final decisions and the direction of the work. To officers of the Atlantic Fleet he could say, much to the distress of certain admirals:

>   This is an unprecedented war and, therefore, it is a war in one sense for amateurs. . . . Somebody has

got to think out the way not only to fight the submarine, but to do something different from what we are doing.

We are hunting hornets all over the farm and letting the nest alone. None of us knows how to go to the nest and crush it. . . . I have come here to say that I do not care where it comes from, I do not care whether it comes from the youngest officer or the oldest, but I want the officers of this Navy to have the distinction of saying how this war is going to be won. . . . We have got to throw tradition to the wind. As I have said gentlemen, . . . every time we have suggested anything to the British Admiralty the reply has come back that virtually amounted to this, that it had never been done that way, and I felt like saying, "Well, nothing was ever done so systematically as nothing is being done now. . . ."[8]

And Wilson himself acted with directness and thoroughness. It was Wilson who chose Pershing and set him free of ordinary command chains. It was Wilson who ruled against the "volunteer" regiments that had characterized America's previous war, and who told the swashbuckling Teddy Roosevelt that he could not go overseas. It was Wilson who decided in favor of the expensive and much-debated North Sea mine net, against the reluctance of the British and the opposition of many of his own Admirals.

But, in the spring of 1918, the focus of decision necessarily turned to France and Pershing. He was dogged in his determination for an American Army, but the crisis of the massive German assaults made it essential for him to detail many divisions for duty under French command. As Canadian historian John Buchan has pointed out, their role was a large one even before they saw action, both because Foch knew how to use them, and because the Germans underestimated them:

> . . . the presence of these great potential reserves . . . enabled Foch to use his seasoned troops

boldly, since material for replacing them was mounting up every day.

It is hard to tell how far Germany was aware of the danger awaiting her in this addition to Allied strength; but whatever her General Staff may have thought, her politicians and her press gave no sign that they realized its gravity. . . . The nation was officially informed that every day saw anti-war demonstrations in New York, and that the weeping and desperate conscripts had to be herded on board the transports by special police. The great American army, said the press, could not swim or fly, therefore it would never arrive; the Americans only shouted to keep warm, and would bring everything to market except their own skins. . . . Even in July boasting continued. One German journal during that month declared that the American millions would be found to be only "soldiers of a child's game, mostly made of paper cuttings. . . ."

Ludendorff was an experienced soldier, and less easily deceived. . . . But he considered that he still had a chance of winning. . . . If . . . [his] operations succeeded, Rheims and the Montagne de Rheims would fall, and the French front would be divided into two parts which would never again be joined.[9]

By the end of May, American troops were playing a crucial role in the front lines, as Erich Ludendorff's Marne offensive swept toward Paris, a mere 50 miles away. On the 28th, the United States First Division, under French command, fought off the Germans in the little village of Cantigny. A week later, the Second Division shared with the French the bloody struggle to smash Ludendorff's main advance. Then, assigned the task of driving the Germans out of a tangled, heavily-defended forest, the Americans began the bloody, week-long assault on Belleau Wood near Chateau-Thierry. Frederick

Palmer has proudly described the spirit of these soldiers and marines:

> When they could locate a gun our men concentrated their rifles upon it. The crackle of bullets passing about the gunners' heads, even if they were not hit, might stop them from firing; but, meanwhile, some other gun was cutting the twigs around the heads of the marksmen. The wounded crawled back behind rocks, or into ravines, or to any place where they could find a dead space. The instinct of our men, caught in such a mesh of fire which was every minute causing a casualty, was to come to close quarters; and they wanted to go free of packs, of blouses, shirts open, rifle in hand, with their faith in their bayonets. Hot cries accompanied the flashing drive of the cold steel through the underbrush. Many bayonets might drop from the hands of the men who were hit, but some bayonets would "get there." And that was the thing—to get there.[10]

There were no more German illusions about "paper soldiers." The official German Army appraisal now read:

> The Second . . . Division must be reckoned a good one and may even perhaps be reckoned as a storm troop. The different attacks on Belleau Wood were carried out with bravery and dash. The moral effect of our gunfire can not seriously impede the advance of the American infantry. The Americans' nerves are not yet worn out. The qualities of the men individually may be described as remarkable. They are physically well set up, their attitude is good, and they range in age from eighteen to twenty-eight years. They lack at present only training and experience to make formidable adversaries. The men are in fine spirits and are filled with naive assur-

ance; the words of a prisoner are characteristic—"We kill or get killed."[11]

When Ludendorff mounted his second great Marne drive near Rheims on July 15, there were more than a quarter of a million Americans with the French, over eighty thousand in the lines. Already their presence had had an electric effect on French morale. Now their presence was felt in steel. They played a crucial part in blunting the offensive by the 19th. By July 21, they had helped the French retake Chateau-Thierry. By the first week in August, the Marne salient had been pinched back to its hilt. On August 10, with the last great German assault destroyed, Pershing assumed personal command of the United States First Army for its own, independent campaign.

For Americans at home this first great war was a riot of victory more than a torture of agony. It was, after all, a brief war. Only between May and November were there large numbers of doughboys involved. There never had been the pall of fear, the dread breath of destruction that Europeans had felt so keenly. America was optimistic, beyond all bounds. It was the Broadway music halls that gave her her war music: "The Yanks Are Coming" and "Over There." There were few somber ballads like the Civil War classic: "Just Before the Battle, Mother."

Partly it was because official propaganda and public spirit combined to weed out of the press and magazines every breath of the pain, death and filth. There was little of the mud and little blood in the newspaper war on which Americans back home lived out their hopes. The War Department telegrams came individually to bring tragedy to isolated homes. There were no eyewitness accounts of the hospital wards. Among Americans there were only heroes; among the Boche only cowardly brutes.

The popular Literary Digest filled its columns weekly with "Letters Home," carefully chosen to make virtue of American toughness, to preach hate and contempt for the Germans. Consider the letter of Private Cecil Elkins—age twenty-one:

We both got to kill some Germans. I killed six myself, three with my rifle and three with a hand-bomb. The Germans are cowards. They won't fight the Americans. They throw up their hands and cry "Kamerad," and then you take them prisoner; while you start to search them they will pull a gun and shoot you. So you see we generally shoot them down like dogs, as they deserve.

The United States marines sure are the heroes now. ... The Germans call us "Devil Dogs." They say we kill all and take no prisoners. Well, we ain't that bad.[12]

The press stories were an Iliad of heroes. The Times told the remarkable tale of Private Lenert:

Seeing that he was alone he thought it best to call off the fighting for a bit. His captors were seventy-eight privates and five officers. They showed great interest in knowing how many Americans were in the attacking party. Lenert told them that eight regiments had attacked and many more were coming after them.

The Germans knew the American barrage behind them had cut off their retreat, and they told Lenert that since so many Americans were coming it was useless for them to fight longer, and they craved the honor of surrendering to Lenert.

Not losing for a moment possession of himself, despite the situation thrust upon him by his overstatements of our forces, Lenert asked for his rifle and got it. Then he ordered the Germans to throw all their arms away, which they did.

Placing himself behind the eighty-three *Boches*, he marched them triumphantly to the rear.[13]

Even when death had to be noted, it was dressed with a hero worship that smoothed its ugly lines.

The atrocity stories matched anything the British propaganda office had ever invented. Even Pershing felt it necessary to deny them when a soldier, sent home to help sell Liberty Bonds, told the American people that the *Boche* gave "poisoned candy to the children to eat and hand grenades for them to play with" and then showed "glee at the children's dying writhings and laugh aloud when the hand grenades explode."[14]

But the humor was often more pointed than the scare propaganda. A few examples:

Those who have become familiar with the Crown Prince through the cartoons will wonder why he is so anxious to save his face. . . .

The Germans are smoking beech and cherry leaves, which probably are some improvement over German cigars. . . .

William the Last has reigned thirty years at an average cost to humanity of $5,000,000,000 a year. It is no joke to call him Bill. . . .

A captured German officer says Germany has just got to have peace. Well, well, he needn't worry any more; we are going to see that she gets it![15]

By mid-August, the peace was being pressed upon Germany and her allies with massive determination. On the tenth, Pershing threw his 550,000 men against the St. Mihiel salient that stuck like a dagger beyond the German lines into France. In a day and a half the salient had been destroyed, and Pershing was ready to drive on Metz. But he was deterred from that great fortress of the German lines by Foch, who insisted instead upon the American assault on the tangled, rough terrain of the Argonne forest. The front was nearly 25 miles long. The grueling battle in the scarred terrain lasted 47 days. It was part of a massive allied advance along 200 miles of fortified front. John Buchan tells the story of Pershing's part:

The problem before Pershing had now become the most difficult of that of any army commander. The German position in the Argonne was nearly invulnerable to frontal attack, and the plan of pressing forward on both sides of the wooded ridge was foreseen by the enemy. . . . [the] front . . . was miserably supplied with roads. . . . The finest transport system in the world must have broken down under such handicaps. But for the engineers to construct a new road system meant delay. . . . if the war was not to drag on into 1919, the splendid fighting stuff of the American infantry must be used in spite of all disadvantages. It was a bold decision for the commander to take, but it was essentially wise, and it was a decisive factor in victory. But the price paid was high. By 28th September the Americans had penetrated seven miles inside the enemy's lines; it took them eleven days to advance two miles more. They were now in direct contact with the Kriemhilde system, and the attack of 14th October . . . failed to break it. On the 15th the 77th Division, on the left, which had been fighting continuously for twenty days in the Argonne woods, entered the town of Grand-Pré, which was finally captured by the 78th on the 25th. Meantime the enemy had evacuated Brieulles on the Meuse, and the divisions on the right of the river were slowly creeping forward. . . . The American First Army had fought a new

Wilderness Campaign which may well rank for valour and tenacity with the old.[16]

The Argonne took more American lives than all the other actions of the war. But it was a crucial part of the vital thrust that drove the German military to its knees. German resistance was crumbling. The reserves were exhausted; the nation faced military collapse; the people were disillusioned at last; the flu epidemic—nonpartisan in a terrifying manner—was taking heavy tolls in German as well as Allied ranks. On September 16, Austria-Hungary had formally asked for peace. On October 4, Archduke Rupprecht, commander of the Bavarian Army, wrote: "I do not think we can hold on throughout the coming winter."[17] Ludendorff was nursing a last hope that an armistice would allow orderly withdrawal and the chance to fight again if the terms proved unacceptable. Even the Kaiser was making last-minute gestures. On September 30, he accepted his Chancellor's resignation. He chose to head the new government Prince Max of Baden, widely known as a liberal and advocate of democracy. The next day, General Paul von Hindenburg himself demanded peace overtures. On the 5th of October, Prince Max made the first of several overtures to President Wilson for an armistice on the basis of the President's well-known Fourteen Points. Wilson valued the role of peacemaker, but he was careful. As the German terms developed, it became clear that they would steal from the Allies the military advantage momentarily gained. By the 14th of October, Wilson had made his basic demands clear: Germany must discontinue her inhuman and illegal practices; the Allies must be sure that they were no longer dealing with the kind of "arbitrary power" that had unleashed the war. His warning was widely interpreted as a demand that the Kaiser abdicate. And finally, he declared, the military terms of the armistice were for the generals to decide.

Ludendorff now balked. He preferred a struggle to the death to such ignominy. But there was no longer room for brutal heroics. C.R.M.F. Crutwell tells the story of the collapse behind the German lines:

> This despair was not merely due to the events at the front, but to the swift spread of revolution at home. The mutineers at Kiel, some 40,000 armed men, were moving by warship, lorry, and rail, all carrying the red flag, over north-east Germany, setting up soldiers' and sailors' councils after the Russian fashion. By the 6th they already controlled Hamburg and Bremen. Next day Hanover, Brunswick, and even Cologne had fallen into their hands. On this day also the insurrection, born of the fear of invasion, had broken out independently at Munich, where the King of Bavaria was the first crowned head to be toppled unresistingly from his throne....

> Berlin remained in tense expectation.... On November 9th the crowds came out into the streets and the crack Jäger battalions, whose fidelity was deemed secure, fraternized with them instantly....

> William had just reached the unconstitutional and unpractical decision of abdicating as Emperor but not as King of Prussia when he was rung up for the last time on the morning of November 9th by the Chancellor. ... The receiver was ... disconnected to avoid the further importunity of the Cabinet. Prince Max immediately announced in Berlin the Kaiser's unqualified renunciation of the throne and handed over the Chancellorship to Ebert, the saddler's son, a staunch, imperturbable, upright man.... At 2 P.M., that day Scheidemann on his own initiative proclaimed the Republic.... Very early the next morning the Kaiser fled in his car to the Dutch frontier....

While all these things were being done, the Armistice Commission had crossed the lines (November 7), had been received by Foch, and presented with terms.[18]

And, while all these things had been done, Colonel House had been negotiating frantically with the British and French governments on behalf of Wilson. The Fourteen Points loomed large; there was much dispute about their meaning. The British balked sharply at Freedom of the Seas, as Americans defined it. The French had other concerns. Out of the welter of negotiations, House brought agreement. The Armistice would be on the basis of the Fourteen Points; Germans would consequently always consider them an essential part of a contract. But there would remain a fateful haggling about the import of their broad and general terms.

And on November 9, Americans would begin to read in their newspapers the unfolding story of Armistice. On November 11, there was final news:

WITH THE AMERICAN ARMY IN FRANCE, Nov. 11—They stopped fighting at 11 o'clock this morning. In a twinkling, four years of killing and massacre stopped as if God had swept His omnipotent finger across the scene of world carnage and had cried "Enough."

WITH THE BRITISH ARMIES IN FRANCE, Nov. 11 —Last night, for the first time since August in the first year of the war, there was no light of gunfire in the sky, no sudden stabs of flame through darkness, no spreading glow above black trees where for four years of nights human beings were smashed to death. The Fires of Hell had been put out.[19]

Later, the French author Joseph Deteil would write:

In the early hours of the morning, a final interview takes place in the famous drawing-room on the train. All is over. Secretaries draw up texts—one last ironing out of Victory. Time waits. Erzberger's head sinks between his shoulders. Foch, motionless, looks at the ceiling.

Time waits. It is endless; apparently no one cares to put an end to it. No one dares speak, move a chair, budge. A slowness of movements falls upon these men, the slowness of centuries. Now is an hour when events crush man. Outside, little by little, a gleam is born. A vague yellowish light like a dog's paws. A dirty dawn, heavy, dismal.

At last the documents are ready. Erzberger advances. He is given a pen. For a second he looks at this pen. His hand trembles. He feels the sting of pins and needles in his fingers. He ... But suddenly the pen falls from his hand, slashing the air, splashing ink on the carpet. Erzberger blushes, stammers an apology. Another pen is passed him. He bends over all this red tape, signs his name. The scratch of his pen explodes in the white silence. ...

It is 5 o'clock in the morning.

To the end of all time, I imagine men will hear the scratch of that pen.

The same day, at 11 o'clock sharp, the Poilu fired the last shot of the war. He was an excellent marksman. The Boche was 20 yards away. He fired. He missed.

Man had just found his heart once more.[20]

NOTES, CHAPTER 13

1. Thomas A. Bailey, **Woodrow Wilson and the Lost Peace** (N.Y.: The Macmillan Company, 1944), p. 13.
2. Preston W. Slosson, **The Great Crusade and After** (N.Y.: The Macmillan Company, 1930), pp. 49–52.
3. Frederick Palmer, **America in France** (N.Y.: Dodd, Mead and Company, 1919), pp. 306–08.

4. Frederic Paxson, **America at War, 1917–1918 (American Democracy and the World War,** Boston: Houghton Mifflin Company, 1939, Vol. II), pp. 94–96.

5. Charles Seymour (ed.), **The Intimate Papers of Colonel House** (Boston: Houghton Mifflin Company, 1926–28), III, 438–39.

6. Ray Stannard Baker, **Woodrow Wilson: Life and Letters** (N.Y.: Doubleday, Doran and Company, 1927–39), VIII, 18.

7. Ernest R. May, "Wilson (1917–1918)," in **The Ultimate Decision: The President as Commander in Chief** (ed. by E. R. May) (N.Y.: George Braziller, 1960), pp. 111, 113, 129–131.

8. R. S. Baker and W. E. Dodd (eds.), **The Public Papers of Woodrow Wilson** (N.Y.: Harper and Brothers, 1925–27), V, 83–84, 86.

9. John Buchan, **A History of the Great War** (Boston: Houghton Mifflin Company, 1923), IV, 273–74.

10. Palmer, **op. cit.,** p. 259.

11. Slosson, **op. cit.,** pp. 48–49.

12. **Literary Digest,** August 31, 1918.

13. **Literary Digest,** July 13, 1918.

14. Baker, **op. cit.,** VIII, 274.

15. **Literary Digest,** July 6, August 3, August 31, 1918.

16. Buchan, **op. cit.,** pp. 386–87.

17. Stephen Bonsal, **Unfinished Business** (N.Y.: Doubleday, Doran and Company, 1944), p. 234.

18. C. R. M. F. Cruttwell, **A History of the Great War, 1914–1918** (2nd edition; N.Y.: The Clarendon Press, 1936), pp. 587–89.

19. **New York Times,** November 11, 1918.

20. Joseph Deteil, **The Poilus** (translated by Jacques LeClercq) (N.Y.: Minton, Balch and Company, 1927) as quoted in **Armageddon** (edited by Eugene Lohrke) (Jonathan Cape and Harrison Smith, 1930), pp. 655–56.

For Woodrow Wilson the war had always been a tragic prologue to the drama of peace. The great essential was to chart the path of peace while there was still time.

The problems of peace, as Wilson saw them, were moral problems; the challenge of peace was the creation of a just, moral and stable world. As always, the matter became for Wilson, a crusade against evil. That there were deep underlying economic problems he knew. That war had come to America over a harsh clash of interests, he also knew. But, if peace were to be just, the objectives of war itself must be just. Propaganda and deep moral purpose combined to make him sell the war to the American people as a crusade "to make the world safe for democracy."

Yet, as he preached to Americans their role as a selfless arbiter of peace and justice, he served also the deep compulsions of his own character. As Richard Hofstadter has explained: "Woodrow Wilson had changed his means before, but in accepting war he was forced for the first time to turn his back upon his deepest values. The man who had said that peace is the healing and elevating influence of the world was now pledged to use 'Force, Force to the utmost, Force without stint or limit.' Having given the nation into the hands of a power in which he did not believe, he was now driven more desperately than ever in his life to justify himself, and the rest of his public career became a quest for self-vindication. Nothing less than the final victory of the forces of democracy and peace could wash away his sense of defeat."[1]

The dilemma ran deep, as Henry May has pointed out: "Like many of his countrymen, Wilson demanded both practical results and a clear conscience."[2]

Wilson had made a League of Nations the cornerstone of his peace program long before the United States had been committed to war. He had not worked alone. British groups were already drafting plans for a society of nations. "The League to Enforce Peace," led largely by Republican statesmen, had long worked to dramatize for the American people the dream of international organization. In fact, it was at a League meeting in Washington on May 27, 1916, that both Wilson and Senator Henry Cabot Lodge had chosen to make their firm commitment to a League of Nations. As Ruhl J. Bartlett explains:

> The senator ... declared that voluntary arbitration agreements had gone as far as they could go and that the next step was the one proposed by the league, the use of force behind international peace. ... He admitted that there would be objections to the league program. "I know," he said, "the difficulties which arise when we speak of anything which seems to involve an alliance. But I do not believe that when Washington warned us against entangling alliances he meant for one moment that we should not join with the other civilized nations of the world if a method could be found to diminish war and encourage peace." Thus Senator Lodge took a strong stand in favor of the principles as well as the proposals of the league.[3]

And the President responded:

> We believe these fundamental things: First, that every people has a right to choose the sovereignty

under which they shall live. . . . Second, that the small states of the world have a right to enjoy the same respect for their sovereignty and for their territorial integrity that great and powerful nations expect and insist upon. And, third, that the world has a right to be free from every disturbance of its peace that has its origin in aggression and disregard of the rights of peoples and nations.

So sincerely do we believe in these things that I am sure that I speak the mind and wish of the people of America when I say that the United States is willing to become a partner in any feasible association of nations formed in order to realize these objects and make them secure against violation. . . . an universal association of the nations to maintain the inviolate security of the highway of the seas for the common and unhindered use of all the nations of the world, and to prevent any war begun either contrary to treaty covenants or without warning and full submission of the causes to the opinion of the world—a virtual guarantee of territorial integrity and political independence.[4]

As war came, Wilson faced the challenge of turning the unity of a hate-disciplined nation into the service of a proper peace. He wished a nonpartisan quest for peace, and early in January, 1918, he announced the Fourteen Points that he hoped would provide a just basis for an early armistice. He hoped also that they would unite the American people as an irresistible force against the old power system of Europe. The united force of American morality and selflessness was the only force strong enough to curb the deadly rivalries of the great nations:

> The program of the world's peace, therefore, is our program; and that program, the only possible program, as we see it, is this:

I. Open covenants of peace, openly arrived at, after which there shall be no private international understanding of any kind but diplomacy shall proceed always frankly and in the public view.

II. Absolute freedom of navigation upon the seas, outside territorial waters, alike in peace and in war. . . .

III. The removal, so far as possible, of all economic barriers and the establishment of an equality of trade conditions among all the nations. . . .

IV. Adequate guarantees given and taken that national armaments will be reduced to the lowest point consistent with domestic safety.

V. A free, open-minded, and absolutely impartial adjustment of all colonial claims, based upon a strict observance of the principle that in determining all such questions of sovereignty the interests of the populations concerned must have equal weight with the equitable claims of the government whose title is to be determined.

VI. The evacuation of all Russian territory and such a settlement of all questions affecting Russia as will secure the best and freest cooperation of the other nations of the world in obtaining for her an unhampered and unembarrassed opportunity for the independent determination of her own political development and national policy and assure her of a sincere welcome into the society of free nations under institutions of her own choosing. . . .

VII. Belgium, the whole world will agree, must be evacuated and restored. . . .

VIII. All French territory should be freed and the invaded portions restored, and the wrong done to France by Prussia in 1871 in the matter of Alsace-Lorraine, which has unsettled the peace of the world for nearly fifty years, should be righted. . . .

IX. A readjustment of the frontiers of Italy should be effected along clearly recognizable lines of nationality.

X. The peoples of Austria-Hungary, whose place among the nations we wish to see safeguarded and assured, should be accorded the freest opportunity of autonomous development.

XI. Rumania, Serbia, and Montenegro should be evacuated; occupied territories restored; Serbia accorded free and secure access to the sea; and the relations of the several Balkan states to one another determined by friendly counsel along historically established lines of allegiance and nationality; and international guarantees of the political and economic independence and territorial integrity of the several Balkan states should be entered into.

XII. The Turkish portions of the present Ottoman Empire should be assured a secure sovereignty, but the other nationalities which are now under Turkish rule should be assured an undoubted security of life and an absolutely unmolested opportunity of autonomous development, and the Dardanelles should be permanently opened as a free passage to the ships and commerce of all nations under international guarantees.

XIII. An independent Polish state should be erected which should include the territories inhabited by indisputably Polish populations, which should be assured a free and secure access to the sea, and whose political and territorial integrity should be guaranteed by international covenant.

XIV. A general association of nations must be formed under specific covenants for the purpose of affording mutual guarantees of political independence and territorial integrity to great and small states alike.[5]

The reaction throughout the world was electric, but, as Thomas Bailey has explained, the very things that made the Points effective, made them also deeply dangerous in the practical maneuvering for peace:

THE PATH OF PEACE 251

In short, the Points were idealistic enough and vague enough to make a splendid platform for waging the war; but they were too illusory and contradictory to make an adequate platform upon which to construct the peace. "He [Wilson] could have preached a sermon on any one of them," writes John Maynard Keynes, "or have addressed a stately prayer to the Almighty for their fulfilment; but he could not frame their concrete applications to the actual state of Europe." ...

Wilson not only preached ideals which were clearly unrealizable in this our world, but those who re-preached them grossly "oversold" them. ... More than sixty million leaflets, pamphlets, and booklets—largely featuring "Wilsonisms"—were showered upon Latin America, the Far East and Europe. They were translated into a veritable babel of tongues. A volume of Wilson's speeches became a "best seller in China"; a leaflet containing one of his addresses was adopted as a textbook in a Madrid school. Always it was the thunderbolts of President Wilson.

Ominously, this great crusade began to arouse Messianic hopes—and President Wilson was the Messiah. In far-away Poland, starry-eyed university students met on the streets, clasped hands, and uttered one word: "Wilson." ... A member of the American Embassy in Rome saw in some barracks an improvised altar, on which burned four candles, above which hung a poster of Wilson, and before which the soldiers were constantly kneeling. ... Among the highly nationalistic Poles, Czechs, and Slavs of Germany and Austria-Hungary the rainbow of self-determination aroused hope, then resistance, and finally rebellion. The winged words of Woodrow Wilson were worth armies. ... As the great conflict roared into its final stages, and as German morale began to crack, increasing numbers of hungry Germans began to ask themselves: would not a negotiated peace based upon the principles of the Fourteen Points be far better than the continuance of this fruitless struggle?

One of the greatest weaknesses of the Fourteen Points as a peace platform was that they lent themselves to sloganizing. ... they were made to mean what their readers wanted them to mean. This was splendid —as long as the Points were used to arouse the Allies and seduce the enemy. But a day of reckoning was bound to come.

Obviously no mortal man this side of the millenium could have hoped to bring about all the things that the world came to expect of Wilson.[6]

Even at the moment there were difficulties that could not be ignored. For one thing, the Points had been designed, rather hastily, as a tactical maneuver to help keep Russia in the war. Their immediate purpose failed. Wilson had tried to understand this Russian Revolution, had tried to be sympathetic, as Charles Madison has indicated:

Soon after the March revolution Wilson ... sent to Russia a commission headed by Elihu Root. The Russian radicals did not trust the conservative Americans, and the latter failed in the mission to strengthen the Russian will to fight the Germans. Yet Wilson did not lose faith in the new republic. Even after the Bolsheviki had seized power [in October, 1917] he remarked that Russia would "go through deep waters but she will come out upon firm land." When Lenin and Trotsky began to negotiate with the Germans, Wilson sought to prevent the Allies from sending an army to northern Russia ostensibly to keep the war material from falling into German hands. Personally, however, he abhorred Lenin's radical doctrines and was violently repelled by the Bolshevik repression and bloodshed.

It was largely to offset the Russian publication of the Allied secret treaties and Lenin's demand for a peace without reparations and annexations that Wilson addressed Congress on January 8, 1918, for the purpose of discussing the war aims and peace terms of the United States.... His comments on Russia were deliberately sympathetic....

Wilson's fair words toward Russia did not lessen his difficulties with that country. In February, 1918, he wrote to Senator John Sharp Williams, "I do not know that I have ever had a more tiresome struggle with quicksand than I am having in trying to do the right thing in respect to our dealings with Russia." Not long afterwards, continuing to adhere to "the principle of Russian territorial integrity and political independence," he advised General Tasker Bliss that Allied military action in Murmansk or elsewhere "should proceed, if at all, upon the sure sympathy of the Russian people." In his own mind still resisting such invasion as late as July, he wrote to House: "I've been sweating blood over the question what is right and feasible to do in Russia."[7]

On January 25, 26, and 28, 1918, the secret treaties were published in the New York Evening Post. On March 3, 1918, the Treaty of Brest-Litovsk was signed. The Russian revolutionaries had not only exposed the most gross and cynical plans of the Allies, but had also led their war-weary people out of this struggle among imperialists. Germany would be free to concentrate upon France and Britain. And it would be all too easy to sketch Wilson's promises as empty bombast or cynical demagoguery, once the President himself had become reluctantly committed to an invasion of Russia by American troops. By August, 1918, there would be 10,000 United States troops in Vladivostok, sent to the aid of Czech prisoners of war. But, as the tangled situation developed, they would find themselves in cooperation with other allied troops whose main purpose was to strengthen the White Russian resistance against the Bolshevik regime.

Difficult in another way were the ambitions of the suppressed nations of Europe. In some cases, domestic politics had strengthened Wilson's natural humanitarian feelings to a dangerous degree. A recent study has summarized, for example, the development of his policy on Poland:

> Wilson first began to take interest in Poland in 1915, when the problem of relief aroused and frustrated the desire of the American people to help the starving people in Eastern Europe. . . .

When Paderewski visited Wilson for the first time, the president was already "Polish-minded," primarily because of Colonel House's influence. It did not take long for the pianist to influence Wilson, this time politically, by telling him of the "shocking crime of the Polish partitions." Wilson, true product of 19th-century liberalism was most sympathetic. . . .

As the presidential elections approached, Wilson's humanitarianism and liberalism became intertwined with his own political ambition. In the Polish question he saw an opportunity to use his already well-known attitude for his own benefit. Thus, up to the election, he grew more openly pro-Polish, and this indirectly affected American public opinion on the Polish problem. . . .

Wilson's awakening came during the Peace Conference. The territorial ambitions of the Poles, their open disavowal of Wilson's own principles of self-determination, their forceful incorporation of non-Polish territories, and their persecution of minorities within their own borders gave proof of the bankruptcy of his political philosophy.[8]

Lansing, experienced in the details of diplomacy, would be lamenting by the end of 1918: "The phrase [self-determination] is simply loaded with dynamite. It will raise hopes which can never be realized. . . . What a calamity that the phrase was ever uttered! What misery it will cause!"[9]

But much more pressing early in 1918 were the burgeoning dangers of partisanship and revenge. In his greatest moments, Wilson had always sought a bipartisan approach to peace, but there had been moments when he had clearly forecast how rigid he would be with any opposition that threatened his bipartisan pose. As early as August, 1917, he had told a congressman: ". . . friends and enemies both will admit that my 'jaw' has proved adequate in past struggles!"[10] And there were already some who saw mere partisanship in his pose of nonpartisanship. President Taft protested with quiet bitterness: "He recognizes no obligations of partnership or of decent courtesy. He thinks he is running the whole show himself. . . . Sometimes I feel like bursting, but as Theodore does the bursting, perhaps I can pursue some other function."[11]

And Theodore was bursting, with impatience, outrage, and personal bitterness. In the columns of the Outlook, in his incessant speeches, he demanded action, vengeance, and an end to idealistic nonsense. But perhaps even more dangerous was the growing anger of Henry Cabot Lodge, who, if the Republicans ever controlled the Senate, would, in turn, control its approval of any peace treaty the President might negotiate. Wilson detested Lodge. They were much alike in their pride of intellect, in their personal vanity, in their need to lead. Lodge, in turn, appraised Wilson sharply as early as October, 1912 ". . . he is a man of ability, but he has no intellectual integrity at all."[12] By January, 1917, Lodge could write: "I am inclined to think that in the back of his mind lurks the desire for a third term, and if he was not hopelessly cowardly at heart our damage would be greater than it is."[13]

Wilson himself did little to build bridges with even Republican friends, to say nothing of Roosevelt and Lodge. He complained to Colonel House: "The thing I wanted particularly to see you about ... was the folly of these League to Enforce Peace butters-in. We must head them off one way or another."[14] Both Wilson and House were conscious of the need to keep the movement for a League of Nations under presidential control. Wilson tended to put the matter on strong tactical grounds: "My own conviction, as you know, is that the administrative constitution of the League must grow and not be made. . . . Any attempt to begin by putting executive authority in the hands of any particular groups of powers would be to sow a harvest of jealousy and distrust which would spring up at once and choke the whole thing. . . . Why begin at the impossible end when there is a possible end and it is feasible to plant a system which will slowly but surely ripen into fruition?"[15]

But House was blunt: "The sentiment is growing rapidly everywhere in favor of some organized opposition to war and I think it essential that you should guide the movement. . . . It is one of the things with which your name should be linked during the ages."[16]

Early in July, 1918, Wilson sought to strengthen his cause with a speech containing four, somewhat simplified, planks for peace:

I. The destruction of every arbitrary power anywhere that can separately, secretly, and of its single choice disturb the peace of the world. . . .

II. The settlement of every question, whether of territory, of sovereignty, of economic arrangement, or of political relationship, upon the basis of the free acceptance of that settlement by the people immediately concerned. . . .

III. The consent of all nations to be governed in their conduct towards each other by the same principles of honor and of respect for the common law of civilized society that govern the individual citizens of all modern states in their relations with one another. . . .

IV. The establishment of an organization of peace which shall make it certain that the combined power of free nations will check every invasion of right. . . .

These great objects can be put into a single sentence. What we seek is the reign of law, based upon the consent of the governed and sustained by the organized opinion of mankind.[17]

Meanwhile, Colonel House submitted a draft of "A World Constitution" upon which his aides had been working since 1915. Root and Taft made suggestions, and Wilson used it, with mild revisions, as the basic draft of his League of Nations. House wanted to use the draft to build public opinion. There was good reason. As the summer's fighting progressed, the forces of bitterness and violence that Wilson himself had helped unleash were making a deeper mark upon the American people. Typical of the trend to revenge was the Washington Post editorial of August 8: "There will be no secure freedom of nations if the Allies do not impose their will on Germany. They must dictate the terms of peace, and Germany must accept what they dictate. If Germany should be treated with the magnanimity that is due to a chivalrous enemy, the savages in control of that empire would twist the concession into a dagger with which to stab their benefactors."[18] As Germany weakened, Wilson's own concept of a liberal peace would be certain to appear more and more like a compound of dangerous concessions.

The demand for vengeance, the rising Republican enmity, the need to avoid detailed discussion of specifics were only three sides of Wilson's complicated

problem in the summer of 1918. A fourth was the con-
gressional election impending in November. John Blum
has described the situation:

Republican criticism of the conduct of the
war hurt the President and his party much less than did
the voting record of those Southern Democrats in key
congressional posts who had consistently obstructed
such war legislation as the draft. Their policies, some
progressive, some parochial, won the Republicans new
friends. This was true of taxation. For the conservative
bill of the administration, the Southern agrarians substituted their own. It imposed heavy, purposefully re-
distributive income, inheritance and excess-profits taxes,
taxes designed to minimize the need for federal borrow-
ing, to take the private profit out of war and incidentally
out of the sections where most of the profit was being
made. This equitable measure solidified the Republican
hold upon the industrial East. So equally did the successful Southern support of wartime prohibition, ana-
thema to most urban workers, Republican or Democrat, and especially to the Democratic machines, whose
captains never forgave the rural evangelicals for the
long thirst imposed upon them and their constituents.
No less outraged were Western farmers, normally Republican but in 1916 a source of Democratic victory.
Jealous of the price of wheat, which the Lever Act empowered Wilson to control, impatient when he would
not raise the price, they particularly resented the inflated
price of cotton which Southern votes had spared from
regulation. On this alone the Republicans could attract
the vote west of the Mississippi.

So the coalition that had elected Wilson crumbled.
The liberal fervor of 1912, the progressivism of 1916 had
faded away, and with them the basis for success. . . .
Only the South remained completely loyal to the party
and its leader. But the South was not enough to win

elections, especially in 1918, when Republican resurgence gained impetus from the weariness of people with meatless days and wheatless days, with manless homes—the weariness of war.

Northern Democratic leaders, recognizing their liabilities, concluded that they might retain control of Congress only if Wilson would endorse the Democratic candidates, endow them with his personal and presidential prestige. But Wilson, concentrating on global matters, more than ever impatient with local politics, had declared with gross inaccuracy that politics were adjourned. The Republican assault upon his foreign policy changed his mind. . . . Democratic leaders in Congress, the cabinet, and the national committee, many themselves obsessed with a hatred of all things German, urged the President to insist on drastic terms for an armistice. . . . Wilson refused to let the exigencies of the election warp a policy he considered just and wise.[19]

But Wilson must do something. His decision was to make a public plea for the election of Democratic congressmen. It was partly his belief in party responsibility and leadership that drove him to it. It was partly that he had no doubts. The American people, he was certain, were with him. But it was partly also to meet the hard-pressed appeals of his supporters that he wrote to the people:

If you have approved of my leadership and wish me to continue to be your unembarrassed spokesman in affairs at home and abroad, I earnestly beg that you will express yourselves unmistakenly to that effect by returning a Democratic majority to both the Senate and the House of Representatives. . . . The return of a Republican majority to either House of Congress would . . . certainly be interpreted on the other side of the water as a repudiation of my leadership.[20]

Wilson's mood was optimistic. His assurance was reinforced by the increasing pace of the German peace appeals. By election day, November 5, armistice was at hand, an armistice brought by the direct negotiations of the President of the United States. He would go to the Peace Conference with the strong mandate of the American people; he would go as a prophet of peace: On November 4, Austria-Hungary surrendered. On November 5, election day, Secretary of the Interior Franklin K. Lane wrote of Wilson: "He is certainly in splendid humor and in good trim—not worried a bit. And why should he be, for the world is at his feet, eating out of his hand. No Cæsar ever had such a triumph!"[21]

And on November 5, 1918, the American people returned heavy Republican majorities in both houses of Congress.

Wilson might have been expected to foresee the possibility. Midterm elections frequently go against the President, and frequently on local issues and personalities. Presidential intervention in congressional elections is bound to create resentment. But he had single-handedly and recklessly created a referendum where no referendum could, in fact, exist. He had asked for a mandate; his defeat was certain to appear a repudiation. Had there been a parliamentary government, Woodrow Wilson would have been out of office. Had he followed his own plan so carefully worked out in case of defeat in 1916, Woodrow Wilson would have resigned. But, with his commitment made, the whole force of conscience, duty and pride drove Wilson on. He could only hope the blunder would be forgotten.

Six days later the Armistice was signed. The hysteria of victory pushed aside the election news, but only for a moment. The cost of war had been high. Four and a half million Americans engaged; over 330,000 casualties; a money cost of over forty-one and a half billion. The figures were not soon known, but their general dimensions were deeply felt. The mood of revenge was still strong. The opposition was soon feeding America's hunger for vengeance, and denying Wilson's right to speak for her cause. Theodore Roosevelt put it bluntly: "Our allies and our enemies and Mr. Wilson himself should all understand that Mr. Wilson has no authority whatever to speak for the American people at this time. His leadership has just been emphatically repudiated by them."[22]

In March, the Republicans would organize the Senate, by a margin of one vote. And their Chairman for the Foreign Relations Committee would be Henry Cabot Lodge. Already Lodge was moving sharply away from his vague commitment to the League, and even more sharply away from any proposition his enemy in the White House might negotiate. Ten days after the November election, he wrote to an English friend: "I cannot believe that victory will be thrown away at the peace arrangements. They must be of such a nature that Germany can never break out upon the world again."[23] A month later, he briefed one of his Republican friends carefully on the prospects: "I think it would be a mistake to admit that the league was a good thing, but I think we should make a mistake if we met the proposition with a flat denial. . . . My own judgment is that the whole thing will break down in the conference. . . . If they do form anything that involves control of our legislation, of our armies and navies, or the Monroe Doctrine, or an international police force, and that sort of thing, then our issue is made up and we shall win."[24]

Yet he was unwilling to leave the matter to chance. In mid-December, he went to Theodore Roosevelt's hospital room in New York. Together the dying ex-President and the bitter, haughty Senator charted their party's strategy. "The decision had been taken—and the League doomed—before ever the Peace Conference began."[25]

The President's own plans made the prospect of a fight beyond all doubt. He could not meet on even polite terms with either Lodge or Teddy Roosevelt. He could no longer go halfway to the Senate, as he had once done for his domestic program. As early as March, 1918, he had refused a harried appeal from Tumulty to use his influence with certain Senators on behalf of the Women's Suffrage Amendment: "I would weaken my influence in a score of directions if I were to depart from the rule I have set myself and send for Senators, but I am eager to advise them to vote for the amendment if they will themselves give me an opportunity to do so."[26]

If Wilson could not go halfway to the enemy, neither would he stand aside for others to take the initiative. Long before the armistice, he had decided to lead the peace delegation personally. Interest, duty, pride and enthusiasm were madly mingled in the decision. No one else, he felt, could be trusted to represent the nation's idealism. No one else could deal toughly with old masters of maneuver like David Lloyd George and Georges Clemenceau. No one else could appeal to the hearts of people everywhere as he could. Besides he yearned for the task, and he yearned for the historic greatness it could bring. His friends were deeply disturbed. Nothing could make the peace more partisan. Besides, the President had no diplomatic experience. The very weight of the business—detailed negotiations, carrying on the ordinary business of government, the interminable speeches and tours and personal appearances—might kill the man, at least distract him from the main objectives of his crusade. Felix Frankfurter protested to House that "by leaving the White House where he could thunder from Sinai from time to time, he was giving up a great advantage of being a deus ex machina. Not only that. He was throwing away the great advantage our commissioners would have of saying, 'Oh, we have to refer that back to the President . . . . .' [and] he in all ways enters upon a process of negotiation in which a person like Lloyd George can out-trump him every time because Wilson hasn't got the agility and flexibility that negotiation allows. He's a great fellow for laying down postulates and avowing principles, but not for translating them into the myriad variants into which general principles can be translated."[27]

And Wilson's old friend Frank Cobb wrote bluntly: "Instead of remaining the great arbiter of human freedom he becomes merely a negotiator dealing with other negotiators. . . . The President, if he is to win this great battle for human freedom, must fight on his own ground and his own ground is Washington. Diplomatic Europe is all enemy soil for him."[28]

House himself came to share their misgivings. He was prepared to go on, as he always had, as Wilson's quiet shadow and alter ego, preparing the way, testing out the President's thinking, gently prodding. But when he boosted his courage and relayed the warnings to Wilson, the President was adamant: "The suggestion that I should not sit as a delegate . . . seems to me a way of pocketing me. I infer that the French and British leaders desire to exclude me from the Conference for fear that there I might lead the weaker nations against them."[29]

For Wilson the issue was a blend of obligation and personal pride. There was no discriminating between the two. As a recent student has suggested: "He had always wanted—needed—to dominate. . . . He had always been interested in ordering the political relations of men. . . . Now, in sponsoring the League, he saw an opportunity to write nothing less than a constitution for the whole world."[30]

So Wilson would go. But he might have hedged against the enemy in the choosing of his delegation. He might have sealed the crusade as an American crusade with a bipartisan commission. The Republican party abounded with potential delegates to lend not only wisdom but prestige to the treaty. Even if he could not bring himself to take Henry Cabot Lodge, or to court the humiliation of a refusal from this petulant old enemy, Wilson might have appointed ex-President Taft, or perhaps the distinguished Elihu Root, or anyone of a score of others. Instead, he chose a commission so evidently docile as to seem ridiculous: the Secretary of State; a professional army officer; his own aide, Colonel House; and one Republican, Henry White, a former career diplomat, personally liked by everyone, but completely without distinction, prestige or power in the Republican party. Taft's remark was acid: "[The Commission] is a cheap lot of skates. I could swear if it would do any good."[31] George Harvey put the matter bluntly in his widely-circulated national magazine:

Name	Occupation	Representing
Woodrow Wilson	President	Himself
Robert Lansing	Secretary of State	The Executive
Henry White	None	Nobody
Edward M. House	Scout	The Executive
Tasker H. Bliss	Soldier	The Commander-in-Chief[32]

For Wilson himself, the matter was different. It was his responsibility. There must be no fighting in the rear ranks while the battle went on. There must be no subversion of "the right" from within his own camp.

On December 2, 1918, the President announced to Congress his intention of going personally to the Peace Conference. On December 4, he sailed for Europe on the George Washington, with his hand-picked delegation, with an army of experts, with Mrs. Wilson. He had carefully left no time for argument of the matter. For better or worse, it would be a Wilson peace.

NOTES, CHAPTER 14

1. Richard Hofstadter, **The American Political Tradition and the Men Who Made It** (Vintage Edition; N.Y.: Alfred A. Knopf, Inc., 1948), pp. 271–72.
2. Henry F. May, **The End of American Innocence** (N.Y.: Alfred A. Knopf, Inc., 1959), p. 383.
3. Ruhl F. Bartlett, **The League to Enforce Peace** (Chapel Hill, N. C.: University of North Carolina Press, 1944), pp. 50–51.
4. Arthur Walworth, **Woodrow Wilson** (London: Longmans, Green and Company, 1958), II, 38–39.
5. U. S. 65th Congress, 2nd Session, **House Documents** (Washington, D. C.: 1918), No. 765, pp. 3–7.
6. Thomas A. Bailey, **Woodrow Wilson and the Lost Peace** (N.Y.: The Macmillan Company, 1944), pp. 26–29.
7. Charles Madison, **Leaders and Liberals in 20th Century America** (N.Y.: Frederick Ungar Publishing Company, 1961), pp. 112–14.
8. Louis L. Gerson, **Woodrow Wilson and the Rebirth of Poland, 1914–1920: A Study in the Influence on American Policy of Minority Groups of Foreign Origin** (New Haven, Conn.: Yale University Press, 1953), pp. 138–39.
9. Bailey, **op. cit.**, p. 18.
10. Walworth, **op. cit.**, p. 150.
11. H. C. F. Bell, **Woodrow Wilson and the People** (N.Y.: Doubleday, Doran and Company, 1945), p. 247.
12. John A. Garraty, **Henry Cabot Lodge: A Biography** (N.Y.: Alfred A. Knopf, Inc., 1953), p. 295.
13. Walworth, **op. cit.**, p. 78.
14. Ray Stannard Baker, **Woodrow Wilson: Life and Letters** (N.Y.: Doubleday, Doran and Company, 1927–39), VIII, 38.
15. **Ibid.**, pp. 43–44.
16. Charles Seymour (ed.), **The Intimate Papers of Colonel House** (Boston: Houghton Mifflin Company, 1926–28), IV, 20–21.
17. Ray Stannard Baker and William E. Dodd (eds.), **The Public Papers of Woodrow Wilson** (N.Y.: Harper and Brothers, 1925–27), V, 233–34.
18. **Washington Post**, August 8, 1918.
19. John Blum, **Woodrow Wilson and the Politics of Morality** (Boston: Little, Brown and Company, 1956), pp. 152–54.
20. Baker and Dodd, **op. cit.**, pp. 286–87.

21. Anne Wintermute Lane and Louise Herrick Wall (eds.), **The Letters of Franklin K. Lane, Personal and Political** (Boston: Houghton Mifflin Company, 1922), p. 298.

22. **Kansas City Star,** November 26, 1918.

23. Garraty, **op. cit.,** p. 343.

24. **Ibid.,** p. 347.

25. Ruth Cranston, **The Story of Woodrow Wilson** (N.Y.: Simon and Schuster, 1945), p. 279.

26. Baker, **op. cit.,** p. 22.

27. Felix Frankfurter, **Felix Frankfurter Reminisces: Recorded in Talks with Dr. Harlan B. Phillips** (Anchor Edition; N.Y.: Doubleday and Company, 1962), p. 190.

28. Seymour, **op. cit.,** IV, 210–11.

29. Bell, **op. cit.,** p. 266.

30. Alexander L. and Juliette L. George, **Woodrow Wilson and Colonel House** (N.Y.: The John Day Company, 1956), pp. 197–98.

31. Bailey, **op. cit.,** p. 87.

32. **Ibid.,** p. 93.

Wilson sailed for Europe with deep hopes, with few doubts. He was convinced that peoples everywhere cried out for permanent and just peace. He would be their prophet in an epic battle against the reactionary and selfish governments of Europe. He would cut through the shadows of vengeance, of greed, of power struggle, cut through the crust of old custom to a new era of peace. At Paris the Fourteen Points would be applied; and they would be applied scientifically with the aid of the greatest collection of technical experts every yet assembled for a Peace Conference. Almost two years before, Colonel House had assembled a staff—which he came to call "The Inquiry"—to chart out the dimensions of world peace. House and his aides had been hard at work in Paris since the early fall. And Wilson was taking with him to Europe a vast research and idea factory of his own: bright young historians like Charles Seymour, distinguished older scholars such as Charles Haskins, thoroughgoing and reliable public servants of the stature of Bernard Baruch and Herbert Hoover, and brilliant, youthful idea men like Walter Lippmann. Wilson begged them: "Tell me what's right and I'll fight for it."[1]

But there would be severe difficulties. The staff was excellent, the potential great, but there was no American master plan, no prepared agenda, nor prior detailed consultation between the President and his fact factory. Eventually the tensions and pace of the Conference

would set barriers between them that would make communication virtually impossible. The careful studies
would lie unused; the President would be forced to make
his decisions on hunch, snap judgment and partial
information. Even at the moment, as Thomas Bailey
has explained, the whole staff arrangement seemed to
some people a ponderous joke:

> One New York journal irreverently described
the whole organization as "Colonel House's troupe of
performing professors." William Allen White, another
journalist, wrote:
> "Down the gangplank walked this Yankee knight
errant followed by a desperate crew of college professors
in horn-rimmed glasses carrying text-books, encyclopae-
dias, maps, charts, graphs, statistics, and all sorts of literary crowbars with which to pry up the boundaries of
Europe. . . ."[2]

It would prove as difficult for Wilson to use his colleagues on the delegation as it was for him to tap the
vast resources of information he had brought with him.
Among them, only House was close to his plans. But
House had long since learned that his rapport with the
President might be broken at any moment. In mid-Feb-
ruary, when the President returned briefly to the United
States, Stephen Bonsal would record in his diary an incident that illustrated dramatically the limits and dangers
of House's authority:

> February 13th
> Today, on the eve of his departure, the President
gave House, and in my presence, very definite instructions for his guidance while he was away. He said: "During my unavoidable absence I do not wish the questions
of territorial adjustments or those of reparations to be
held up." I would have concluded from these words that
the President left House in control, but House did not

so interpret them. "The President does not mean that I am authorized to definitely settle anything," he explained, "but he does hope that I will get the problems, one and all, in such shape that on his return they can be submitted to him for final judgment. . . .

"Of course . . ." commented House, "I would like to have specific instructions in writing, but as the 'Governor' never gives them we can dismiss that idea."[3]

As for the others, they were soon out of Wilson's confidence—embarrassed men, facing responsibility without power, restless men, sitting uselessly through the long months in Paris. Arthur Walworth has described the situation:

Lansing, to whom the President had paid little attention, was thinking of resigning. Sitting alone at his desk, hour after hour, the secretary of state recorded his dissents in a diary in a copybook hand. He was scornful of Wilson's deficiencies as an international lawyer. . . . Told by Henry White of Lansing's pique at the President's preference for the counsel of House, Wilson said, "It never occurred to me," . . .

Like Lansing, General Bliss had strong views of his own. Gruff, very shy of personal publicity, a man who always carried a Latin text in his pocket, studied Oriental botany, and swore beautifully, Bliss craved peace. He saw, perhaps more vividly than any of the military men at Paris, the handwriting on the sky of the future. He was distressed by the vagueness of the President's remarks on policy and by the casualness of the meetings of the American Commission; and he put more emphasis than his chief on the necessity for disarmament. Bliss was to prove a valiant lieutenant, rarely volunteering advice, quickly supplying information when it was called for. Wilson thought him "a real thinking man who takes the pains to think straight."

The President could depend, too, on the disciplined loyalty of Henry White, a diplomat of fine old vintage with a bouquet of quality and tradition, commanding both respect and affection as he limped into the Crillon from his daily walk, his cheeks apple-red under thick white hair, in one hand a proper cane and in the other a tall black hat with a broad band around it. Wilson became fond of the old gentleman. A master of French and of diplomatic protocol, gallant with the ladies, White did his best to create teamwork among his compatriots and liaison with Europeans. He hinted to Wilson that he be detailed to make the personal contacts that his experience had taught him were necessary. Not encouraged, he presumed no further, but sought the confidence and help of Edith Wilson. At first lukewarm toward the President's league ideal, he grew to appreciate Wilson's character and his purposes, and wrote appreciatively of them to his Republican friends at home—"affectionately" to "Dear Cabot."[4]

Yet Wilson's problems with his own aides were petty as compared with the challenges that he came only slowly to see once he had embarked on the hard business of the moment. For one thing, his own nation was moving rapidly into a postwar letdown. Transfixed with his sense of mission, his intuitive feeling of public support, Wilson failed to sense how rapidly his own people were drifting into reaction. Perhaps it was because he gave too little time those days to the domestic problems of the nation, to reconversion, to economic readjustment, to domestic reform. Abandoned by their leader, the American people sought out familiar, comfortable paths to the future. In the process they were driven increasingly within themselves as they faced the tangled web of readjustment. During 1919, over four million men were out of work in strikes or lockouts at one time or another. Inflation burgeoned rapidly. The

High Cost of Living was the major complaint every-where. In New York City prices had risen 79 percent since 1914. The government offered no guidance. The War Industries Board went out of business on January 1, 1919. Other governmental controls and agencies were rapidly dissipated. There had been no planning for peace. Wilson apparently assumed an easy return to the prewar patterns. But adjustment was not merely economic. In mid-January, the war-sped prohibition amendment was proclaimed. The nation was caught up in a monumental Red Scare. There were race riots in Chicago and Washington in July. In September there was a general police strike in Boston. The spirited enthusiasm of the war months was dissipated daily by the divisive issues of domestic policy.

But Wilson's eyes were on the problems of Europe, which seemed so urgently more pressing. One was the threat of Bolshevism. His doctor later wrote: "I used to beg him to slacken a little the pressure under which he worked, and he would answer: 'Give me time. We are running a race with Bolshevism and the world is on fire.' "⁵ Another was the haunting spectre of hunger, which Wilson had moved quickly to dispel. Late in February, 1919, Congress voted $100 million for European relief, and early in March the President appointed Herbert Hoover as Director of the American Relief Administration. As Hoover later said: ". . . unless Europe could be fed, pestilence stopped and reconstruction started, there could be no peace made in Paris."⁶

Quite as threatening as instability and hunger in the conquered nations was the drastic drift of public opinion among the conquerors. Everywhere, in England, France, and Italy, there were demands for revenge, deeply underlined by fears for the future. Wilson would never realize the sad extent to which he underestimated the selfishness of people everywhere. He would never realize the extent to which the tough politicians at

Versailles were directed and inhibited by the demands of their people. But he would soon face the impact of the matter. It could not be a peace without victory, without revenge. Nothing had made this more clear than the publication by the Russians of the Secret Treaties that already bound the Allies.

The world already knew that Britain had made a deal with the Czar to swap Russian possession of the Dardanelles for a British special interest in the Middle East, that France and Britain had agreed to give Russia a free hand in Poland. And the world already knew that Britain had bought Italian alliance at a monumental price—a great swath of territory down the eastern shore of the Adriatic. Italy could expect to make the Adriatic an Italian lake, to seal off Austria-Hungary from the sea, to rule over 200,000 Germans and hundreds of thousands of Slavs, Albanians, Greeks, and Turks. Other deals were reluctantly unveiled as it became necessary during the Conference. Soon Wilson would know that Romania had been promised large areas populated by Hungarians, Ruthenians and Slavs, that France and Britain had made intricate deals to divide the Middle East between them, that Britain and Japan had plans for parceling out Germany's Pacific Ocean islands. The Secret Treaties made a mockery of the Fourteen Points. The shock was all the greater because some of the deals had been made after the Allies had formally agreed to Wilson's principles.

But the lowering problems were not all of European making. Wilson himself had created some with the essential vagueness and impracticability of his Fourteen Points. It was soon clear that "Open covenants, openly arrived at" could not mean diplomacy in a fishbowl. There was haggling with Britain particularly on the meaning of "Freedom of the Seas." "A free, open-minded, and absolutely impartial adjustment of all colonial claims" proved to be a meaningless spate of words. By what standards? By whose judgments? What territory was French and what German, after a century and a half of shifting boundaries? There was ambiguity aplenty.

But also there was impracticability. The Fourteen Points proposed one principle for drawing national boundaries: the "autonomous development of the peoples." But unhappily, in all the difficult areas, the "peoples" were sadly mixed. And there were other considerations Wilson had overlooked—natural boundary markers like mountains and rivers, economic units that could not be split and still live healthily, problems of access to the sea. How to free the Slavs of the Austro-Hungarian empire without entrapping large groups of Germans? How to separate Austria and Hungary without destroying both economically? How to give Poland access to the sea without putting Germans in Poland? How to set up any Poland without trapping under alien governments some Russians, or Poles, or Czechs, or Germans or Slovenes? How to assure stability at all for liberated peoples who had lost their governing institutions and traditions a century or more before?

In general the Points had ignored the fundamental economic issues of the twentieth century. They had been too simple. And, of all the problems Wilson would face at Paris, the very complexity of the issues would be the greatest. He had proposed moral and neat and attractive answers. But unhappily there was no neat or completely moral answer for the problem of Poland, of the Balkans, of the Rhineland, of the colonies.

Yet perhaps the gravest of the problems Wilson himself had created was his centering of the whole process around his own personal decisions. His confidence in his judgment was serene; his confidence in his ability to sway the peoples of the world was overpowering; and yet he came as a President repudiated by his own people, and constantly overshadowed by the necessity of getting his treaty through a hostile Senate. And gradually his personal diplomacy, his personal busyness, cut him off from his advisers, cut him off from criticism, entangled with his own personality and prestige every line of the Treaty.

It would soon become clear that Wilson could not have everything. He developed his own scale of priorities. The League of Nations stood at the top. Whatever the faults of the treaty, the real hopes lay in a respected public forum for the future adjustment of frictions. Only a step down the ladder lay his concern for justice to the subject peoples of Europe. He could not, in haste and confusion, deal rightly at every point. But he would fight hard for the independence of Poland, for the self-determination of Central European peoples against the grasping ambitions of their victorious neighbors. Some of the matters closest to his heart must be postponed hopefully for future development under the League: free seas, disarmament, the emergence of self-government of the colonial peoples. But far down on his list, submerged beneath his priorities, would remain the question of justice to the enemy. He would have to bow, perhaps, to the spirit of revenge.

Some of the most crucial obstacles to peace were matters that seemed merely technical at the moment. One was the delay of the conference because of the need to prepare, the need to await elections in England and France, the desire to await stable governments in Germany and Austria with which to make terms. But, as Thomas Bailey has said:

> . . . the results were highly unfortunate. The nationalistic aspirations of France and especially of Italy were given time to develop in an overblown fashion. . . .

Public opinion began to lose faith in the negotiators —the "dawdlers of Paris." Everywhere there was a mounting impatience to get the thing over with and "bring the boys back home," ... the frittering away of the costly weeks in December and January meant that the work of the Conference had to be rushed forward with frantic speed in April, when a number of hasty and regrettable decisions were made.

The selection of Paris as the site of the Conference was one of the cardinal misfortunes of the negotiation. The atmosphere of the shell-shocked city—"gashed to her very soul"—was the complete reverse of that serenity which should surround the making of great and lasting decisions. . . .

One of the worst things ... was the clatter of the corrupt and corruptible French press. A dozen or so sheets responded to the commands of the government with servile precision. . . .

Another reason why Paris was an unfortunate choice was that it gave to the nerve-wracked French a disproportionate control of the program and machinery of the Conference. The able but domineering Clemenceau became Chairman.[7]

Wilson arrived in France December 14. The reception was tumultuous—a fête for a Cæsar. And while he awaited the calling of the Conference, the President set out on a triumphal tour of Europe, designed to strike the rapport with the common people upon which he so heavily relied. There was Christmas with the troops at the front. There were five days in England, four days in Italy. Everywhere the crowds were great. A man with Wilson's sensitivity could not help but return to his task with the belief that he had struck the hearts of these Europeans, just as he had always been able to do with his American crowds. But he misunderstood the enthusiasm of victory for the deeper emotions of faith. Englishmen and Italians might toast and cheer the symbol of their joint achievement; but they would not desert their own statesmen to follow the inspired slogans of a casual outsider. And he misunderstood the people themselves. In England, he preached little sermons, filled with overtones of American superiority. He hurt both French and British by failing to make clear his deep sympathy at their frightful losses. Late in December, Clemenceau "appeared before the Chamber of Deputies, and with a sneering reference to Wilson's noble candeur ('noble simplicity') came out four-square for the old balance of power—with France the dominant end of the balance. He was resoundingly supported by a vote of confidence, 380–134, the greatest of his tempetuous career. Tactfully, the compositors of the official record of the debates changed noble candeur to noble grandeur."[8]

Herbert Bell describes Wilson's visit to Italy:

Rome received the President and Mrs. Wilson by hanging out not only its flags, but its emblazoned tapestries; and cascading its guests with mimosa and violets. . . . Wilson was pleased to find the crowds dense and demonstrative; pleased again when he received the freedom of the city, with the right to say "Civis Romanus sum." But the visit was sadly marred by . . . the Italian Government's decision to prevent the new Civis Romanus from satisfying his heart's desire by addressing his fellow citizens in the streets. A passage from [Gino] Speranza's diary seems worth quoting:

"I wish I could record . . . all the obstructive measures taken by the Italian Government to prevent the President from speaking to the people. . . . The officials in charge of the visit even lied to him. They told him that on the way to the Chamber of Deputies, his motor would stop in the Piazza Venezia, so that he might speak to the people, but instead they whisked him off to Montecitorio. When he asked if it were there that he was to speak to the citizens, they replied, 'No, it is now too late.' Meanwhile the Ambassador in his car and thousands of persons were waiting in the Piazza. Even the plan for the President to stop a moment in the Piazza on his way to the reception at the Capitol was frustrated; and finally, on the evening of his departure, as he started to go out on the balcony of the Quirinal, from which it had been arranged for him to say a few words, he was informed that there was no audience—quite true, for a cordon of troops on the Piazza in front of the palace prevented anyone from coming into it. After the President left Rome, the Government circulated reports that Wilson had a *fobia* of crowds; also that it feared someone might throw a bomb. All rot. The people really trust Wilson, almost too much, I think."

Mrs. Wilson describes the President as "blazing with anger," and adds: "He expressed himself in no uncertain terms both to the press and to the officials who tried to explain." Wilson made a number of speeches before he left Italy, at Genoa, Turin and Milan. From a balcony he told forty thousand Milanese, packed into the great square, that he had "never known such a greeting" as theirs, and that it had brought tears to his eyes. But he was not the sort of man to forget the incident at Rome. One may imagine that his jaw was firmly set when he got back to Paris on January 7.[9]

When the victors did sit down to work on January 12, it was in an atmosphere of almost unparalleled confusion and indecision. Bailey describes it clearly:

It is difficult to find an eyewitness who was not impressed by the indescribable confusion and disorganization at Paris. . . . Harold Nicolson speaks of "that sense of riot in a parrot house."

The explanation is not far to seek. There were twenty-seven Allied and Associated Powers, plus the five British Dominions, and each of the thirty-two was entitled to send delegates. The American contingent alone, counting various kinds of subordinates, totaled about 1,300. The British delegation occupied five hotels. . . .

The Conference set up more than sixty different commissions to deal with territorial, economic, and other problems. These groups held over 1,600 meetings, worked more or less in the dark, and often at cross purposes with other groups, whose functioning they were only dimly aware of. . . . The right hand seldom knew what the left hand was doing; sometimes the right hand did not even know what the right hand was doing. . . .

Several years ago the present writer asked a distinguished American expert—one who had had a large hand in the drafting of the League Covenant—for some information about the Conference. "I do not know anything about it," he smiled. "I was only there." . . . They were like soldiers in a campaign who know only their part of the trench on the battlefield; they are unable to glimpse the general plan of battle. . . . [And] Every one of the heads of governments at Paris had to spend a considerable part of his time looking after the home front. Wilson had to peck out his message to Congress on his portable typewriter at odd moments before and after the regular meetings of the Council of Four. The sheer fatigue resulting from such numerous and oppressive duties undoubtedly contributed to some of the unfortunate decisions at Paris. . . .

The machinery of the Conference was gradually perfected by trial-and-error methods. A great body of several hundred delegates was too unwieldly, too dilatory, too loquacious, and too leaky for the efficient dispatch of business. So the plenary sessions became rubber stamps for the smaller groups.

The Supreme Council, or the Council of Ten, which evolved from the Allied Supreme War Council, at first did the most important work. It consisted of the two ranking delegates from each of the five great powers: Great Britain, France, Italy, Japan, and the United States. President Wilson and Secretary Lansing represented the United States.

The Council of Ten proved in turn to be too cumbersome and too leaky, but it was not until March, 1919, when the Conference came squarely to grips with the problem of Germany, that it gave way to the Council of Four—the Big Four—which more or less usurped authority.... It consisted of Wilson for the United States, Lloyd George for Great Britain, Clemenceau for France, and Orlando for Italy. Some of the time it was the Council of Three, for Orlando was not infrequently absent. At the early meetings there were neither secretaries nor written records. Three lone men in a room deciding the destiny of the world! ...

Harold Nicholson attributes many of the woes of the Paris Conference to the "marsh of imprecision"—and properly so. If ever a conference needed a carefully worked-out program, as well as a precise definition of terms, this one did.... It may well be argued that ... [Wilson's] greatest error was not in going to Paris but in going without a plan....

As it was, the discussions ... drifted along from day to day like a rudderless ship, with the powers combating one another's proposals, and forming combinations against one another. Then, when it became clear that the race between chaos and peace would be perilously close, the Conference buckled down and in a spasm of work gave birth to a treaty that was as ill coordinated as its parent.[10]

Compounding the confusion for Wilson was the character of his tough, experienced adversaries. Winston Churchill would later describe the whole situation as the "turbulent collision of embarrassed demagogues."

David Lloyd George, the British Prime Minister, was an attractive, dynamic person; a fighter born to the trade, and also a master of the half-truth and the slippery maneuver. And, as Bailey makes clear, Lloyd George came to the Peace Table loaded not only with secret promises of the Treaties, but also the all too glibly made public promises of a hot election campaign:

In the general election of 1918 the welkin had rung with cries of "Hang the Kaiser"; "Make Germany pay to the last pfennig"; and "Search their Pockets." Sir Eric Geddes had cried: "We will get out of her all you can squeeze out of a lemon and a bit more. I will squeeze her until you can hear the pips squeak." George Creel relates that Lloyd George came to Paris grinning, as if it were all a huge joke. "Heaven only knows what I would have had to promise them if the campaign had lasted a week longer."[11]

The French premier, Georges Clemenceau, was more predictably tough, less devious of maneuver, but a terrifying and domineering personality. He had the fresh and firm mandate of his nation. As Bailey describes him:

The Tiger was the incarnation of the Old Order—of Europe as it had been. Wilson was the incarnation of the New Order—of Europe as he hoped it would be.... [Clemenceau] called Wilson "Jupiter," sneered at his "elevated simplicity," and made cutting remarks about the "Fourteen Commandments." He told Colonel House: "I can get on with you. You are practical. I understand you, but talking to Wilson is something like talking to Jesus Christ!" ...

There were few who did not fear Clemenceau's withering tongue. His bons mots were the talk of France, and there are few enduring epigrams from the Conference that are not attributed to him, whether correctly or not. He loved the racy phrase, the biting epigram, the sarcastic sally, and when one came to him, whether at the expense of friend or foe, he seemed powerless to hold it back. His voice was penetrating, and his terrible audibility frequently brought blushes to the cheeks of all his hearers. At one session of the Council of Four, a Japanese delegate made some remark. Clemenceau understood English, but not Japanese-English, so he turned and in a loud stage whisper, "*Qu'est-ce qu'il dit, le petit?*" (What's the little fellow saying?)—as if a small child had spoken out of turn at the dinner table.

Dogged, domineering, honest, courageous, realistic, and narrow—this was the Tiger. Wilson respected him because one could tell where he stood—back in 1871. There was no deceit or equivocation about the man: he had the courage to meet his problems head on. If he seemed to be dozing at some of the sessions, there could be no doubt as to his vigilance when the interests of France were concerned. And here, as the record reveals, he yielded remarkably little.[12]

Wilson could frequently match Clemenceau, in both retort and temper. When the Premier protested to Wilson: "You have a heart of steel," the President swiftly replied: "But I have not the heart to steal." The Old Tiger complained once in anger: "How can I talk to a fellow who thinks himself the first man in two thousand years to know anything about peace on earth?"[13] But, in the end, Wilson and Clemenceau would leave the Conference with a mutual respect that no other of the delegates could share.

Some of the lesser figures were also difficult: Orlando, Premier of Italy, given to tears and sudden angers, playing only a small role among the Big Four, but pushing relentlessly for the fulfillment of his nation's ambitions; the careful Japanese, smartly timing their demands to take advantage of the most hectic quarrels among the Big Four. Perhaps the most objectionable to Wilson personally was the eccentric, hard-boiled Imperialist from Australia, William H. Hughes. He was, as Paul Birdsall says, the "living embodiment of everything that was anti-Wilsonian." He mounted a savage assault on Wilson's " 'intolerable' claim 'to dictate to us how the world should be governed.' " Hughes was the kind of man to shock Wilson's deepest instincts. Once, when Lloyd George asked whether Australia had any objections to accepting missionaries in its proposed mandate of New Guinea, the Aussie Prime Minister calmly explained: " 'Of course. The natives are very short of food and for some time past they have not had enough of missionaries' ... to eat."[14]

But what disturbed Wilson most deeply at Paris was not the tough, impervious, slippery maneuvering of his opponents, or the crass materialism of a Hughes, but his own deep inner doubts. He feared above all else that his sympathies for the French people would trap him into the hatred for Germany that dominated their thinking. When the French wanted him to visit the devastated areas, he refused, and later confided to his friends: "They want me to see red, and I can't afford to see red. To whip myself into a passion of rage would be to unfit myself for the present task. I know well enough the wrong that Germany has done, and Germany must be punished, but in justice, not in frenzy."[15] When he did visit the American wounded, it was almost more than he could manage.

Throughout January and early February, the discussions went on loosely, without result and without much form or direction. But by February 14, Wilson was able to mark one great victory. On that day he presented to the full conference the Covenant of the League of Nations. The Conference had authorized its drafting on January 25. Wilson had been made chairman of the commission. And the draft was largely his, modified in some details by combination with a British draft, influenced somewhat by the ideas of South Africa's Jan Smuts, by the suggestions of House and some others. But essentially it was the draft he had brought from home, much to the distress of his own experts, who were only infrequently and hastily consulted. It provided a machinery for regular conferences of the great and small powers alike. It admitted into the Council of the League representatives of some of the smaller powers. It provided in Article X the machinery for identifying threats to peace, and for consultation to recommend appropriate preventive measures to the various nations. It provided a concept of mandates, control of undeveloped areas by nations responsible for their record to the League—a halfway station, in theory at least, between colonies and independence. Sacrifices had to be made on all sides. Wilson had to give up a cherished freedom of religion clause. House regretted the lack of procedures for compulsory arbitration. The colonial powers bowed to Wilson's insistence on mandates. France had to give up her strong insistence upon an international army, when Wilson protested that the United States Constitution would not allow him to commit American forces. It was weaker than some might have desired. It was as strong as it might well be if it were to be accepted by the governments generally. For Wilson, it was a great victory. He had given up nothing essential to his plan. He had forced the conference to make the Covenant an integral part of the treaty. It was a dramatic moment that William Allen White described on February 14:

His day of glory was typically Wilsonian. That is to say, toned down, understated, gray, shadowless, misty with a certain luminosity characteristic of a February day in Paris. In mid-afternoon lights flicker in the Place de la Concorde; honking carriages like great birds of passage flit in and out of the hazy mist. Inside a gray government building across the Seine from the Place de la Concorde is a large room perhaps sixty by forty feet in area—a high-walled room, stiff, formal, French to the last tip of the gilded tail on the gilded flea on the gray wing of the putty-colored angels that jump out from the perfectly proportioned walls. Gray, putty-colored cupids and gray apprentice angels crawling out of the designs hover dangerously with their little potbellies filled with diplomatic east wind, over a group of sober gentlemen, mostly bald or gray, wearing black, three-buttoned cutaway coats, white vests, and pin-striped trousers. They are seated in gilded chairs upon a bright-red carpet—seated around a U-shaped, green-baize-covered table, two or three score of them, middle-aged, middle-class, dominated by a keen-eyed, yellow-skinned, bald little old man in gloves—always in gloves —the peace delegates and Clemenceau. The four walls, the cornices, and the ceiling are smeared with gilded wreaths, gilded leaves, and gilded flowers. Golden incrustations rise to the ceiling in a veritable chaos of ornate golden flopping of palm leaves and gilt gewgaws about a large gold clock, a clock which really keeps time; and from the clock the hall takes it name—The Hall of the Clock; a fussily over-decorated room, in the manner of the ancient French monarchs. . . . Here in this Hall of the Clock would seem to be no place for two doddering schoolmasters like Clemenceau and Wilson. Here's a place for bewigged gentry in pink breeches, blue coats, yellow waistcoats, to disport themselves. . . . Nothing in this room speaks of democracy. . . . Everything the room stands for . . . a weary God has thrown into the scrap-heap. Amid this rococo grandeur, beneath the bloated little apprentice angels and the putty-colored figure above the clock, sat the delegates to the Peace Conference around their green-baize-covered table; a drab splotch in the middle of the gorgeous room. . . . Down the whole length of the green-baize table, between the two prongs of the U, sat Mrs. Wilson. Beside her stood Admiral Grayson, who gleamed a full-panoplied Apollo on guard, with his hand on her chair of state. She was in her wine-colored purple cloth suit, with her purple hat and purple plume.

Without ceremony or introduction, the President of the United States of America rose. He smiled across the room at Mrs. Wilson. . . . He read slowly, in an even voice which carried throughout the room, and which reporters outside, peering through open double doors and standing on a string of chairs and tables in an adjacent chamber, could hear perfectly. He read without emotion or emphasis. . . . The import of the thing grew. . . . words of tremendous import it seemed, for we were hearing for the first time the Covenant of the League of Nations as the President read it to the Peace Conference. He droned on with as little intonation as if he were reading a list of goods at a receiver's sale. The light outside in the gray mist faded. The lamps inside danced in crystal chandeliers. And he read on to the end with no climactic tone or timbre in his voice.

Then he began speaking. What he said was well said. It was spoken from the heart, only a few typewritten headings in his hand guiding him. He improvised his paragraphs, and the stenographers took them down. Almost with a studied casualness he took the dramatics out of the day and scene. He was setting the oratorical pace of the occasion, and setting it deadly low. When he finished, not even a flutter of applause greeted him. . . . So the League of Nations was born.

It was a typical Wilsonian performance; a great thing done insignificantly. . . . It was his last public appearance as the ruler of the world. . . . Behind him lay all his glory.[16]

The next day Wilson sailed for home, to consult with

the Senate Foreign Relations Committee, to revive the flagging interest of Americans generally, to deal with the accumulated paper work of the presidency. He sailed west through winter seas. And, although he could not know it, he sailed a course that would lead eventually to disaster.

NOTES, CHAPTER 15

1. Thomas A. Bailey, **Woodrow Wilson and the Lost Peace** (N.Y.: The Macmillan Company, 1944), p. 110.
2. Ibid., pp. 108–09.
3. Stephen Bonsal, **Unfinished Business** (N.Y.: Doubleday, Doran and Company, 1944), pp. 49–50.
4. Arthur Walworth, **Woodrow Wilson** (London: Longmans, Green and Company, 1958), II, 236–38.
5. Cary T. Grayson, **Woodrow Wilson: An Intimate Memoir** (N.Y.: Holt Rinehart and Winston, 1960), p. 85.
6. Herbert Hoover, **The Ordeal of Woodrow Wilson** (N.Y.: McGraw-Hill Book Company, 1958), p. 89.
7. Bailey, **op. cit.**, pp. 121–22.
8. Ibid., p. 112.
9. H. C. F. Bell, **Woodrow Wilson and the People,** (N.Y.: Doubleday, Doran and Company, 1945), pp. 278–80.
10. Bailey, **op. cit.**, pp. 134–38, 142.
11. Ibid., pp. 243–44.
12. Ibid., pp. 154–56.
13. Grayson, **op. cit.**, p. 79; Bailey, **op. cit.**, p. 221.
14. Paul Birdsall, **Versailles Twenty Years After** (N.Y.: Reynall and Hitchcock, 1941), pp. 51–52, 69.
15. Grayson, **op. cit.**, pp. 70–71.
16. William Allen White, **Woodrow Wilson: The Man, His Times, and His Task** (Boston: Houghton Mifflin Company, 1924), pp. 404–11.

16. THE TARNISHED DREAM

Wilson, someone said, had been born "half way between the Bible and the dictionary." He believed in "the power of words."[1] He was going home to use this favorite of all his weapons in the great cause. But already his friends were worried. They did not doubt his ability to inspire the American people. But the Senate was a different matter. It was in hostile hands. The Foreign Relations Committee was dominated by Henry Cabot Lodge, and it was a proud and stiff-necked committee. Wilson himself should have known the dangers. Long before he had gone to the White House he had written:

Particularly in its dealings with the President has the Senate shown its pride of independence, its desire to rule rather than to be merely consulted, its inclination to magnify its powers and in some sense preside over the policy of the government. . . .

The President has not the same recourse when blocked by the Senate that he has when opposed by the House. When the House declines his counsel, he may appeal to the nation, and if public opinion respond to his appeal the House may grow thoughtful of the next congressional elections and yield; but the Senate is not so immediately sensitive to public opinion and is apt to grow, if anything, more stiff if pressure of that kind is brought to bear upon it.

But there is another course which the President may follow, and which one or two Presidents of unusual political sagacity have followed, with the satisfactory results that were to have been expected. He may himself be less stiff and offish, may himself act in the true spirit of the constitution and establish intimate relations of confidence with the Senate on his own initiative. . . . The policy which has made rivals of the President and Senate has shown itself in the President as often as in the Senate. . . . If he have character, modesty, devotion, and insight as well as force, he can bring the contending elements of the system together in a great and efficient body of common counsel.[2]

Yet Wilson was unwilling, perhaps unable, to follow his own prescription. Long before he had left Paris, he had decided to fight rather than adjust. House was particularly worried and undertook, as he told Stephen Bonsal, to argue the matter with Wilson:

I told him I was already counting noses and as that made him laugh I went into details. I urged the President to extend some courtesies, to even extend an olive branch to Hoke Smith, the Senator from Georgia, with whom, as I knew, he had been "feuding" for some years. . . . "If you whistle Hoke will not come to heel," I suggested, "but if you ask him to come to the White House and assist you he will come and stay with you."

"I shall do nothing of the sort!" answered the President, and for a moment his eyes blazed with anger. "That man is an ambulance-chaser. I scorn to have any relations with him whatsoever"

Aghast, I inquired for details, and the strange story of the feud came out. It seems that, unhappy coincidence, Hoke Smith and Wilson hung out their law-office shingles in Atlanta in the same month and the same year. . . . As I see it Smith was a hustler and Wilson a Southern Gentleman inclined to stand on his dignity. Smith got a few clients, perhaps he did chase ambulances, but Wilson got none . . . so Wilson soon returned to academic life and Smith went on his way to the Senate.

"But, 'Governor,' " I insisted, "this man's vote is important, it may be vital. If he did chase ambulances thirty years ago, do not ostracize him. Let him, too, help save civilization."

The President laughed now, and that was a good sign. "I don't think his vote will be important, and I'm sure it will not be decisive. I shall receive him, of course, as the Senator from Georgia, if he calls, but, House, no nosegays, no olive branches in that direction. . . . I have found that you get nothing in this world that is worth while without fighting for it."[3]

Wilson went to the people first, and in Lodge's home state. He landed in Boston, February 24. It was an emotional, fanatically enthusiastic reception. And Wilson's were inspiring words that day:

I do not mean any disrespect to any other great people when I say that America is the hope of the world. And if she does not justify that hope, results are unthinkable. Men will be thrown back upon bitterness of disappointment not only, but bitterness of despair. All nations will be set as hostile camps again. . . .

But I talk as if there were any question. I have no more doubt of the verdict of America in this matter than I have doubt of the blood that is in me. . . . The nations of the world have set their heads now to do a great thing, and they are not going to slacken their purpose. And when I speak of the nations of the world I do not speak of the governments of the world. I speak of peoples who constitute the nations of the world. They are in the saddle, and they are going to see to it that if their present governments do not do their will some other governments shall.[4]

No Massachusetts man could have mistaken the gauge laid down that day to Senator Lodge: "Any man who resists the present tides that run in the world will find himself thrown upon a shore so high and barren that it will seem as if he had been separated from his human kind forever."[4]

Two days later, the Senate Foreign Relations Committee came to the White House. Wilson was cordial. They were polite. There was deep and long discussion. The President's plea was passionate with his sense of righteousness and duty. There was even a touch of humor:

> As he sat down and leaned back in his chair, something fell out of his pocket and bounced loudly on the floor. It was the horse chestnut that he had treasured since Princeton days, for good fortune and because he liked to run his sensitive fingers over its velvety surface. When a congressman retrieved it and handed it to him, he reddened and looked sheepish. "It's my good-luck buckeye," he explained with a smile. "I keep it in my pocket to ward off the rheumatism." The roar of laughter that followed seemed to unify the group.[5]

But no one was convinced. The isolationist William E. Borah remained firmly "irreconcilable" to any League. Wilson's old enemy Lodge remained frosty. The President turned from the White House door even more rigidly committed to the fight. Two days later, Lodge made a sharp, uncompromising attack on the League. On March 2, he presented in the Senate his "Round Robin," a petition designed to serve notice on the world that Wilson did not have the necessary support. As John Garraty describes the dramatic moment:

> For it to be presented, voted upon, and defeated would have destroyed a good deal of its psycho-

logical value, if not of its actual importance. In this delicate position, Lodge placed his faith in the impetuousness of the Democrats.

It was nearly midnight when he rose to speak. His voice was steady, but his hand, holding the resolution shook perceptibly.

Mr. Lodge. Mr. President, I desire to take only a moment of the time of the Senate. I wish to offer the resolution which I hold in my hand, a very brief one:

". . . *Resolved* . . . That it is the sense of the Senate that while it is their sincere desire that the nations of the world should unite to promote peace and general disarmament, the constitution of the league of nations in the form now proposed to the peace conference should not be accepted by the United States; and be it *Resolved further,* That it is the sense of the Senate that the negotiations on the part of the United States should immediately be directed to the utmost expedition of the urgent business of negotiating peace terms with Germany . . . and that the proposal for a league of nations . . . should be then taken up for careful consideration."

I ask unanimous consent for the present consideration of this resolution. This was the crucial point. . . . He was not disappointed.

Mr. Swanson. I object to the introduction of the resolution.

Mr. Lodge. Objection being made, of course, I recognize the objection. I merely wish to add, by way of explanation, the following: "The undersigned Senators of the United States . . . hereby declare that, if they had had the opportunity, they would have voted for the foregoing resolution. . . ."

And he proceeded to read off the names of the thirty-seven signers. . . .

When the Democratic leader of the Senate, T.S. Martin of Virginia, suggested . . . that a two-thirds majority for the Covenant might be difficult to muster, Wilson said to him heatedly: "Martin! Anyone who opposes me in that, I'll crush!" Since the Republicans had control of the new Senate, this might seem no more than empty bluster, but Wilson had his foes in a terrible dilemma. No Senate action could separate the Covenant from the Versailles Treaty. Therefore the opposition could not reject the League without also destroying the Treaty and delaying the peace which every American so desperately desired. "I shall consent to nothing," Wilson told the French Ambassador. *"The Senate must take its medicine."*[6]

It was only two days after the "Round Robin" that Wilson told the nation in his farewell speech:

> The first thing that I am going to tell the people on the other side of the water is that an overwhelming majority of the American people is in favor of the League of Nations. I know that that is true. . . . I am amazed—not alarmed but amazed—that there should be in some quarters such a comprehensive ignorance of the state of the world. These gentlemen do not know what the mind of men is just now. Everybody else does. . . . the forces of the world do not threaten, they operate. The great tides of the world do not give notice that they are going to rise and run; they rise in their majesty and overwhelming might, and those who stand in their way are overwhelmed.[7]

Wilson had sensed the feeling from the crowds, from the press. In fact, even Lodge was secretly admitting it. But actually, Wilson returned to Paris considerably sobered. The people did seem to be with him. In another month the Literary Digest would publish the results of a poll indicating overwhelming support for the League. It was crude, but it was the only one available. Yet Wilson also knew that there was strong doubt about endangering the Monroe Doctrine, about obligating the nation to a colonial mandate, about methods of getting out of the League, once in, and about the danger of League-meddling in domestic affairs of the nation. Despite the rigidity of his speeches, Wilson now faced the prospect of asking the Allies for changes in the Covenant that he himself had drafted. Frederic Paxson describes the result:

Leading Republican supporters of the League were invited to suggest to the President amendments the adoption of which might help obtain consent by the Senate, and the President acted on the advice thus given.... [But] other delegations felt as free to ask for compensation.

France reverted to the conviction that Article X, too strong to please senators, was too weak to produce security for France; but the President found it hard to yield. Eventually, however, he and Lloyd George prepared with France a separate treaty by which Great Britain and the United States agreed to come to the rescue in the event of an attack on France. He found it necessary, too, to resist the plea which Japan pressed again: a plea for the guarantee of racial equality....

It was difficult to procure the insertion of a withdrawal clause in the Covenant, or clarification respecting domestic policies. The clarification, based on a suggestion by Taft, added the sentence: "If the dispute between the parties is claimed by one of them, and is found by the council, to arise out of a matter which by international law is solely within the domestic jurisdiction of that party, the council shall so report, and shall make no recommendation as to its settlement." But it was very difficult to phrase a sentence which would at one stroke free the Monroe Doctrine without at the same time freeing many other special policies with which some of the Allies were concerned.... A new article was drafted to allay American fears without conceding too much:

"Nothing in this Covenant shall be deemed to affect the validity of international engagements, such as treaties of arbitration or regional understandings like the Monroe Doctrine, for securing the maintenance of peace."

Yielding to the President in matters relating to the League, the delegations permitted the insertion of the amendments for which he had to ask. But the fact that he asked weakened him for the remaining tasks of the Conference, since it was an open admission that he was unable to command a continuing effective support from all the leaders of even his own party. Before the League of Nations Commission gave final approval to the amended Covenant the Italian crowds which, in January, hailed him as messiah were denouncing him as a traitor.[8]

And Wilson's problems were complicated seriously by three other factors—haste, a deepening and permanent break with Colonel House, and illness. House had been managing negotiations during his absence in the United States. When the Colonel reported to Wilson aboard the George Washington on his return, the President was suddenly crushed. His wife later wrote:

He smiled bitterly. "House has given away everything I had won before we left Paris. He has compromised on every side, and so I have to start all over again and this time it will be harder, as he has given the impression that my delegates are not in sympathy with me. His own explanation of his compromises is that, with a hostile press in the United States expressing disapproval of the League of Nations as part of the Treaty, he thought it best to yield some other points lest the Conference withdraw its approval altogether. So he has yielded until there is nothing left."[9]

Paul Birdsall explains the interaction of these problems in the case of the French demands:

From that day [March 29] until about the second week in April, practically all negotiations were at a standstill. Wilson was seriously ill from April 3 to April 8, and, on the morning of April 7, dispatched the order to bring the George Washington to Brest. From all sides and from every commission came the same complaints of French obstruction and delay, and during the evenings of April 10 and 11, Bourgeois and Larnaude prolonged the sessions of the League of Nations Commission to register their objections to the Monroe Doctrine amendment as destructive of French security, not because they really objected but because it was "a good thing to bargain with." It is now clear what they were bargaining for—French aims in the Rhineland.

During this period Colonel House sided strongly with the French on most of their demands, saying privately that President Wilson had made a great mistake in coming to Paris at all. He yielded entirely to the French view on Reparation on April 5, during Wilson's illness, and consistently urged Wilson to yield to French demands in the Rhineland and Saar. The President's intimate friend Ray Stannard Baker bitterly remarked that "The Colonel would make peace quickly by giving the greedy ones all they want!" and Lloyd George complained directly to Colonel House, "You and I do not agree as well as the President and I agree."

The French ultimately won considerable concessions to their demand for military occupation. . . . On April 14, Clemenceau came down in his demands from a thirty-year period of occupation to fifteen, even though he realized that he would have to fight Foch and other generals of the French army. "The President made a wry face over some of it," wrote House, "particularly the three five-year periods of occupation, but he agreed to it all...."

...Yet Clemenceau was still afraid of his generals, and he had one more card to play.... he told Wilson he had no assurance that the Senate would ratify the guarantee treaty. Since France had sacrificed so much of her Rhineland program for the sake of that guarantee, what then became of French security. Wilson agreed that the difficulty was real, but it raised a "delicate question." By April 29, he had agreed that the date of evacuation might be delayed at the end of fifteen years if by that time guarantees against unprovoked aggression by Germany were not sufficient.[10]

There were equally bitter problems with Italy, and with Japan. As Frederic Paxson describes them:

The Italian case was complicated by the fact that at the moment only the German peace was being arranged, whereas the demands of Italy affected Austria ...and the enlarged Serbia.... So it was now the territory of an ally which Italy was demanding. Wilson protested in vain that the secret treaties lost their validity with the default of Russia, and that they were inconsistent with the new world order. Italy clung to its claim.... protesting editors complained in many tongues that the legitimate needs of the European Allies were being ignored while the Conference tinkered with the Covenant to please the American Senate.... the technical advisors assured the President that Fiume was indispensable to Yugoslavia. He held his ground, and on April 23 appealed to the world over the heads of the Italian delegation, in an attack upon the demands with which Italy was holding up the peace.

Orlando ... hurried back to Rome in the crisis, and the Big Three proceeded to go ahead without him or Italy. The Italians came back to the Conference in a few days.

... the Japanese plea reached its crisis almost at the time when other matters were at their worst. Orlando led his Italian delegation back to Rome on April 24. The German delegation began to assemble ... in Versailles on April 25. The Covenant was ... voted into the treaty on April 28. Two days later Japan's face was saved by permission to remain in Shantung after Japan had given a secret promise to withdraw on its own initiative. On May 4 Italy's face was saved by a cordial invitation to return.... Compromise and something resembling legal fiction were the price which Wilson had to pay for acceptance of his program.[11]

There were many other compromises with reality: a divided and segmented Germany, to create a viable Poland and Czechoslovakia; a mandate provision that barely concealed the tough realities of imperialism; and later, there would be a division of Austria and Hungary that would create immense economic problems. Perhaps most forbidding, however, was Wilson's reluctant retreat on reparations. The Allies gave themselves a blank check, and Wilson had to endorse it. It was, in the end, a peace of the victor, and a peace of vengeance.

For Wilson himself the answer to the dilemma was always the League. Much could be sacrificed now, if necessary, in the interest of future peace. A strong League would apply salve to the wounds, could redress in more peaceful times the hasty, vengeful balances of Versailles.

For the Germans, it was a moment of humiliation. Scarcely given time to study the 440 articles of the Treaty, their delegates were hailed to the formal signing in the Hall of Mirrors at Versailles—a handful of civilian politicians surrounded by bitter and vengeful ranks of allied officers and statesmen. They signed. But they would later remember that they had sued for armistice on the basis of Wilson's ideals, that they had been summoned to sign a dictated peace filled with the gall of defeat.

For others there would always be mixed emotions. Some, like John Maynard Keynes, would blast the lack of idealism and economic good sense at the Peace Table. American liberals would shout treason at the desertion of Wilson's simple idealism. Paul Birdsall, studying the Conference many years later, would point out:

> The issue of realism at Paris is mainly the question of the short-term as against the long-range view. The pressures of national demands, made effective and menacing through diplomatic strategy in the League of Nations Commission, made immediate and pressing by the danger of delay in pacifying the turbulent and disintegrating Europe, necessitated a degree of compromise. The realists of the American Delegation lost their perspective under such pressure and were ready to throw away all their cargo in the scramble for the lifeboats. The cargo consisted of the Fourteen Points. . . . Colonel House felt that if the boat were lightened sufficiently, it would still carry the League of Nations. . . . In this atmosphere, one concession was an argument for the next. . . .

Naturally, President Wilson looked stiff and unrealistic when viewed through the eyes of such men, at the very time when William Bullitt was resigning from the American Delegation in protest at Wilson's sacrifice of principle, and others were grumbling that the treaty was thoroughly bad. To the former group he seemed rigid and uncompromising, to the latter weak and uncertain in his stand on principle. A careful study of the record reveals an extraordinary consistency in Wilson's fight for his program under overwhelming difficulties, as well as a high degree of political intelligence in translating the abstract principles of his program into concrete details of application. . . .

Throughout the conference Wilson maintained his stand on principle as the only safe guide in a welter of conflicting interests, as the sole safeguard against laying foundations for future conflict.... The record clearly shows that on every major question but that of Reparation, the Treaty of Versailles would have been a worse treaty had Wilson remained in Washington. With all his mistakes, he emerges as the only man of real stature at Paris.[12]

For Colonel House there were only sad regrets:

How splendid it would have been had we blazed a new and better trail! However, it is to be doubted whether this could have been done, even if those in authority had so decreed, for the peoples back of them had to be reckoned with. It may be that Wilson might have had the power and influence if he had remained in Washington and kept clear of the Conference. When he stepped from his lofty pedestal and wrangled with representatives of other states upon equal terms, he became as common clay....

To those who are saying that the Treaty is bad and should never have been made and that it will involve Europe in infinite difficulties in its enforcement, I feel like admitting it. But I would also say in reply that empires cannot be shattered and new states raised upon their ruins without disturbance....

And yet I wish we had taken the other road, even if it were less smooth.... We would at least have gone in the right direction.[13]

For Wilson himself there was, on occasion, the deep foreboding of disaster:

Before leaving Paris, Clemenceau and Lloyd George had been urging the President to return to Europe after a while, to which the President replied: "That is practically out of the question. Lincoln one time told the story about a little girl who had some blocks with letters on them. She was learning her ABC's with the use of those blocks, and one night before going to bed she was playing with them. When she got into bed she started to say her prayers, but she was so sleepy that all she could say was—'Oh, Lord, I am too sleepy to say my prayers. Here are the blocks and the letters, you spell it out!' "[14]

Years later, Winston Churchill would write of this war and this peace: "Governments and individuals conformed to the rhythm of the tragedy, and swayed and staggered on ever-increasing scales, till injuries were wrought to the structure of human society which a century will not efface, and which may conceivably prove fatal to the present civilization.... Victory was to be bought so dear as to be almost indistinguishable from defeat. It was not to give even security to the victors."[15]

NOTES, CHAPTER 16

1. Thomas A. Bailey, **Woodrow Wilson and the Lost Peace** (N.Y.: The Macmillan Company, 1944), p. 150.
2. Woodrow Wilson, **Constitutional Government in the United States** (N.Y.: Columbia University Press, 1908), pp. 138–41.
3. Stephen Bonsal, **Unfinished Business** (N.Y.: Doubleday, Doran and Company, 1944), pp. 59–60.
4. Ray Stannard Baker and William E. Dodd (eds.), **The Public Papers of Woodrow Wilson** (N.Y.: Harper and Brothers, 1925-27), V, 436–37, 439.
5. Arthur Walworth, **Woodrow Wilson** (London: Longmans, Green and Company, 1958), II, 270–71.
6. John Garraty, **Henry Cabot Lodge: A Biography** (N.Y.: Alfred A. Knopf, Inc., 1953), pp. 353–55.
7. Baker and Dodd, **op. cit.**, V, 446–47.
8. Frederic Paxson, **Postwar Years (American Democracy and the World War**, Berkeley, Calif.: University of California Press, 1948, Vol. III), pp. 61–62.

9. Edith Bolling Wilson, **My Memoir** (Indianapolis, Ind.: The Bobbs-Merrill Company, 1939), p. 246.
10. Paul Birdsall, **Versailles Twenty Years After** (N.Y.: Reynall and Hitchcock, 1941), pp. 212–14.
11. Paxson, **op. cit.**, pp. 63–65.
12. Birdsall, **op. cit.**, pp. 292–93, 295.
13. Charles Seymour (ed.), **The Intimate Papers of Colonel House** (Boston: Houghton Mifflin Company, 1926–28), IV, 488–89.
14. Cary T. Grayson, **Woodrow Wilson: An Intimate Memoir** (N.Y.: Holt, Rinehart and Winston, 1960), pp. 89–90.
15. Winston Churchill, **The World Crisis** (N.Y.: Charles Scribners' Sons, 1923–29), II, 1–2.

17. THE TRIUMPH OF THE TRIVIAL

Fatigued by tedious months of negotiations, disturbed deeply by the compromises he had been compelled to make, separated for the first time from the firm bulwark of Colonel House's friendship, Woodrow Wilson returned to face the most crucial challange of his career. And he returned with a mind more rigid, a mood more threatening than his friends had seen since the bitter last days at Princeton. He faced a Republican Senate. Yet he had no inclination to woo them. He would go to the people. With their help, he would crush the foes of truth and of peace. On July 10, 1919, he presented the Treaty to the Senate, but his speech was a call to the hearts of Americans everwhere:

It was universally recognized that all the peoples of the world demanded of the Conference that it should create such a continuing concert of free nations as would make wars of aggression and spoliation such as this that had just ended forever impossible.... The monster that had resorted to arms must be put in chains that could not be broken. The united power of free nations must put a stop to aggression, and the world must be given peace.... The League of Nations was not merely an instrument to adjust and remedy old wrongs under a new treaty of peace; it was the only hope of mankind.... Shall we or any other free people hesitate to accept this great duty? Dare we reject it and break the heart of the world? ...

America may be said to have just reached her majority as a world power. . . . Our participation in the war established our position among the nations and nothing but our own mistaken action can alter it. . . . a new role and a new responsibility have come to this great Nation that we honor and which we would all wish to lift to yet higher levels of service and achievement.

The stage is set, the destiny disclosed. It has come about by no plan of our conceiving, but by the hand of God who led us into this way. We cannot turn back. We can only go forward, with lifted eyes and freshened spirit, to follow the vision.[1]

. . The country was probably with him: "A poll of 17,000 Protestant, Catholic and Jewish clergy gave all but 800 votes for the Treaty; and another, held at hundreds of universities and colleges, showed nearly two thirds of 150,000 voters demanding ratification with mild reservations or none at all. . . . From chambers of commerce, from the American Federation of Labor, from railroad brotherhoods, from women voters, from granges, the same demands came in."[2]

But, as W. Stull Holt has pointed out, the Isolationist bloc and Senator Lodge's tough core of professionals had other plans:

> With the Committee on Foreign Relations safely under their control the irreconcilables faced the future with greater confidence than ever before. . . . it became increasingly clear during the debates in May and June . . . that the Republicans in the Senate were going to make the treaty an issue for party action. . . . The majority of Republican Senators were being maneuvered into the position of insisting on drastic changes in the treaty while the irreconcilables were not being bound to accept the treaty when changed. Of course the unity of the Republicans in the Senate was by no

means certain. . . . Much would depend on the course of public opinion, on what Wilson and the Democrats would do, and on the ability of the Republican leaders in the Senate to hold their followers together. . . . Their control of the committee enabled them to keep the treaty from the Senate for two months. Delay was essential to their cause, for the state of public and senatorial opinion was such that prompt action would be fatal. Several years later one of them, Senator Moses, asserted that if the rules of the Senate had permitted a quick decision "the Versailles treaty would have been ratified without reservation." Time was needed to arouse a hostile public opinion, to wait for a public reaction against the ideals of the war period, and to work further on the majority of their Republican colleagues in the Senate. . . . First, the long treaty of several hundred printed pages was read aloud line by line. . . . The reading consumed two weeks. Then the committee held public hearings which lasted six weeks more. . . .

The hearings served another purpose in addition to delaying the action of the Senate. . . . Self-appointed spokesmen pled the causes of Ireland, China, India, Albania, Sweden, Czechoslovakia, Egypt, Hungary, Italy, Jugoslavia, Esthonia, Latvia, Lithuania, Persia, and Ukrainia. . . . Stirring up opposition to the treaty among the foreign elements of the United States was a natural policy for the irreconcilables.

The majority report of the Committee on Foreign Relations that reached the Senate on September 10, made several things certain. The irreconcilables no longer entertained any hope of persuading the Republicans in the Senate to unite on a policy of complete rejection. . . . Following the advice of Lodge they proceeded "by way of amendment and reservation," and with Lodge, Harding and New recommended forty-five amendments, many covering the same point, and four reservations. . . . Three . . . possibilities remained. The

Republicans might be held together on a program of reservations that could be supported by all of them, even by the mild reservationists. Or by offering to accept less severe reservations, Wilson and the Democrats might reach an understanding with the mild reservationists that would detach them from the other Republicans. With them—and their numbers were likely to be augmented once party lines were definitely broken—the necessary two-thirds vote might easily be secured. Or by resolutely refusing any concessions, the Democrats might yet win completely through the votes of some Republican senators who would be willing to sacrifice their desires for mild reservations, rather than have the treaty rejected and the league of nations crippled at birth by the absence of the United States.

This last alternative was the one which the Democratic leadership publicly insisted could and would be attained. . . .

Publicly, Wilson gave no hint that he contemplated the slightest concession. Privately, he gave to Senator [Gilbert] Hitchcock . . . an outline of the interpretive reservations he would accept if necessary. But . . . the President took no steps to meet the advances of the mild reservationist group among the Republicans. No bid was made for their support until after they had come to terms with the other Republican senators.[3]

Instead, Wilson tried to persuade them to his position, and to meet the attacks of the Foreign Relations Committee with polite and reasonable explanation:

> For a month after his return he constantly invited senators of both parties to consult with him at the White House. He was told again and again that these conferences were producing excellent results. But Senator Lodge was also at work. On August 12, after three months of comparative silence, he attacked the

Treaty in a two-hour speech on the floor of the Senate. He cleverly borrowed Wilson's *leitmotiv* of service. America, he said, must have freedom to pursue her task of serving all the world. He managed to make this plea a basis for demanding reservations which virtually eliminated Article X, and made other important changes in the Covenant. What was more, he demanded that our ratification of the Treaty should not go into force until these reservations were accepted by four (that is to say all) of the other great Allied and Associated Powers. . . .

The President's appearance before the Committee, on August 19, was not technically a part of the hearings, and took place at the White House. . . . At ten o'clock in the morning a very tired President sat down in the East Room, with Messrs. Lodge and Knox within arm's length, and Messrs. Borah and Brandegee across from him. Able Democrats of the Committee did their best to defend the President; but all the advantages lay with the prosecution, in strategic position as well as in numbers. They had been able to decide beforehand what questions should be asked and who should ask them. Mr. Fall even had written a list of twenty, which the President would be permitted to answer at leisure—and the newspapers to print at once. Some of them were tricky and technical, some wide of the main issues, and some apparently designed . . . to disgust the newspaper-reading public with the peace settlement.

Generally speaking, the President's performance was admirable. At all times, and under much provocation, he was extremely courteous and seemed composed. . . . The inquisition itself had been very far from jovial. . . . Thanks to the fact that the senators asked Wilson for little "information"—and that little mostly on matters already covered by others—it did not, in fact, get much. But it got some misinformation that was infinitely damaging. . . .

Wilson asserted emphatically that he had not been

THE TRIUMPH OF THE TRIVIAL 307

informed, officially or unofficially, prior to his arrival in Paris, about any of the secret treaties between the Allies. It was an astounding statement, contradicting a mass of evidence, some of which the members of the Committee must have had. . . .

In the words of one who especially studied the President's statement, there are just two possibilities: "that the President lied" or that, "not remembering the time and circumstances of his learning of the treaties, he felt that he was telling the truth."[4]

The mask of sweet reason became increasingly difficult for the President to hold in the face of Senator Lodge's cool contempt. At one point, Lodge observed: "Perhaps I do not regard the drafting committee with . . . veneration. . . . I do not think their intellect or position in the world are so overpowering that we cannot suggest amendments to this league."[5]

Infuriated, Wilson told the Democratic National Committee: "If I could really say what I think about them, it would be picturesque. . . . The President . . . is liable some day to burst by merely containing restrained gases. . . . When the lid is off I am going to resume my study of the dictionary to find adequate terms in which to describe the fatuity of these gentlemen with their poor little minds that never get anywhere but run around in a circle and think they are going somewhere. I cannot express my contempt for their intelligence."[5]

The encounters with congressmen during the summer drove Wilson to take his case to the great court of the people. He sought little advice. His wife and his doctor were deeply fearful. But his secretary, Joseph Tumulty, reinforced the President's own deep commitment to making a personal crusade. As John Blum describes it:

Tumulty planned the tour carefully. . . . He concentrated on the Midwest and Far West, avoiding the Democratic South and Republican East. The itinerary he proposed called for ten thousand miles of travel in twenty-six days, with twenty-six major stops. He also allowed for twelve short, rear-platform speeches daily. In spite of Wilson's fatigue few changes were made in this schedule. . . .

Tumulty cultivated the appearance of nonpartisanship, taking care that some Republicans were on all the local committees and in evidence at all the large meetings. Nonpartisanship in fact, however, was far from his mind. McAdoo sent him a list of Democratic politicians in Columbus, Portland, San Francisco, and Los Angeles for whom a presidential handshake was mandatory. Much of Tumulty's time en route was given over to Democratic committees. Even Wilson did his best to be a "good mixer."

The presidential party left Washington on September 3. For almost a month they were to live on wheels, a small, closely confined group, plagued by dust and cinders, finding little relief in the commercial hotels and amidst the noisy crowds at their places of call. Tumulty took it upon himself to enliven his fellow travelers. He started the trip on a jocular note by substituting a colored messenger from the executive offices, whom Wilson knew, for the railroad's porter. On the train, every evening after dinner, with Grayson as his "end man," Tumulty amused the President and Mrs. Wilson with his unfailing Irish wit.

Wilson needed these diversions. To add to the discomfort of travel, he received, through Tumulty, discouraging reports from Washington. Billy Cochran informed Tumulty that the West was confused and upset about the British Empire's six votes to the United States' one. Rudolph Forster . . . telegraphed that the Democrats needed definite proposals endorsed by the President for interpretive reservations. Democratic Senator Pomerene of Ohio, reporting that Lodge was negotiating with the mild reservationists, feared that the Democrats would have to choose between rejection and hurtful amendments unless they reached an agreement with the mild reservationists at once. Vance McCormick warned Tumulty that the treaty could not be ratified without reservations. . . . He was particularly unhappy about Wilson's attacks on the Senate.[6]

And there were other, grave problems, as the President's doctor, Admiral Grayson, has written:

For him the journey was a prolonged agony of physical pain; for Mrs. Wilson and me an unceasing agony of anxiety. . . . The terrific strain which he had been under for more than a year was telling, and his exertions on the western trip were sapping his vitality very fast. With it all he was under enormous emotional strain because he felt that he was fighting the fight of future generations. Again and again as we rode through the crowded streets of western cities he would look intently at the lines of school children on the pavements and say: "I am the attorney for these children."

From the time we reached Montana the President suffered from asthmatic attacks and severe headaches, which seriously interfered with his rest. Frequently I was summoned during the night to give him necessary aid and to assist him in breathing. It was necessary for him to sleep a good part of the time sitting up, propped up with pillows in a chair.[7]

Yet this was for Woodrow Wilson the very deepest of all satisfactions: the politician come home to his people; the great preacher opening his heart to the beloved parish of his choice.

There was little eloquence, in the old Victorian sense. There were few of the great phrases that ring on for generations. In the deadly routine of repetition, there was little hope to reach for phrases that would stand with Jefferson's or Lincoln's. But Wilson, for the moment, reached for ordinary peoples' hearts, and for their common sense.

In Omaha, on September 8:

> They do not like the way in which the Monroe Doctrine is mentioned. Well, I would not stop on a question of style. The Monroe Doctrine is adopted. It is swallowed, hook, line and sinker. . . . When I came back to this country in March I brought the first draft, the provisional draft, of the Covenant of the League. I submitted it to the Foreign Relations Committee of the Senate of the United States. . . . They made a number of suggestions. I carried every one of those suggestions to Paris, and every one of them was adopted. Now apparently they want me to go back to Paris and say, "We are much obliged to you, but we do not like the language."[8]

In Sioux Falls, the same day:

> I find some gentlemen so nervous about doing right that their eyes rest very uneasily on the first article of the Covenant of the League of Nations, and they say, "That says that we can get out after two years' notice, if we have fulfilled all our international obligations at that time. Now, we want to make it perfectly clear that we will get out when we want to." . . . You cannot choose the seat by the door and keep fumbling with the knob without creating the impression that you are going to get out in a minute . . . that you are by constitution and disposition a scuttler! If America goes into this thing, she is going to stay in, and she is going to stay in in order to see that justice is done.[9]

And at Bismark: "I do not recognize this Covenant when I hear some other men talk about it. . . . I am told *that plain sentences which I thought were unmistakable English terms mean something that I never heard of and that nobody else ever intended as a purpose."*[10]

At Helena, he appealed to both the heart and the purse:

Suppose we did not have any hearts under our jackets. Suppose we did not care for these people. Care for them? Why, their kinsmen are everywhere in the communities of the United States, people who love people over there are everywhere in the United States. . . . . Our hearts are theirs, but suppose they were not. Suppose we had forgotten everything except the material, commercial, monetary interests of the United States. You cannot get those markets away from Germany if you let her reestablish her old influence there. . . . If you are going to trade with them, you have got to go partners with them.[11]

In Pueblo, near the end of this great crusade, he asked the people to share both his humor and his deep sense of moral guilt:

Why gentlemen should fear that the Congress of the United States would be advised to do something that it did not want to do I frankly cannot imagine because they cannot even be advised to do anything unless their own representative has participated in the advice . . . we are not obliged to take any advice except our own, which to any man who wants to go his own course is a very satisfactory state of affairs.[12]

[And then], Why, my fellow citizens, should they pray God to bless me? I advised the Congress of the United States to create the situation that led to the death of their sons. . . . Why should they weep upon my hand and call down the blessings of God upon me? Because they believe . . . and rightly believe, that their sons saved the liberty of the world.[13]

But above all, Wilson warned the people that they stood helpless in the fist of a fate that would not relent: "The facts are marching, and God is marching with them. You must either welcome them or subsequently, with humiliation, surrender to them."[14]

Then came the supreme moment of indignity, of relentless, crushing helplessness. As Admiral Grayson later wrote on September 25, 1919:

All day the President had such a splitting headache that, as he expressed it, he could hardly see. Leaving the Pueblo auditorium he went directly back to the train. He was very tired and suffering when he entered the car. . . . the President was scheduled to make an address the following morning. He was very desirous of retiring after dinner to get some rest, but at the first stop, Rocky Ford, Colorado, a large crowd surged about the car and shouted for him to come out and shake hands with them . . . the President came out on the platform and grasped the hands of those who were closest to the rear end of the train. . . .

Early the next morning I was awakened from my sleep and told that the President was suffering very much. I went at once and found that he was on the verge of a complete breakdown. . . . It was with great difficulty that I could persuade him to turn back to Washington and omit the remainder of the itinerary. He insisted that he must go on saying: "I should feel like a deserter. My opponents will accuse me of having cold feet should I stop now." . . .

Mrs. Wilson added her pleas to my urgent medical advice, and at last he turned to me and said sadly: "I suppose you are right"; and tears ran down his cheek as he added: "This is the greatest disappointment of my life."

We arrived in Washington on Sunday, the 28th of September. . . . On the evening of October 1st he seemed quite bright and cheerful. . . . But early next morning the crash came. He fell stricken with a thrombosis.[15]

It was one of the most fateful moments in the history of the Republic. Wilson had made his appeal to the nation. There could never be another. The Senate, in the next two months, would decide the fate of the Treaty, and, if United States support were crucial, the fate of the League of Nations. Wilson's enemies stepped up their partisan bawling. His ancient foe George Harvey wrote: "He has had his say. He has shot his bolt. He has done his worst. He is no more to be considered. Now let the Senate act."[16]

And, at this fateful moment, the President was nearly isolated from the world whose fate lay in his hands. As John Blum has written:

From October, 1919, until his death, Wilson was a sick man. . . . For days he was in a coma. It was a wonder and a tragedy that he lived. . . .

There is no question but that for at least a month Wilson was incapacitated within the meaning of the Constitution. He considered no legislation, made no appointments to office, issued no proclamations. For at least another month his capacity was doubtful. . . . For a month the United States had no President; for many months the country had only a shell of a President. . . . Congress and the public . . . were not told the truth about Wilson. Nor did the Cabinet receive any direct word. . . .

The secrecy, imposed in part to avoid alarm, was necessary primarily because Mrs. Wilson directed that the

President was not to resign; he was too ill himself to make any decision. She, putting her duties as a wife above her duties as a citizen, refused to endanger her husband by upsetting him emotionally. Wilson's physicians were bound to secrecy by their professional oaths.... Throughout October and most of November the Presidency was held by a regency. Mrs. Wilson then and later had great power, for she alone decided what business could be brought before her husband. He was given very little.... By the middle of December there were eight major diplomatic vacancies and over a dozen important unfilled offices in the executive branch.... When Wilson was again able to transact some business, the situation improved, but for two crucial months his wife, his Secretary, and his Cabinet attended as best they could to the duties of the President's office.[17]

There was no chance of liaison between the stricken President and his Democratic leaders in Congress who must manage the party's tactics on the treaty votes. Before his speaking tour, the President had been apparently ready for some compromise—if necessary. Now Senator Hitchcock, the Democratic leader, could no longer argue the point. He was allowed to see Wilson twice, but commanded not to upset the President. He tried to persuade Wilson that some adjustment was essential. "Let Lodge compromise," Wilson responded.[18] And Lodge, too, was becoming more frosty. Stephen Bonsal, trying to mediate between the two proud, tough-minded leaders, later reported the Senator's appraisal of the League Charter: "As an English production it does not rank high.... It might get by at Princeton but certainly not at Harvard."[19]

Wilson himself had to undergo the indignity of receiving a Senate Committee, chosen to ascertain whether the President was competent to act. His resentment was deep, as he later told friends: "After the Com-

mittee had . . . discovered that I was very much all
there, the Committee turned to leave. Senator Fall
paused a moment and said: 'Mr. President, I want you
to know that I am praying for you.' . . . If I could have
got out of bed I would have hit the man. . . . He must
have known that God would take the opposite view
from him on any subject."[20]

By mid-November, the Republican leadership was
ready for its test. It was united in intent—to capture
the League issue for the Republicans. It was divided in
the substance of the matter. Senator William E. Borah
sounded the trumpet of the irreconcilables:

> Sir, we are told that this treaty means peace.
> Even so, I would not pay the price. Would you pur-
> chase peace at the cost of any part of our independence?
> We could have had peace in 1776—the price was high,
> but we could have had it. . . .
> But your treaty does not mean peace. . . . The people
> in whose keeping alone you can safely lodge the power
> of peace or war nowhere, at no time and in no place,
> have any voice in this scheme for world peace. . . .
> Can you hope for peace when love of country is
> disregarded in your scheme, when the spirit of national-
> ity is rejected, even scoffed at? . . . With a ruthlessness
> unparalleled your treaty in a dozen instances runs
> counter to the divine law of nationality. Peoples who
> speak the same language, kneel at the same ancestral
> tombs, moved by the same traditions, animated by a
> common hope, are torn asunder, broken to pieces,
> divided, and parceled out to antagonistic nations. And
> this you call justice. This, you cry, means peace. . . . No;
> your treaty means injustice. It means slavery. It means
> war.[21]

Senator Warren G. Harding described the position of
the reservationists in the murky prose that would soon
be issuing from the White House itself:

We are content to give you your league of nations, doubtful as we are about the wisdom of the great experiment. . . .

If this ratification is made with the reservations which have been adopted, there remains the skeleton of a league on which the United States can, if it deems it prudent, proceed in deliberation and calm reflection toward the building of an international relationship which shall be effective in the future. . . .

. . . I speak for one who is old-fashioned enough to believe that the Government of the United States of America is good enough for me. . . . you can tell to the people of the United States of America and to the world that the Senate of the United States has once more reasserted its authority, and representative government abides.[22]

Henry Cabot Lodge had drawn his various Republican groups together to support fifteen reservations. These would assure, in insultingly specific language, the specific approval of Congress before the United States would undertake any obligations to enforce peace, any mandate, any interference with American foreign trade, any contribution to the League's support, any limit on armaments. They would make the United States the sole judge of its right to withdraw from the League, of the domestic questions from which League action was barred. They would insist on American immunity from all League action, until the United States had the same number of votes as the whole British Empire. And, in deference to domestic politics, they would insist upon Irish admission to the League of Nations.

Wilson stood unmoved. He would accept no changes to spell out the obvious, no excuses for other nations to reopen negotiations. It would be the treaty he had brought home, or the issue would be taken directly to the people.

It was a day of drama and tragedy, as Thomas Bailey described it:

... the day was November 19, 1919—one year and eight days after the Armistice. The Senate of the United States, with galleries packed and long lines standing out in the corridors, was convening to vote on the treaty.

The country was weary of debate; the Senate was even more weary. . . .

Last-minute maneuvers had already taken up a part of the morning. The Democrats had just met together in secret caucus, and Wilson's letter now being published in the newspapers, was read to them. The great President had asked them to vote down the Lodge reservations, and they would follow the leader. He had taken from their shoulders the grave responsibility of having to make this decision themselves.

The Republican "irreconcilables" had their final hour in court. Brandegee condemned the "pipe dream" of the League, and declared that he would consider himself as "candidate for the madhouse" if he were to vote for it. . . . Sherman denounced the "boiling hell" of the treaty, and castigated the Covenant as the charter of an "international homicide club." He brought a ripple of laughter from the galleries when he said that he was pleased to follow the advice of Wilson and vote against the pact—the first time he had supported the administration since the Armistice.

Senator Hitchcock presented the final case for the Democrats. He went down the line to show that there was no wide gulf between his reservations and those of Lodge. . . .

The "mild reservationists" resented both Hitchcock's remarks and Wilson's tactless letter. . . .

It was now 5:30 in the afternoon, and five and one-half hours had been consumed in final debate. The

Senate was impatient for action, and as McCumber took his seat cries of "Vote," "Vote," "Vote," arose from all over the chamber.

The question before the Senate was on approving the treaty with the Lodge reservations attached. The crowded galleries sat in tense silence as the roll was called, and as each senator responded to his name.

The result was announced: 39 ayes, 55 nays. A murmur swept through the galleries. The treaty with its reservations had lost.

The Republicans (with four independently minded Democrats) had voted for the Lodge resolution of ratification. The Democrats, aided by thirteen Republican "irreconcilables," had voted as a body against it.... Hitchcock's motion that the treaty be reconsidered with his reservations was ... defeated 41-50.... Lodge, still in the driver's seat, then surprised the opposition by permitting another vote on the treaty with his reservations. This time he lost 41 to 51, as compared with 39 to 55 on the first vote. Three more Democrats, faced with the appalling prospect of a complete defeat of the treaty, joined the four who had already bolted.

Lodge then permitted Senator Underwood ... to move approval of the treaty without any reservations. The motion was defeated 38 to 53....

Now that the Democrats had themselves defeated the treaty with the Republican reservations attached, Lodge made good on his threat that he would permit no further compromise. And he held the whip hand. Senator Swanson (a Democrat) walked over to him and, according to one press report, pleaded:

"For God's sake, can't something be done to save the treaty?"

"Senator, the door is closed," replied Lodge. "You have done it yourselves."[23]

The great wave of public protest on which Wilson

depended never came. There was no clear issue, as W. Stull Holt explains: "If the Republican party in the Senate had joined the irreconcilables, public opinion might have operated as Wilson had expected, but the majority of the Republicans insisted they wanted to enter the league with a few reservations to protect American interests."[24]

Yet there was protest from the press that sparked a new mood of compromise. As Holt has noted: "It seemed absurd that the national policy adopted should be the one advocated by only 17 senators. Common sense revolted at seeing the votes of 78 senators to enter the league nullified because they could not agree among themselves on the terms of entry."[25]

Throughout the winter, Republican and Democratic "reservationists" worked toward a compromise. They had no help from Wilson or Lodge, or the irreconcilables. The only hope was that both groups of moderates would break free of party discipline. Lodge held his men in line. Republican moderates would not threaten to bolt their party; Republican irreconcilables did and, in the end, they had their way. Wilson was equally adamant. Early in January, in his message to the Jackson Day Dinner, he made the matter a party issue, challenged the Senate to battle, and called for a "great and solemn referendum" in the election of 1920.[26] He should have known that no presidential election can be a referendum on any single issue; he had been given, only a year and a half before, a crude practical lesson in the matter of elections. But this remained his unalterable position to the end of his career. The people must decide. Party leaders and old friends sought their way through the protective barriers Mrs. Wilson had erected and pled for compromise. Bernard Baruch was one, and he later told of his experience:

> I begged him to accept some of the reservations proposed, saying, "If we can at least get the spirit

of the Covenant ratified, we can make it work."

He stopped me; his voice sharp. "No. They are not reservations, they are nullifications. No, I shall not accept. If I did, I would be false to every young man who lies in Flanders."

The interview was over. I walked from the room, certain that the President believed I had deserted him. . . . Mrs. Wilson later told me that after I had gone he had murmured, "And Baruch, too."[27]

The much-respected, now retired British Foreign Secretary, Sir Edward Grey, hastened to the United States to let the President know that the old Allies would rather have United States participation with reservations than no participation at all. The President would not receive him. On Janaury 16, the League Council met for the first time in Paris, at the call of the President of the United States. There was no American delegate. On March 19, at long last, the Senate made its final deferential bow to public opinion with a series of new test votes on the Treaty. It was clear that the people supported a league of some sort.

Again enough Democrats deserted party leadership to provide a clear majority for Lodge's reservations—49-35. But a two-thirds vote was needed. Again Wilson threw his strength against any change, and twenty-one party regulars, largely from the South, stood fast. If seven of them had deserted, there would have been a Treaty with reservations. Again the pure Wilson treaty was voted down by a combination of reservationists and irreconcilables, Democratic and Republican alike. The dream had been killed—by Lodge's politicking, by the unholy alliance between the League's sworn enemies and the League's firmest friends. Wilson had killed his own child, it was said, out of stubbornness, ignorance and selfish ambition.

The President himself was stunned. Late that night he turned to the familiar Scriptures:

> We are troubled on every side, yet not distressed;
> We are perplexed, but not in despair; Persecuted, but not forsaken; cast down, but not destroyed.[28]

Borah and his isolationist friends were delighted. And Lodge was beside himself with glee, as he wrote of Wilson: "I think on the whole we have done very well.... His personal selfishness goes beyond what I have ever seen in any human being. It is so extreme that it is entirely unenlightened and stupid."[29]

The toll was deadly, as Thomas Bailey writes: "It gave new comfort to the forces of disorder everywhere. It left the United States discredited, isolated, shorn of its prestige, and branded as a hypocrite and renegade."[30]

1920 might have been the year of a great enlightenment. In fact, it celebrated the triumph of the trivial in America.

NOTES, CHAPTER 17

1. Ray Stannard Baker and William E. Dodd (eds.), **The Public Papers of Woodrow Wilson** (N.Y.: Harper and Brothers, 1925–27), V, 547–52.
2. H. C. F. Bell, **Woodrow Wilson and the People** (N.Y.: Doubleday, Doran and Company, 1945), p. 363.
3. W. Stull Holt, **Treaties Defeated by the Senate** (Baltimore, Md.: The John Hopkins Press, 1933), pp. 279–83, 285–86.
4. Bell, **op. cit.**, pp. 334–35, 337–39.
5. Alexander L. and Juliette L. George, **Woodrow Wilson and Colonel House** (N.Y.: The John Day Company, 1956), p. 237.
6. John Blum, **Joe Tumulty and the Wilson Era** (Boston: Houghton Mifflin Company, 1951), pp. 209–10.

7. Cary T. Grayson, **Woodrow Wilson: An Intimate Memoir** (N.Y.: Holt, Rinehart and Winston, 1960), pp. 96–97.
8. Baker and Dodd, **op. cit.**, VI, 38–39.
9. Ibid., pp. 52–53.
10. Ibid., p. 97.
11. Ibid., p. 126.
12. Ibid., p. 409.
13. Ibid., p. 413.
14. Ibid., p. 64.
15. Grayson, **op. cit.**, pp. 97–100.
16. **Harvey's Weekly**, October 4, 1919, p. 2.
17. Blum, **op. cit.**, pp. 214–16.
18. John Garraty, **Henry Cabot Lodge: A Biography** (N.Y.: Alfred A. Knopf, Inc., 1953), p. 377.
19. Stephen Bonsal, **Unfinished Business** (N.Y.: Doubleday, Doran and Company, 1944), p. 275.
20. Bell, **op. cit.**, p. 353.
21. U. S. **Congressional Record** (Washington, D. C.), LVIII, Part 9 (November 19, 1919), pp. 8783–84.
22. Ibid., pp. 8791–92.
23. Thomas A. Bailey, **Woodrow Wilson and the Great Betrayal** (N.Y.: The Macmillan Company, 1945), pp. 187–92.
24. Holt, **op. cit.**, p. 290.
25. Ibid., p. 298.
26. Baker and Dodd, **op. cit.**, VI, 455.
27. Bernard M. Baruch, **The Public Years** (N.Y.: Holt, Rinehart and Winston, 1960), p. 138.
28. Grayson, **op. cit.**, p. 106.
29. Garraty, **op. cit.**, p. 390.
30. Bailey, **op. cit.**, p. 285.

18. MANTLE OF A PROPHET

As Americans turned in upon themselves, the deep spirit of dedication was soon dissipated. The gnawing concerns of the immediate took its place. Mounting inflation, disillusionment, fatigue—the need to earn a living, the yearning to be left alone: these were the keynotes of life in the new decade.

Government all but ignored the urgent problems of a nation in transition. The Attorney General and large segments of the American population distracted themselves with the crusade against the "Reds." The chief concern of the New York Legislature that spring was the expulsion of five Socialist members. Congress played games with the public interest. Republicans ignored the President's requests for legislation and spent their time accumulating material for the fall campaign. This was the springtime of investigations, as congressional committees unearthed the odds and ends of scandal and carelessness that might seal the Democratic fate in November. Democrats, reduced to the defense, leaderless and uncertain, spent their time in fruitless rebuttals of Republican charges. And the war was still on. Doughboys still kept a restless Wacht am Rhein. The President vetoed a joint resolution ending the war without a treaty. He remained aloof. He was more active now, more involved in his work, but he was no longer leader of the party or of the nation. Wherever he could, he insisted that the 1920 Campaign must be a great referendum on the League. Consider, for example, this letter to a Democratic County Chairman:

> I think it imperative that the party should at once proclaim itself the uncompromising champion of the Nation's honor and the advocate of everything that the United States can do in the service of humanity; that it should therefore endorse and support the Versailles Treaty and condemn the Lodge reservations as utterly inconsistent with the Nation's honor and destructive of the world's leadership which it had established and which all the free peoples of the world, including the great powers themselves, had shown themselves ready to welcome.[1]

He declared war on Congress:

> In the light of the record of the present Congress, I have no reason whatever to hope that its continuance in session would result in constructive measures for the relief of the economic conditions to which you call attention. It must be evident to all that the dominating motive which has actuated this Congress is political expediency rather than lofty purpose to serve the public welfare.[2]

And, pathetically enough, he cherished a hope for a third nomination. But he had the support neither of his party nor of the nation. And he had no organization. When the Democratic National Convention met in San Francisco on June 28, there was an enthusiastic demonstration for the President—but nothing more. The men he had hoped would lead the way never found the opportunity.

Calloused Republican bosses had already imposed on their convention a team of "safe" nominees: for President—the stalwart, ambiguous, handsome, but small-gauged Senator from Ohio, Warren G. Harding; for Vice-President—the quiet Governor of Massachusetts, Calvin Coolidge, whose reputation had been made at the moment when he had lashed out against the Boston police strike, safe in the knowledge that it was already broken. Coolidge was a master of brevity and platitude—Silent Cal. Harding's speeches were wondrously opaque and ungrammatical. But both were expected to keep quiet and let the landslide of reaction carry them in.

Now Democrats sought to match the mood. Out of the trading and confusion came the ticket to lead Wilson's "solemn referendum": James M. Cox, Governor of Ohio, the darling of the organizations, virtually unknown to the American people, a more intelligent, less handsome Harding—a man of great integrity, but little popular appeal; for Vice-President, Franklin D. Roosevelt, Assistant Secretary of the Navy, a "progressive," personally dynamic, attractive, a man who might carry the votes of the old Wilsonians.

Cox and Roosevelt accepted Wilson's challenge. They made the hopeless crusade for the League. But they could never make the issue precise. Wilson might support them, as he did on October 4, with a statement to the press: "This election is to be a genuine national referendum. . . . Do you want your country's honor vindicated and the Treaty of Versailles ratified? Do you in particular approve of the League of Nations as organized and empowered in that Treaty? And do you wish to see the United States play its responsible part in it? . . . The whole world will wait for your verdict in November as it would wait for an intimation of what its future is to be."[3] Cox and Roosevelt might take the issue to the country with a vigor that amazed the whole nation.

But Republicans confused the League issue mightily. Republicans like Borah told the nation that to vote for Harding would kill the League. Republicans like Hoover and Taft and Hughes said that the best way to assure

American entry into the League was to vote for Harding. Harding himself said all things to all men. By the end of the campaign, it was possible to quote him for the League, for some kind of a league, and against all leagues.

Voters went on to reflect their fatigue with crusade, their boredom with Democrats and with Wilson, their desire above all else to be left alone. The American people never had their chance to speak on the League issue. But they swept into the White House with a massive landslide the handsome, white-haired champion of do-nothing government, the eloquently ambiguous master of the meaningless cliché.

Lodge, as John Garraty has said, interpreted the election "as being the 'solemn referendum' both he and Wilson had wished it to be."[4] Wilson could only carry on through the long four months remaining to him with the dignity and restraint his deep sense of propriety demanded. On December 10, he received from Europe the recognition his own nation had denied him: the Nobel Prize for Peace in 1919 was awarded to him. On March 4, he would ride with dignity beside Warren G. Harding from the White House to the Capitol. There he would stump painfully to the President's room, complete his last official chore of signing documents. There he would meet for the last time Henry Cabot Lodge.

Then, as cheers rose for Harding, Edith and Woodrow Wilson drove away to the house on S Street where he would live out his days, to watch as the war was ended at last, by joint resolution of Congress, and then by simple treaties, without obligations.

As John Blum has written:

>   The failure was complete—the grand vision gone; the treaty dead; the election lost; the party dis-

abled; the leader fallen, and with him his associates. Most of them never recovered from the shock. Yet in the distant perspective the mechanics of failure appear less shocking. Wilson came to power with the support of an uneasy alliance of organization Democrats and crusading liberals, joined, after his nomination, by Southerners who distrusted both. He conquered in 1912 a divided opposition. Defeat reunited his opponents while the fruits of victory gradually destroyed his coalition. The liberals, after accomplishing their purpose— the purpose of their generation—had left neither the energy nor the imagination to cope with the problems of America which, intensified during war, came into focus by 1920. By 1916 they had lost their program, by 1918 their organization. Meanwhile the organization Democrats of the North and South, never compatible, drifted further and further apart. Openly hostile by 1918, they were by 1920 dueling venomously over the sorry issues of patronage, prejudice, and prohibition. Not until 1932, and then only in time of crisis, could a new generation of liberals with a new leader restore the still uneasy triple alliance. . . .

The failure was complete and shocking, but the process of failure is clear in retrospect. The defeat of the League no longer shocks for it is now also clear that an international organization in itself cannot guarantee peace. Yet the shock persists because the grand vision of continuing peace through international organization . . . is precious still to men who would believe . . . that in a good world reasonable human beings can solve amicably and finally the problems of living together. . . . Men were shocked, for they had founded their hopes on a dream.[5]

Yet Wilson himself never lost his commitment to the dream and he never lost his hatred for its enemies. His old friend Bliss Perry, found both still strong as he visited the faltering invalid:

> He sat at the right of the fireplace in his library, slumping a little in his chair, and holding a cane. His head, which he had always carried high, was bent, as if he had been bludgeoned. His voice was distinct, but low, slow, and without animation. His mind, however, seemed to me as clear as ever, though not so alert. We talked a little of the old days at Princeton thirty years before, when we used to discuss Stevenson and Walter Bagehot. He spoke of the Peace Conference. . . . He asked me about the political situation in Massachusetts, and spoke grimly of Henry Cabot Lodge. No Scotch-Irish Presbyterian ever found it easy to forgive his enemies! And then, with a sudden flash of that indomitable religious faith which lay deeper than anything else in his nature, he assured me that a revival of moral idealism was bound to come to our American people.[6]

And he still had his sense of humor. When he was asked to write his autobiography, he could reply: "I have always acquiesced in the joke that there are three kinds of personal memoirs,—biographies, autobiographies, and ought-not-to-biographies. And whether mine ought to be or not, they will not be."[7] His doctor would record numerous incidents of the lingering lightness of his native humor: ". . . as I turned a light on his eyes he asked me what I was up to and I said: 'I am examining your pupils.' To which he replied: 'You have a large order, as I have had a great many in my day.'" When Wilson found it difficult to eat, he was fond of quoting a limerick:

> "A wonderful bird is the pelican
> His bill will hold more than his bellican.

He can take in his beak enough food for a
    week
I wonder how in the hell-he-can."[8]

And when the Senate passed a pious resolution of
hope for the ex-President's recovery: "He chuckled and
said: 'Think of them passing it and not meaning it....'
He then repeated this limerick:

> 'There was an old man of Khartoum,
> Who kept two black sheep in his room,
> To remind him, he said,
> Of two friends who were dead,
> But he never would specify whom.'[9]

There was no humor in Lodge's attitudes. As late
as April, 1921, he could write to an old friend: "You
speak of Harding's English.... Perhaps I am less sensitive about it because I have been through eight years
with a man who wrote English very well without ever
saying anything."[10]

On Armistice Day, 1923, there was a last tribute to
Woodrow Wilson, and a last flash of the old idealism, of
the old contempt for the enemy. William Allen White
reported:

For six months he had been growing weaker.
Armistice Day, 1923, a crowd gathered uptown in Du
Pont Circle. Joe Tumulty had hired a "scratch" band,
and Victor Murdock headed a procession that walked
out to "S" Street. It was not the elite of Washington,
nor the elect of the Government, but the simple people,
department clerks, young boys and girls, a few straggling
colored people on the edge of the crowd, which ...
swept along the street, some on the sidewalks, some in
the center of the pavement.... As the crowd ... came
nearer to Wilson's home, some of the Really Best People joined it. The ex-service men in the crowd were
placed at the head of the procession. Respectfully it

gathered about the door of the Wilson house. . . . When the band had ceased playing, the expectant eyes of the crowd saw an old man come out leaning heavily on his cane. Supporting him stood Senator Carter Glass, of Virginia, who read a prepared introductory address. The old man beside the Senator lifted his face, and they saw the kindly smile that Wilson was wont to bestow upon the populace in his happier days, the last gleam of the lamp from the hall of the Irish Kings. Amid the cheers were tears in the eyes that saw the waning smile. . . . He recited his speech carefully in a voice unexpectedly clear. Then he paused. . . .

"That's all I can do." The crowd broke into sturdy, supporting cheers. He seemed to have finished. The police were busy whacking camera-men—dragging a snap-shooter from an elm tree opposite. The band seized the silence. They were about to break away when he began again. The band had to be squelched. Then he finished his speech. It was not a particularly notable utterance . . . but it held high and unshaken the torch of his faith. He smiled again, waved his free hand, and so turned almost jauntily from the crowd forever, to face the messenger who had been calling him through his declining years.[11]

His tone had been somber: ". . . we turned our backs upon our associates and refused to bear any responsible part in the administration of peace, or the firm and permanent establishment of the results of the war. . . . This must always be a source of deep mortification to us."[12] And his tone had been defiant: "I have seen fools resist Providence before and I have seen their destruction, as will come upon these again—utter destruction and contempt. That we shall prevail is as sure as that God reigns."[12] The next day, the New York Times carried a three-column headline: "HITLER FORCES RALLYING NEAR MUNICH."[13]

Six weeks later, Grayson had finally to tell his distinguished patient and intimate old friend that the road they had traveled together was nearing its end. Wilson was staunch, though his voice was weak: "The machinery is worn out. I am ready."[14]

On February 3, 1924, Woodrow Wilson died.

Henry Cabot Lodge sat down to write: "At this moment, of course, there is a great outburst from the people who admired him, and that is all as it should be and very natural, but he will now pass into the keeping of history, and there . . . he will be justly judged."[15] Wilson would have agreed. He himself had only recently written: "Don't worry. The truth is not a cripple; it can run alone."[16]

Many years before he had come to Washington, he had written what perhaps would be his own best epitaph:

> Our slow world spends its time catching up with the ideas of its best minds. . . . in almost every generation men are born who embody the projected consciousness of their time and people. Their thought runs forward apace into the regions whither the race is advancing, but where it will not for many a weary day arrive. A few generations, and that point, thus early descried, is passed; the new thoughts of one age are the commonplaces of the next.[17]

History might judge him justly, but with some confusion. That he had lived in the grip of tragedy is beyond dispute. A great leader of the crusades, he was fatefully inept at essential compromise, disastrously rigid under attack. A warm and vibrant master of crowds, he was cold and awesome with individuals, never able to charm to his support the powerful leaders whose aid he must have. A shrewd analyst of American government, he proved incapable of practicing his own lessons. A great dreamer, he proved sadly inadequate in making dreams come true. He helped lead his party in the progressive path of the future, but he fell short of solving its basic dilemma. He sensed only vaguely what Arthur Schlesinger Jr., has called the "fatal gap" in his party's ideology since the Age of Jefferson and Jackson: how to protect the public interest against entrenched minorities and at the same time to keep government weak, and moderate and decentralized? A great personal leader, he failed as a party leader. He left the Democracy a divided and leaderless hulk, more deeply shattered than he had found it. And he presided over a transition to reaction that outraged everything for which he had fought. A great prophet of the profound, he watched, a helpless prisoner in the White House, as the cult of the trivial engulfed his nation.

The tragedy was deeply personal. The man who had yearned to be great sat out his days repudiated, defeated, a hapless invalid, pathetically turning the pages of picture magazines, unable longer to see the words that had once been the life's blood of his career, incapable of concentrating upon the ideas that had once been the purpose of all existence.

And the tragedy was deeply moral. After a life of searching, Wilson had found in the League of Nations the great contribution to human welfare that fate had marked him to make. Yet, as the light faded, and the shadows grew deeper within the house on S Street, he must sit with the conscience of failure—failure to the duty, and the truth, and the right, failure to the obligation for which he had been chosen.

Others would be more gentle with him than Wilson himself was. William Allen White noted: "Woodrow Wilson lost the peace because it could not have been won; not the peace he envisioned. Humanity was not ready for it."[18] Historians generally would draw his dreams with nobility; sketch his motives with integrity; paint his tragedy with the full colors of Greek drama. This was no petty man, stumbling ineptly. This was a noble mind, a great talent, a deep moral conscience, reduced to destruction by the chance of circumstance and the frailty of human personality. Some would stress the impossibility of the tasks he assayed: to unite a deeply divided party; to maintain progressivism when the cycle was already trending downward; to maintain neutrality in a world where there could be no neutrals; to bring a noble peace from a war that had fed upon hate, ambition and vengeance. Some would stress the impact of accident, the dictates of circumstance. Some would blame his illness for the last and greatest of his tragedies.

But more and more frequently historians would look to the deep personal dilemmas that set Woodrow Wilson at war with himself. Alexander and Juliette George, attempting the dangerous business of psychoanalyzing the dead, would conclude:

> Not only did Wilson grow up with a taste for achievement and power; he must exercise power alone. He could brook no interference. His will must prevail, if he wished it to. He bristled at the slightest challenge to his authority. Such a characteristic might well have represented a rebellion against the domination of his father, whose authority he had never dared openly to challenge. Throughout this life his relationships with others seemed shaped by an inner command never again to bend his will to another man's. . . . He must dominate, out of fear of being dominated.[19]

John Garraty would put the matter more gently, and perhaps more soundly:

> No man ever needed the protection of human warmth and understanding more, but some

inner insecurity drove him from his fellows. He lived too much within himself, drawing reassurance from absolutes—God, duty, justice. He set himself standards beyond human attainment, and, unable to admit his inevitable inadequacies, fled from his limitations into pitiable self-deception.

His life was full of achievements and honors. He ruled a great university, a great state, and a great nation. Vast crowds cheered his name. He dined with kings, and sat with the most powerful men of his age to remake the map of the world. His tragedy was that he never learned to live at peace with himself.[20]

Yet, if Wilson was more often a great failure than a great victor, he wore, as he left this world of tragedy, the mantle of the prophets. For, even as he erred, he had moved his nation in the path of the future. His words had revived the American faith in democracy. Though he never saw it clearly, his domestic policies had charted the first exploratory paths toward a new land where the power of government would stand at the service of the people in their battle against irresponsible private power. The enthusiasm of experiment and the necessity of war had made his administrations a vast proving ground for the techniques of the future. A whole generation of young men had learned the techniques in Wilson's administration—and they had learned the meaning of deep moral commitment. In varying specifics, with varying challenges, the heart and mind of Wilson would be carried into another age by Herbert Hoover and Franklin D. Roosevelt, by Felix Frankfurter and Bernard Baruch, by the scores of young men who served their apprenticeship with a great schoolmaster, and committed their own master-craftsmanship to F.D.R.'s Age of Action.

But above all, it was the prophecy of peace that Wilson left to a younger generation. The shadow of Wilson haunted the oval study in the White House as another President dealt with the desperate challenge of German aggression. It was the Fourteen Points that reechoed from the American tradition as Roosevelt and Churchill signed the Atlantic Charter. If Woodrow Wilson needed vindication, it came when the nations of the world sat down in San Francisco in 1945, under American leadership, to chart out the dimensions of a new and more hopeful League of Nations.

A prophet is not known in his own time.

NOTES, CHAPTER 18

1. Ray Stannard Baker and William E. Dodd (eds.), **The Public Papers of Woodrow Wilson** (N.Y.: Harper and Brothers, 1925–27). VI, 483.
2. **Ibid.**, p. 496.
3. **New York Times,** October 4, 1920.
4. John A. Garraty, **Henry Cabot Lodge, A Biography** (N.Y.: Alfred A. Knopf, Inc., 1953), p. 399.
5. John Blum, **Joe Tumulty and the Wilson Era** (Boston: Houghton Mifflin Company, 1951), pp. 256–57, 259.
6. H. C. F. Bell, **Woodrow Wilson and the People,** (N.Y.: Doubleday, Doran and Company, 1945), p. 377.
7. Ray Stannard Baker, **Woodrow Wilson: Life and Letters** (N.Y.: Doubleday, Doran and Company, 1927–39), I, xxv.
8. Cary T. Grayson, **Woodrow Wilson; An Intimate Memoir** (N.Y.: Holt, Rinehart and Winston, 1960), pp. 108–09.
9. **Ibid.**, pp. 134–35.
10. Garraty, **op. cit.**, p. 395.
11. William Allen White, **Woodrow Wilson: The Man, His Times, and His Task** (Boston: Houghton Mifflin Company, 1924), pp. 466–68.
12. Baker and Dodd, **op. cit.**, pp. 540–41.
13. Alexander L. and Juliette L. George, **Woodrow Wilson and Colonel House** (N.Y.: The John Day Company, 1956), p. 314.
14. Grayson, **op. cit.**, p. 139.
15. Garraty, **op. cit.**, p. 424.
16. Baker, **op. cit.**, p. xxv.

17. Woodrow Wilson, **Leaders of Men** (Princeton, N. J.: Princeton University Press, 1952, p. 55.
18. White, **op. cit.**, p. 436.
19. George and George, **op. cit.**, pp. 11–12.
20. John Garraty, **Woodrow Wilson: A Great Life in Brief** (N.Y.: Alfred A. Knopf, Inc., 1956), pp. 194–95.

INDEX

G

H

VOLUMES IN SOCIAL SCIENCE
FROM DELL